THE MBA TOOLKIT

The MBA Toolkit

Walter R. Hilker

Erin Preston Gee

CHILTON BOOK COMPANY
RADNOR, PENNSYLVANIA

Copyright © 1985 by Walter R. Hilker and Erin Preston Gee
All Rights Reserved
Published in Radnor, Pennsylvania 19089, by Chilton Book Company
No part of this book may be reproduced, transmitted or
stored in any form or by any means, electronic or mechanical,
without prior written permission from the publisher
Designed by Jean Callan King/Metier Industrial, Inc.
Manufactured in the United States of America

Library of Congress Cataloging in Publication Data
Hilker, Walter R.
  The MBA toolkit.
  (Chilton's better business series)
  Bibliography: p. 222
  Includes index.
    1. Decision-making—Handbooks, manuals, etc.
2. Industrial management—Handbooks, manuals, etc.
I. Gee, Erin Preston. II. Title. III. Series.
HD30.23.H54 1985   658.4'033   84-45164
ISBN 0-8019-7517-4 (pbk).

1 2 3 4 5 6 7 8 9 0   4 3 2 1 0 9 8 7 6 5

To our wives and our shared quests

Contents

Acknowledgments

We wish to thank:

Diane L. Hilker and Janice A. Gee, our wives, for their encouragement, support, patience, humor, and love.

Our children Ryan, Tiffany, Matthew, and Scott Gee, and Kenneth, Kristin, Stephen, and Daniel Hilker, who showed those same enviable attributes.

Brigham Young University, which gave us, and continues to give us, far more than just our graduate degrees.

Dr. Paul Timm at BYU, who voiced encouragement at all the right times.

Dr. Gil Frisbie, at Bowling Green State University, and Dr. Roger Clarke at BYU, who provided solid suggestions.

Jason Stewart, who gave sage advice in the very BASIC matters.

Karen Johnson and Shauna Robertson, who typed the manuscript.

THE MBA TOOLKIT

Introduction

While we slaved individually and, at times, collectively in graduate school to earn our MBA degrees, the thought occurred to us: wouldn't it be convenient to have a little handbook that contained all the formulas, theories, and definitions that our textbooks have, without the detailed explanations and derivatives? The beef without the fat? The idea probably occurred during one of the many times that we were deeply entangled in a case analysis, surrounded by well-worn texts open to heavily underlined, dog-eared pages, and by dustier tomes that, due to lack of use, wouldn't stay open at all.

The value of the handbook idea has been confirmed over and over, in our own experiences as well as in others'. We can cite several people who, in the midst of their own business school studies, have begged us to hurry with the book, or at least pass them a draft of certain chapters. And in our own careers, we have continued to feel the need for such a handy reference.

The value of the idea is confirmed. Now you can test the value of the product. *The MBA Toolkit* is designed to provide convenient access to the most frequently used and cited business formulas, theories, statistical tables, and definitions. These are the tools of your trade. The book is designed for easy use. *The MBA Toolkit* does not teach you the formulas.

It briefly illustrates them and often provides a short explanation of how they are used. The tone is light and, we hope, humorous at times, to make it all the more palatable.

One thing this handbook does *not* do: Businesspeople and students alike often have a tendency to apply formulas and theories indiscriminantly, like the little kid with the new toy hammer who bludgeons everything in sight. This book will not tell you when to use the hammer, the buzz saw, or the drill press: that is your task, and the task of textbooks, teachers, and other managers. When you have a bag of nails and you decide you need a hammer, *The MBA Toolkit* will help you find it and start pounding.

One further note: If you have a personal computer, you may want to use it for easy access to the book's formulas. To help, we've included a number of Basic language programs beginning on page 160. Or perhaps you'd rather just buy a disk. For information on *The MBA Toolkit* computer disk, send a self-addressed stamped envelope to MBA Toolkit Disk, P. O. Box 26, Newbury Park, CA 91320. Please specify whether you want an Apple or IBM-compatible version. Write to us at the same address if you have ideas for improving or adding to *The MBA Toolkit*. We look forward to hearing from you.

Without further ado, we give you *The MBA Toolkit*. Here are the tools—you supply the materials.

1

Operations

Operations managers look at business through blue-collared glasses. Operations, people say, is where you *really* get your hands dirty. This is the realm of inventory control, production scheduling, determining the size and timing of orders—overall, it is the study and design of the process itself.

Some say operations first came into its own in the 19th century with Frederick Winslow Taylor, whose pioneering yet demeaning treatment of workers led to much research in effective scheduling and worker incentive programs. Others say England's Henry VIII perfected operations, when he found himself overbooking the henchman and needed improved time management. Still others insist operations was begun by Noah, who formulated the Economic Order Quantity model (which, incidentally, was shown to be 2, with no safety stock but plenty of reordering).

This chapter contains the following formulas, theories, and procedures:

Forecasting methods
    Simple moving average
    Weighted moving average

Exponential smoothing

Linear regression

Stock reordering

Economic order quantity

Reorder point (units or time)

Total cost

Safety stock

Time study and learning curve

PERT and CPM

Forecasting Methods

We wholeheartedly subscribe to a brilliant description of forecasting reported in Philip Kotler's *Marketing Management: Analysis, Planning and Control:*

> *Forecasting is like trying to drive a car blindfolded and following directions given by a person who is looking out of the back window.*

With forecasting, you turn history's events into eternal truths, then project them into the future as a basis for making decisions related to production, sales, and distribution, to name a few. Forecasting sounds like a great mistake. But the only bigger mistake is not forecasting. Use forecasting for what it is: a source of ballpark figures.

Say you are projecting demand for toys (a classic example for depicting seasonality) and you're forecasting sales for the coming months of January, February, and March. If you're not careful, you'll be basing those forecasts on sales that occurred in October, November, and December—the three months when over half of the year's toy sales are made. And you'll be in extra trouble, as the months January, February, and March are typically dogs in the toy industry.

The point of all this? Forecasts are guidelines, not gospel. The following forecasting methods are guidelines as well, so modify them to fit your purposes. In the toy example, you might use a weighted average method that gives more weight to the sales from the previous January—

March period. Choose the method that meets your needs and use good judgment in applying it, and you'll have a more satisfactory forecast.

The following data base will be used for demonstrating the forecasting methods that follow:

Month (M)	Actual Demand (D)
January	4,200
February	4,080
March	3,960
April	4,020
May	4,180
June	4,320
July	4,480
August	4,530
September	4,700
October	4,790
November	4,810
December	4,720

Simple Moving Average

The simple moving average is simple, all right, and because it is simple, it is a commonplace in business applications. However, the method is to forecasting what the *Kitty Hawk* is to manned flight, a great idea that has since been vastly improved upon.

There are two steps to the method:

1. Identify the number of months of historical data that will serve as the basis for next month's forecast (F).
2. Find the average of the most recent historical data.

EXAMPLE

No. of months of historical data to be used: 3.
Month to be forecasted: April.

$$D_{Mar} = 3,960 \text{ units}$$
$$D_{Feb} = 4,080$$
$$D_{Jan} = \underline{4,200}$$
$$12,240$$

$$F_{Apr} = 12,240 \div 3 = 4,080 \text{ units}$$

Weighted Moving Average

This method is an improvement over the simple moving average because it allows you to assign varying degrees of importance to each piece of historical data. For example, why not base a January toy sales forecast in part on the previous January, instead of the previous boom month of December? That way, your method would be recognizing the existence of seasonal peaks and valleys. A similar adjustment could be used for forecasting cyclical demand, if you had an accurate estimate of the cycle's duration.

There are three steps to this method:

1. Identify the number of months of historical data that will serve as the basis for the next month's forecast (F).
2. Assign weights to each of the past months, in order to put greater emphasis on some months than on others. It is convenient when the weights add to 1, or 100 percent; *if they do not, divide the sum you reached in step 3 by the sum of the weights.*
3. Multiply the weights by their respective month's data, and then add their products.

EXAMPLE

No. of months of historical data to be used: 3.
Month to be forecasted: April.
Weights assigned: $W_{Mar} = .39$, $W_{Feb} = .34$, $W_{Jan} = .27$.

$$D_{Mar} \times W_{Mar} = 3,960 \times .39 = 1,544.4 \text{ units}$$
$$D_{Feb} \times W_{Feb} = 4,080 \times .34 = 1,387.2$$
$$D_{Jan} \times W_{Jan} = 4,200 \times \underline{.27} = \underline{1,134.0}$$
$$1.00 \quad 4,065.6$$

$$F_{Apr} = 4,065.6 \cong 4,066 \text{ units.}$$

Exponential Smoothing

Exponential smoothing is quite impressive in presentations, what with the alpha (α) value and all. You need not use alpha; any Greek letter will do to project the same level of expertise.

In performing exponential smoothing, you need to keep track of each period's demand in order to forecast the next period's demand. This means that, on the basis of *actual* demand, you can't forecast beyond one period. But if you substitute *forecasted* demand for actual, you can create forecasts, albeit increasingly shaky ones, into the Great Beyond. Just be sure to update your predictions each time actual data becomes available. If you don't, you might do well to update your resume.

You also need to select an alpha value. The alpha factor controls how much a difference between last period's actual and forecasted demand will affect this period's forecast. In other words, the alpha you select determines how rapidly your forecast reacts to changes in demand over time. Experimenting with various values between 0.0 and 1.0 will show you that as your alpha nears 1.0, the resulting forecast will move closer to the actual demand for period 1.

The method has three steps:

1. To calculate a forecast F_M, determine the demand and the forecast for the previous period. That is, find

   a. Demand D_{M-1}

   b. Forecast F_{M-1}

2. Select a value for α between 0.0 and 1.0.

3. Use either of these equations:

   a. $F_M = F_{M-1} + \alpha\,(D_{M-1} - F_{M-1})$
   b. $F_M = (1 - \alpha)\,F_{M-1} + \alpha\,D_{M-1}$

EXAMPLE

Forecast months 2, 3, 4, 5, and 6. $\alpha = .12$, $F_{JAN} = 4,150$, and $D_{MI} = 4,200$.

Using formula (a) and demand data from page 5:

$$F_{FEB} = 4,150.00 + .12\,(4,200 - 4,150.00) = 4,156.00$$

$$F_{MAR} = 4,156.00 + .12\,(4,080 - 4,156.00) = 4,146.88$$

$$F_{APR} = 4,146.88 + .12\,(3,960 - 4,146.88) = 4,124.45$$

$$F_{MAY} = 4,124.45 + .12 (4,020 - 4,124.45) = 4,111.92$$
$$F_{JUN} = 4,111.92 + .12 (4,180 - 4,111.92) = 4,120.09$$

Using formula (b):

$$F_{FEB} = (.88) 4,150.00 + (.12) 4,200 = 4,156.00$$
$$F_{MAR} = (.88) 4,156.00 + (.12) 4,080 = 4,146.88$$
$$F_{APR} = (.88) 4,146.88 + (.12) 3,960 = 4,124.45$$
$$F_{MAY} = (.88) 4,124.45 + (.12) 4,020 = 4,111.92$$
$$F_{JUN} = (.88) 4,111.92 + (.12) 4,180 = 4,120.09$$

Linear Regression

Some calculations should be done nowhere but within the preprogrammed chip of a hand-held calculator. Linear regression is one of them. In fact, it is even better if it's performed by a computer. Of course, sometimes carrying a PC in your briefcase just isn't practical. Try to do it on your calculator; if your batteries poop out, here is the method for paper and pencil.

Linear regression allows you, in effect, to plot historical data, such as sales per month, and derive an equation for a line that "best fits" that data. The equation can then be used in forecasting. In other words, you will have established a linear relationship between two variables, in this case sales and time of year, that can be used to forecast future sales.

The equation that is identified by linear regression will yield a straight line. And, unless you're regressing only two data points, chances are mighty slim that the line you draw on graph paper, based on your equation, will pass through your data points. Don't panic. Instead, calculate your r value (coefficient of correlation), as described in step 5 below.

The method of least squares is probably the most commonly used form of linear regression, and that is the method described here.

The goal is to find values for a and b in the straight line equation:

$$y = a + bx$$

where y = dependent variable, or $f(x)$, such as demand
   x = independent variable, such as time
   a = y intercept
   b = slope
   n = number of data points

The procedure is actually a simple one, and there are five steps to it:

1. Using your historical data, set up a table like the one in Table 1-1. Column 1 contains the values (in this case, number of months in a year), column 2 is the y values (demand in each month), column 3 is the product of x and y, and columns 4 and 5 are the squares of x and y. (Omit column 5 if you do not want to calculate the correlation coefficient, described in step 5.)

2. Now add up each column to get Σx, Σy, Σxy, Σx^2 and Σy^2.

3. Calculate the average of all x values ($\bar{X}$) and y values ($\bar{Y}$).

4. Find your equation by plugging the appropriate numbers into these formulas:

$$b = \frac{\Sigma xy - n(\bar{X})(\bar{Y})}{\Sigma x^2 - n(\bar{X})^2}$$

Table 1-1. LINEAR REGRESSION: LEAST SQUARES METHOD.

(1) x	(2) y	(3) xy	(4) x^2	(5) y^2
1	4,200	4,200	1	17,640,000
2	4,080	8,160	4	16,646,400
3	3,960	11,880	9	15,681,600
4	4,020	16,080	16	16,160,400
5	4,180	20,900	25	17,472,400
6	4,320	25,920	36	18,662,400
7	4,480	31,360	49	20,070,400
8	4,530	36,240	64	20,520,900
9	4,700	42,300	81	22,090,000
10	4,790	47,900	100	22,944,100
11	4,810	52,910	121	23,136,100
12	4,720	56,640	144	22,278,400

$\Sigma x = 78$ $\Sigma y = 52,790$ $\Sigma xy = 354,490$ $\Sigma x^2 = 650$ $\Sigma y^2 = 233,303,100$

$\bar{X} = 6.5$ $\bar{Y} = 4,399.17$

$$a = \overline{Y} - b(\overline{X})$$

$$b = \frac{354{,}490 - 12(6.5)(4{,}399.17)}{650 - 12(6.5)^2} = 79.41$$

$$a = 4{,}399.17 - 79.41(6.5) = 3{,}883.03$$

$$y = a + bx$$

$$\therefore y = 3{,}883.03 + 79.41x$$

5. So now you've got an equation to help forecast future demand. But is that equation any good? Does the line it describes really fit your data well enough to be a predictive tool? The coefficient of correlation (r) is an indicator of how well the equation fits your data.

$$r = \sqrt{\frac{\text{Explained Variance}}{\text{Total Variance}}}$$

Calculate the coefficient of correlation with this formula:

$$r = \frac{\Sigma xy - \dfrac{\Sigma x \Sigma y}{n}}{\sqrt{\left(\Sigma x^2 - \dfrac{(\Sigma x)^2}{n}\right)\left(\Sigma y^2 - \dfrac{(\Sigma y)^2}{n}\right)}}$$

$$r = \frac{354{,}490 - \dfrac{(78)(52{,}790)}{12}}{\sqrt{\left(650 - \dfrac{(78)^2}{12}\right)\left(233{,}303{,}100 - \dfrac{(52{,}790)^2}{12}\right)}}$$

$$r = \frac{11{,}420}{\sqrt{(143)(1{,}071{,}091.7)}}$$

$$r = .92$$

At r as high as .92, you can judge the data to yield a rather good correlation (perfect fit gives an r value of ± 1.0; no fit at all gives an r value of 0.0.)

Stock Reordering

Calculating economic order quantity, or EOQ, is a simple and effective way to find out how much stock to order and how often. Use it when

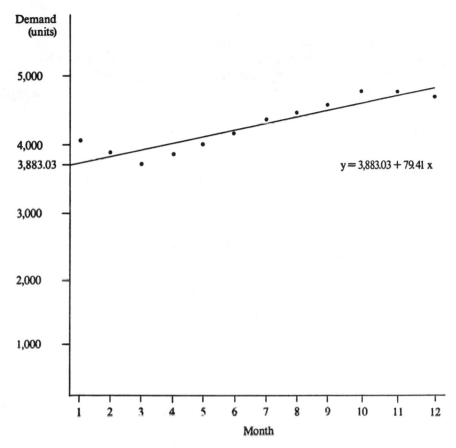

The graph shows demand in units plotted against month, with the regression line $y = 3,883.03 + 79.41\,x$

Figure 1-1. Forecasted demand using linear regression.

demand is reasonably stable. The EOQ formula balances the costs that are incurred when ordering and storing a certain stock keeping unit (SKU). Those costs are:

1. Inventory, or how much it costs you to store it, and
2. Set-up, or how much you have to pay to make and process a purchase order.

EOQ also takes into account your yearly demand. The resulting EOQ figure is the number of units to order each time an order is made.

Of course, you also need to know *when* to order. The reorder point formula tells when to order the EOQ according to inventory levels. The optimal time for ordering, if you prefer to follow a calendar rather than inventory levels, can be determined with another formula.

The total annual cost formula is the whole ball of wax. How much is all this ordering and storing going to cost after one year?

Remember, these formulas apply if your demand is reasonably stable.

Economic Order Quantity

The formula for determining the economic order quantity is:

$$EOQ = \sqrt{\frac{2DS}{H}}$$

where

D = annual demand
S = ordering cost
H = inventory (holding) cost

EXAMPLE

D = 50,000 units per year
S = $200 per order
H = $3 per unit per year

$$EOQ = \sqrt{\frac{2 \times 50{,}000 \times 200}{3}} = 2{,}582 \text{ units per order}$$

Reorder Point

The formula for determining the reorder point according to inventory levels is:

$$R = \frac{D}{365 \text{ days}}(L)$$

where

D = annual demand
R = reorder point
L = lead time for order

EXAMPLE

$L = 3$ days and $D = 50,000$ units (from previous example).

$$R = \frac{50,000}{365} (3) = 411 \text{ units}$$

In other words, order 2,582 units each time your inventory hits 411 units.

Optimal Reorder Time

The optimal time to reorder is given by the equation

$$T = \sqrt{\frac{2S}{DH}}$$

where T is the reorder time and other variables are as defined above.

EXAMPLE

Using quantities from the economic order quantity problem:

$$T = \sqrt{\frac{2 \times 200}{50,000 \times 3}} = \sqrt{\frac{400}{150,000}} = \sqrt{.002667} = .052 \text{ years}$$

$$\frac{.052 \text{ years}}{1} \times \frac{365 \text{ days}}{1 \text{ year}} = 18.98, \text{ or roughly 19 days}$$

$$EOQ = DT = 50,000(.052) = 2,582 \text{ units}$$

Therefore, order 2,582 units every 19 days.

If you already have computed EOQ, then finding the optimal reorder time is greatly simplified:

$$T = \frac{EOQ}{D}$$

In our example this would be

$$T = \frac{2,582}{50,000} = .052 \text{ years}$$

Total Annual Cost

The calculation of total annual cost follows a logical, sensible pattern. Don't get hung up in the number of variables. Instead, spend five minutes to see how nicely the variables work together to find your total cost figure.

$$\text{Given } H = \text{holding cost per unit}$$
$$C = \text{cost per unit}$$
$$D = \text{annual demand}$$
$$Q = \text{order quantity}$$
$$S = \text{ordering cost}$$

$$\text{Total Annual Cost} = \text{Annual Purchase Cost} + \text{Annual Order Cost} + \text{Annual Holding Cost}$$

$$\text{Annual Purchase Cost} = \text{Annual Demand} \times \text{Cost per Unit}$$
$$= D \times C$$

$$\text{Annual Order Cost} = \text{Ordering Cost} \times \text{Number of Orders per Year}$$
$$= S\left(\frac{D}{Q}\right)$$

$$\text{Annual Holding Cost} = \text{Average Inventory on Hand} \times \text{Holding Cost per Unit}$$
$$= \frac{Q}{2}(H)$$

Therefore,

$$\text{Total Annual Cost} = DC + \frac{D}{Q}(S) + \frac{Q}{2}(H)$$

EXAMPLE

$$D = 50{,}000 \text{ units per year}$$
$$S = \$200 \text{ per order}$$
$$H = \$3 \text{ per unit per year}$$
$$Q = EOQ$$
$$C = \$82.50 \text{ per unit}$$

$$TAC = (50,000)(\$82.50) + \frac{50,000}{2,582}(\$200) + \frac{2,582}{2}(\$3)$$
$$= \$4,125,000 + \$3,873 + \$3,873$$
$$= \$4,132,746$$

Safety Stock

Figuring out how much safety stock to have uses confidence levels and a one-tailed test. That is, safety stock protects you from running out, not from having too much. It requires the standard costs and time variables listed below, as well as some historical daily demand figures. Also, you need to choose in advance what level of confidence you want to attain, to protect yourself from stock-outs. In the example, we'll use once again the data base used in earlier examples.

1. Define the following variables:
   D = yearly demand
   $\bar{d}$ = daily demand, average
   d_i = daily demand for days i = 1 to N
   S = ordering or set-up cost
   H = holding or inventory cost
   L = reorder lead time, in days

2. Determine EOQ:

$$EOQ = \sqrt{\frac{2DS}{H}}$$

3. Compute the standard deviation of daily demand, or σd:

$$\sigma d = \sqrt{\frac{\sum_{i=1}^{n}(d_i - \bar{d})^2}{n-1}}$$

4. Calculate the standard deviation of demand during lead time, or the σL value (you must assume that demand from one day to the next is independent).

$$\sigma_L = \sqrt{\sum_{i=1}^{L} \sigma d_i 2}$$

As a practical matter, one almost always assumes that the standard deviation of daily demand does not change from one day to the next, in which case use this simpler formula:

$$\sigma L = \sqrt{L(\sigma d)^2}$$

5. Choose level of confidence for protection against stock-outs. In this step, you are identifying the average demand that must be met while your order for more is being processed ($\overline{d}L$) and adding a little cushion to protect against stock-outs occurring before your order arrives. Choosing a 90% confidence level means that you can be confident that in 9 out of 10 reorders you will not run out of stock during the reorder lead time, and you accept a 10% chance that you *will* run out. Below are commonly used confidence levels and the corresponding reorder formulas:

90% confidence: Reorder point = $\overline{d}L + 1.28\,\sigma L$

95% confidence: Reorder point = $\overline{d}L + 1.645\,\sigma L$

99% confidence: Reorder point = $\overline{d}L + 2.33\,\sigma L$

EXAMPLE

$D = 50{,}000$ units

$\overline{d} = \dfrac{50{,}000}{365} = 136.99$ units

$S = \$200$ per order

$H = \$3$ per unit per year

$L = 3$ days

Determine EOQ:

$$EOQ = \sqrt{\frac{2 \times 50{,}000 \times 200}{3}} = 2{,}582 \text{ units}$$

Compute the standard deviation of daily demand, σd (assuming these daily demand levels: $d_1 = 110$ units, $d_2 = 166$ units, ... $d_{365} = 141$ units):

$$\sigma d = \sqrt{\frac{\sum_{i=1}^{365} (d_i - \overline{d})^2}{364}}$$

$$= \sqrt{\frac{(110 - 136.99)^2 + (166 - 136.99)^2 + \cdots + (141 - 136.99)^2}{364}}$$

$$= 14 \text{ units}$$

Calculate standard deviation of demand during lead time:

$$\sigma L = \sqrt{L(\sigma d)^2}$$
$$= \sqrt{3(14)^2} = \sqrt{588} = 24.25 \text{ units}$$

Choose a 90% confidence level and determine the reorder point:

$$\text{Reorder point} = \overline{d}L + 1.28 \, \sigma L$$
$$= (136.99 \times 3) + (1.28 \times 24.25)$$
$$= 411 + 31$$
$$= 442 \text{ units}$$

The answer tells you three things:

a. When stock hits 442 units, reorder your EOQ (2,582 units);

b. 411 units will be demanded on average between reorder and shipment;

c. 31 extra units will protect you from stock-outs 90% of the time.

Time Study Calculations and Learning Curve

Normal and Standard Time

Time study calculations are usually no more than numbers assigned to subjectively interpreted observations. When properly and skillfully used, however, they can act as guidelines for determining the time necessary to complete tasks. Normal time (NT) is the observed performance time by worker multiplied by a performance rating based on an evaluator's judgment. Standard time (ST) is NT modified to include allowances for coffee breaks, equipment delays, etc.

To determine normal and standard time on a per unit basis, use these formulas:

$$NT = \frac{\text{Time Worked}}{\text{No. of Units Produced}} \times \text{Performance Rating}$$

$$ST = NT (1 + Allowances)$$

or

$$ST = \frac{NT}{1 - Allowances}$$

EXAMPLE

Time worked = 132 minutes

No. of units produced = 60

Performance rating = 80%

Allowances = 15%

$$NT = \frac{132 \text{ min.}}{60} \times .8 = 1.76 \text{ min. per unit}$$

$$ST = 1.76 \times (1 + .15) = 2.024 \text{ min. per unit}$$

or

$$ST = \frac{1.76}{1 - .15} = 2.071 \text{ min. per unit}$$

Learning Curve

Anyone who has learned to type probably performed at a snail's-pace the first few times at the keys. With each successive lesson and each hour of practice, though, familiarity with the location of all the keys increased. After a while, performance on the typewriter leveled out, and probably hasn't increased much beyond that plateau.

The learning curve is the quantified version of that process. Although it is a clever idea it only has limited application. It can show how long it might take to do a process for the nth time, on the basis of knowing how long it took to do it the first time and of knowing a "learning curve factor" expressed as a decimal. The factor is generally determined through observation and reflects this concept: with each doubling of times a process has been completed, the new time required to complete the process *once* is decreased to a percentage of the old time. That percentage is your learning curve factor.

Developing a curve is really quite simple:

1. Determine values for the following variables:

   x = the unit number

K = the number of direct labor hours used to produce the first unit

b = learning curve factor

$$n = \frac{\log b}{\log 2}$$

2. To find out how many direct labor hours will be used to produce unit number x:

$$Y_x = Kx^n$$

EXAMPLE

It took 30,000 hours of direct labor to produce the first unit, so $K = 30,000$. An 85% learning curve factor has been chosen. Therefore,

$$b = .85$$

$$n = \frac{\log .85}{\log 2} = -.234$$

Let's say you want to find out how many direct labor hours will be needed to produce the 10th, 25th, 50th, 75th, 100th, and 125th units. This will allow you to actually plot the curve (Figure 1-2).

$$\text{For } x = 10: \quad Y_x = 30,000(10)^{-.234} = 17,503 \text{ hours}$$
$$\text{For } x = 25: \quad Y_x = 30,000(25)^{-.234} = 14,125 \text{ hours}$$
$$\text{For } x = 50: \quad Y_x = 30,000(50)^{-.234} = 12,011 \text{ hours}$$
$$\text{For } x = 75: \quad Y_x = 30,000(75)^{-.234} = 10,923 \text{ hours}$$
$$\text{For } x = 100: \quad Y_x = 30,000(100)^{-.234} = 10,212 \text{ hours}$$
$$\text{For } x = 125: \quad Y_x = 30,000(125)^{-.234} = 9,693 \text{ hours}$$

PERT and CPM

PERT and CPM are two different planning tools that map out all the activities that comprise a project. PERT (Program Evaluation and Review Technique) was developed by the U.S. Navy Special Projects Office; CPM (Critical Path Method) was developed by J. E. Kelly of Remington-Rand

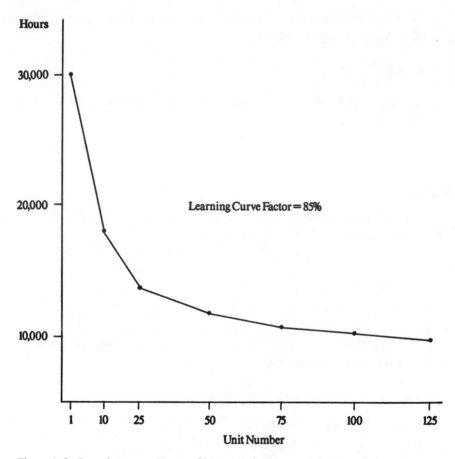

Figure 1-2. Learning curve: Hours of labor required to produce nth unit.

and M. R. Walker of duPont. Both methods map out the order in which activities occur and on what other activities they depend.

The greatest difference between the two systems is that PERT includes a calculation of the probability that the total project will be complete by a given due date. The greatest similarity is that they both resemble the freeway system between Los Angeles and San Bernardino, California.

Here is a key to help in mapping out the activities: In PERT, activities are paths(————) and events are nodes (O). In CPM, activities are nodes (O), and events are not represented.

Steps for CPM

1. Identify and list all activities necessary to complete a project.
2. List them in sequence of occurrence, along with activities they follow.
3. Make time estimates of activities, and from them develop:
   - Early Start time (ES)
   - Late Start time (LS)
   - Early Finish time (EF)
   - Late Finish time (LF)

   Early Start is the earliest possible time an activity can begin; Early Finish is the earliest it can conclude, dictated by schedules of preceding activities. Likewise, Late Start and Late Finish are the latest an activity can begin and end without delaying the total time schedule of the project.
4. Find the critical path, defined as the path where slack time = 0, that is, where Early Start equals Late Start, and Early Finish equals Late Finish. An example of this determination is shown in Table 1-2. A CPM map is shown in Figure 1-3.

Table 1-2. EXAMPLE CPM CRITICAL PATH DETERMINATION.

Activity	Time Estimate	Follows	Early Start (ES)	Early Finish (EF)	Late Start (LS)	Late Finish (LF)	Slack (LF-EF) or (LS-ES)	Critical Path? (0 Slack)
A	8	—	0	8	0	8	0	Yes
B	5	A	8	13	8	13	0	Yes
C	4	A	8	12	13	17	5	No
D	6	B	13	19	13	19	0	Yes
E	2	B, C	13	15	17	19	4	No
F	6	B, D	19	25	22	28	3	No
G	9	D, E	19	28	19	28	0	Yes
H	3	F, G	28	31	30	33	2	No
I	5	F, G	28	33	28	33	0	Yes
J	2	H, I	28	35	33	35	0	Yes

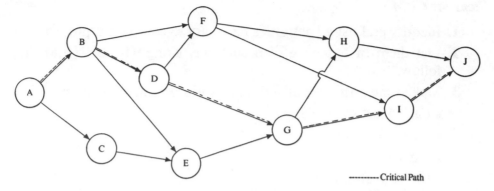

---------- Critical Path

Figure 1–3. CPM activities mapping.

Steps for PERT

1. Identify and list all activities necessary to complete a project.
2. List them in sequence of occurrence, along with activities they follow.
3. Make time estimates of activities:
   - Most optimistic (a)
   - Most likely (m)
   - Most pessimistic (b)
4. Calculate expected time (ET) and variance (σ^2) for each activity:

$$ET = \frac{a + 4m + b}{6}$$

$$\sigma^2 = \frac{(b - a)^2}{36}$$

5. Find the critical path:

   a. Draw a map of activities as shown in Figure 1-4, using lines to represent activities.

   b. At each node, or intersection, develop a "fraction." The numerator shows the cumulative estimated time to complete the project through each activity. If more than one activity feeds into another, the following activity can't start until *all* its predecessors have been completed. In the denominator, work backwards by subtracting

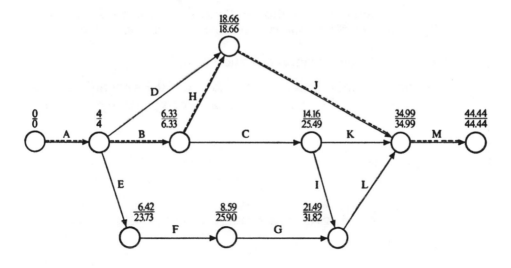

Top number is expected completion
Bottom number is latest allowable completion

Bottom − Top = Slack

----- = Critical Path

Figure 1–4. PERT activities mapping.

activity times from their respective cumulative completion times. The total completion time remains the same—in this case, 44.44 minutes.

The node between C and K shows an 11.33-minute difference between the numerator and denominator, signifying 11.33 minutes of "slack time." At the node preceding activities H and C, the denominator must be $(18.66 - 12.33) = 6.33$ minutes, rather than $(25.49 - 7.83) = 17.66$ minutes. If it were to accommodate the southern route's 11.33-minute slack, it would cause a delay to the northern route, and to the entire process.

c. The path where numerator equals denominator, or where slack is zero, is the critical path.

6. Find probability of completion in a given amount of time:

$$Z = \frac{T_d - T_e}{\sqrt{CP^2}}$$

where
T_d = amount of time allotted for the project (your deadline)
T_e = amount of time for earliest project completion, or length of critical path
CP^2 = sum of the variances on critical path

Use the standard normal tables (Table A in the Appendix, to determine the probability, based on the z value you have calculated.

EXAMPLE

Example calculations and PERT mapping are shown in Table 1-3 and Figure 1-4. The probability of finishing the project in a certain amount of time is determined as follows:

T_e = 44.44 minutes, via critical path A-B-H-J-M

T_d = 48 minutes

$$Z = \frac{48 - 44.44}{\sqrt{2.18}} = \frac{3.56}{1.48} = 2.41$$

Table 1-3. EXAMPLE PERT ANALYSIS.

(IN MINUTES)

Activity	Follows	a	m	b	ET	σ^2	Slack
A	—	3	4	5	4	.11	—
B	A	1.5	2	4.5	2.33	.25	—
C	B	6	8	9	7.83	.25	11.33
D	A	4	5	7	5.17	.25	9.49
E	A	1.7	2.5	2.8	2.42	.03	17.31
F	E	1	2	4	2.17	.25	17.31
G	F	4	6	7.5	5.92	.34	17.31
H	B	10	12.5	14	12.33	.44	—
I	C	6	7	10	7.33	.44	10.33
J	D, H	14	16	20	16.33	1.00	—
K	C	8	9	13	9.5	.69	11.33
L	G, I	1	3	6	3.17	.69	10.33
M	J, K, L	8.3	9.1	12	9.45	.38	—

From Table A, $p \cong 99.2\%$:

$T_e = 44.44$ minutes

$T_d = 41$ minutes

$$Z = \frac{41 - 44.44}{\sqrt{2.18}} = \frac{-3.44}{1.48} = -2.32$$

From Table A, $p \cong 1.0\%$.

2

Accounting

Accountants are the ones who keep track of everything. "Bean counters" as they are affectionately known to some, have the job of getting to the bottom line. The basic rules of accounting are not difficult, although their application may seem complex at times. Perhaps that is what keeps accountants and accounting professors in business. (Just remember, if they can do it with beans, you can do it with a calculator.)

This chapter will deal with some of the basic formulas and formats, specifically:

Six steps of the accounting cycle
Income statement
Balance sheet
Depreciation methods
Inventory methods

Since accounting has its own special terminology, accounting terms are represented extensively in the glossary at the back of the book.

Accounting Cycle

The foundation of the accounting process is the accounting cycle (AC). The cycle, which usually occurs over the course of a year, is the means by which financial transactions are recorded during that year.

The AC involves six steps. We'll review each of them individually, but briefly they are:

1. Record transactions in a journal as they happen.
2. Post debits and credits from the journal to ledger.
3. Prepare a work sheet.
4. Prepare financial statements. These include income statements, balance sheets, and statements of owner's equity.
5. Using the work sheet, enter adjusting and closing entries in the journal. Then these get posted to the ledger accounts.
6. Make an after-closing trial balance to prove ledger is in balance.

The detailed explanation of all of this is beyond the scope of this book. Remember this is a toolkit, not a user's manual. We'll just hit some of the highlights.

For example, let's assume that you are starting a business. You have contracted with a Pacific Island fruit grower to sell exotic fruits like mango, papaya, and breadfruit. For lack of a better name, you call the business Sour Grapes, Inc.

Now, let's run through the accounting cycle with Sour Grapes (we won't be the first). The first transaction is to buy office space for running the business.

Step 1: Journal Transactions

You rent office space in the attic of a local theater. You have agreed to pay the theater owner $150 a month. He has in turn rented you the space and agreed to let you watch two free movies a month. This would be recorded in the journal as shown below.

	GENERAL JOURNAL	PAGE 1	
Date	Account Titles and Explanation	Debit	Credit
198_	Rent Payable	150	
Nov. 15	Cash		150

Each transaction is done in similar fashion, until you have yourself quite a journal.

Step 2: Debits and Credits (Ledger Accounts)

Now the transactions are posted to debit and credit ledger accounts. The most difficult thing about debits and credits is to remember which is which. Below is a key.

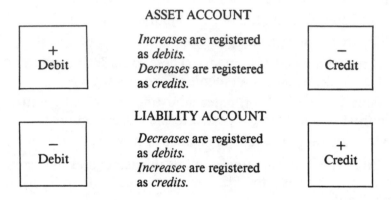

ASSET ACCOUNT

+ Debit

Increases are registered as *debits.*
Decreases are registered as *credits.*

− Credit

LIABILITY ACCOUNT

− Debit

Decreases are registered as *debits.*
Increases are registered as *credits.*

+ Credit

So taking the rental transaction used before, we post that journal entry to the following ledger account:

ASSET

Cash

(+)	(−)
	$150 (1)

LIABILITY

Rent Payable

(−)	(+)
(1) $150	

And so it goes. The number in parentheses indicates the order of transaction in the journal. You create a new ledger or "T" account for each asset or liability account you need. On existing T accounts you just work down, like this:

Cash

(+)	(−)
	$150 (1)
(4) $300	$250 (7)

In this example, you have earned (or somehow acquired) $300 for transaction 4. In transaction 7, you gave $250 for something.

Step 3: Work Sheet

The work sheet is used to run a trial balance of the ledger accounts—in essence it is a sheet that shows all the T accounts. You reconstruct them to assure yourself they balance and to make it easier to prepare the financial statements.

A partial work sheet showing only a couple of selected accounts would look something like what's shown in Figure 2-1.

Step 4: Financial Statements

Financial statements are the hallmarks of the accounting profession. Most of the other documents are used largely for internal use, but the income statement, balance sheet, and other financial statements are viewed by outsiders as well as insiders (if the business is publicly owned). They reflect the financial strength and operations of the firm.

Income Statements
A statement of income shows how the firm arrived at its profit position. The statement usually starts with sales and ends with profit (or loss).

Figure 2-1 PARTIAL WORK SHEET.

ASSETS

	Cash					Accounts Rec	
	$1000						
		$150	(1)	(2)	$1000		
(4)	$300					$700	(6)
		$250	(7)	(11)	$5000		

LIABILITIES

	Notes Payable					Rent Payable	
		$300	(4)	(1)	$150		
(7)	$250						
		$8,500	(13)				

A sample statement for Sour Grapes is shown in Figure 2-2. Though it is simplified, it hits the key points. A more detailed income statement appears in Figure 2-4. As seen here, there are three income figures. The one that is used for reinvestment, or distribution to owners or involved parties, is net income. This is often called the bottom line, and for some firms who lack much of one, it may prove the end of the line.

Balance Sheet
The balance sheet balances assets and liabilities. It is an expansion of the ledger accounts, where we balanced each transaction individually and then in aggregate. A sample Sour Grapes balance sheet is shown in Figure 2-3.

The assets section comprises current and long-term assets. The liabilities and owner's equity section is comprised of current and long-term liabilities, and owner's equity. An expanded version is shown in Figure 2-5.

Step 5: Adjusting/Closing Entries

Once the financial statements are generated, the work sheet is used to enter the adjusting and closing entries to the journal. These are then posted to

Figure 2-2. SIMPLE INCOME STATEMENT.

INCOME STATEMENT
SOUR GRAPES, INC.
PERIOD ENDING DEC. 31, 198_

Sales	$50,000
Less: Cost of Goods Sold	35,000
Gross Income	15,000
Less: Advertising and Marketing	1,000
Rental Expense	900
Salaries	10,000
Additional Movies	500
Operating Income	2,600
Less Taxes	500
Net Income	$ 2,100

Figure 2.3. SIMPLE BALANCE SHEET.

BALANCE SHEET
SOUR GRAPES, INC.
FOR PERIOD ENDING DEC. 31, 198_

Assets		Liabilities and Owner's Equity	
Current Assets		Current Liabilities	
Cash	$ 900	Accounts Payable	$ 2,800
Accounts Receivable	5,300	Wages Payable	3,700
Inventory	3,400	Total Current Liabilities	6,500
Total Current Assets	9,600	Notes Payable (Bank loan)	8,550
Equipment	6,500	Owner's Equity	
		Paid in Capital	1,050
Total Assets	$16,100	Total Liabilities & Owner's Equity	$16,100

the ledger account. One entry that would need an adjusting entry is an unrecorded expense such as the accrual of interest. An example is shown below:

Interest Expense.   36
Interest Payable   36

Step 6: After-Closing Trial Balance

After-closing trial balances are generated to prove that the ledger is still in balance. It is also done to make the necessary preparations for beginning the cycle over again. Fascinating stuff, isn't it?

Income Statement

Figure 2-4 shows an expanded version of an income statement. An income statement depicts how well a firm is utilizing its resources. Sales (or revenues) represent the culmination of converting inputs to outputs and acceptance of those outputs by the community. Income represents how efficiently the entire process has transpired.

Figure 2-4. EXPANDED INCOME STATEMENT.

MBA TOOLKIT
INCOME STATEMENT
YEAR ENDING DEC. 31, 1984
(000)

Gross Sales		$31,400
Less: Returns		1,400
Net Sales		30,000
Cost of Goods Sold		12,900
Gross Profit		17,100
Less: Operating Expenses		
Marketing	6,200	
Sales	2,900	
Development	900	
General and Administrative	2,500	12,500
Gross Operating Income		4,600
Depreciation		560
Net Operating Income		4,040
Add: Other Income		
Royalties		430
Gross Income (EBIT)		4,470
Interest Expense		120
Net Income Before Taxes		4,350
Taxes (48%)		2,088
Net Income		2,262

When interpreting the income statement, the Glossary is the best place to look for definitions of the key terms. The basic framework for an income statement is as follows:

Net Sales — Cost of Goods (direct material, labor, overhead) = Gross Profit

Gross Profit — Non-allocated Expenses (e.g., marketing, indirect overhead, administration, etc.) = Gross Operating Income

Gross Operating Income − Depreciation = Net Operating Income

Net Operating Income + Other Income = Gross Income or EBIT

Gross Income − Interest expenses and taxes = Net Income

Net income is what's available for reinvestment; distribution to owners, employees, and shareholders; retaining in the firm as cash; or financing trips to Aruba.

Balance Sheet

An expanded balance sheet is shown in Figure 2-5. The balance sheet is the firm's score card. It shows in detailed fashion how the firm is doing with the basic "accounting equation," which is:

Assets = Liabilities + Owner's Equity

or

Owners Equity = Assets − Liabilities

In other words the balance sheet depicts the composition of a firm's resources and how "stable" or "unstable" a firm is.

As with the income statement, many of the financial ratios and other tools of financial analysis (which will be explored in Chapter 3) are derived from the balance sheet. Never underestimate the value of the seemingly innocuous balance sheet.

And remember, to paraphrase Orwell, although all these sheets balance, some are more balanced than others.

Depreciation

Depreciation is what happens the minute you drive your new car off the dealer's lot. It is also a very important principle in accounting. Of the two, we will expound further on the latter.

Basically, depreciation is the gradual diminishment of the book value of a physical asset. The inherent value of depreciation lies in the fact that you can use depreciation of an asset to offset the tax burden and improve your net cash flow position.

Figure 2-5. EXPANDED BALANCE SHEET.

MBA TOOLKIT
BALANCE SHEET
PERIOD ENDING DEC. 31, 1984
(000)

Assets

Current Assets		
Cash		$ 1,400
Marketable Securities		950
Accounts Receivable		2,560
Inventories		3,800
Total Current Assets		8,710
Equipment & Machinery	1,100	
Plant	12,750	
Less accumulated depreciation	2,400	
Net Plant and Equipment		11,450
Other Assets		780
Total Assets		$20,940

Liabilities & Owner's Equity

Current Liabilities	
Notes Payable	$ 1,490
Accounts Payable	2,650
Salaries & Wages Payable	560
Income Taxes Payable	740
Total Current Liabilities	5,440
Bonds	2,260
Owner's Equity	
Preferred Stock	810
Common Stock (9,500,000 shares)	9,500
Retained Earnings	2,930
Total Owner's Equity	13,240
Total Liabilities & Owner's Equity	$20,940

There are several methods of depreciating assets. These are selected based on the firm's financial objectives and how much savvy the controller has. Four methods are described below.

Straight Line

Straight line depreciation is the easiest method to use and one of the most commonly used. It is calculated with the following equation:

$$\text{Annual Depreciation Amount} = \frac{\text{Cost} - \text{Salvage Value}}{\text{Years of Useful Life}}$$

EXAMPLE

The annual depreciation on a forklift costing $20,000 with 8 years expected life and a salvage value of $4,000 is

$$\frac{\$20,000 - \$4,000}{8} = \$2,000$$

Units of Output

$$\text{Depreciation per Unit} = \frac{\text{Cost} - \text{Salvage Value}}{\text{Estimated Units of Output}}$$

EXAMPLE

A milk shake maker costs $5,000 with a salvage value of $1,000. Expected productivity is 40,000 shakes.

$$\frac{\$5,000 - \$1,000}{40,000} = \$.10 \text{ depreciation per shake}$$

For each shake you make, you can depreciate the machine by $.10.

Double Declining Balance

Suppose the firm wants to depreciate the asset's value more rapidly than either the straight line or unit output methods permit. (Perhaps the controller is retiring to Monaco in three years and wants to improve cash flow of the firm.) Then the accounting group would probably use one of the "accelerated" depreciation methods, such as the double declining balance method or the sum of year digits method (see next section).

The double declining balance method uses the following equation:

$$\text{Annual Depreciation Percentage} = \frac{2}{\text{Useful Life}}$$

EXAMPLE

An olive-pitting machine costs $2,000 and has a life expectancy of 10 years. This would be depreciated as such:

$$\text{Annual Depreciation Percentage} = \frac{2}{10 \text{ years}} = .20 \text{ or } 20\% \text{ per year}$$

Year	Depreciation Calculation	Depreciation Expense	Total Accum. Depreciation	Book Value
1	(.2 × $2,000)	$400	$400	$1,600
2	(.2 × $1,600)	$320	$720	$1,280
3	(.2 × $1,280)	$256	$976	$1,024
⋮	⋮	⋮	⋮	⋮

As can be seen, this enables the firm to "write off" the value of the asset in an accelerated fashion in the first few years.

Sum of Year Digits (SYD)

Under this method, the accountant sums the total years of an asset's depreciable life. That sum becomes the denominator. The number of remaining years of useful life becomes the numerator. The resultant fraction is then used to calculate the annual depreciation. Trust us, it's easier than it sounds.

EXAMPLE

Your firm buys a paper shredder at a cost of $10,000 with a life expectancy of 4 years. Sum of years equals $1 + 2 + 3 + 4 = 10$:

Year	Depreciation Calculation	Depreciation Expense	Total Accum. Depreciation	Book Value
1	$\frac{4}{10} \times 10,000$	$4,000	$4,000	$6,000
2	$\frac{3}{10} \times 10,000$	$3,000	$7,000	$3,000
3	$\frac{2}{10} \times 10,000$	$2,000	$9,000	$1,000
4	$\frac{1}{10} \times 10,000$	$1,000	$10,000	—

The double declining balance, sum of years digits, and other accelerated schedules do not typically include any salvage or residual value. Accelerated depreciation methods allow the firm or individual to defer taxes in dollars of higher present value. That is to say, one dollar of shielded income today is worth more than one dollar of shielded income tomorrow.

Inventory Methods

Inventory methods are a vital element of accounting because of the impact various methods can have on the reported profits. The most common methods of accounting for inventory are described below.

Average Cost

Inventory value can be computed simply as the average cost per unit times the number of units remaining.

EXAMPLE

Sour Grapes Inc. has 200 crates of mango melon. The cost of goods available for sale (the mango melon) is $10,000.

$$\frac{\text{Cost of Goods Available}}{\text{No. of Units}} = \text{Average Unit Cost}$$

$$\frac{\$10,000}{200} = \$50$$

Beginning inventory: $10,000 (200 crates)
Sales during period: 180 crates
Ending inventory: 20 crates $\times$ $50 = $1,000

The only possible thing that could confuse this simple method is if the mango melon rot. That topic will be discussed in a sequel to this book.

FIFO (First In-First Out)

This is best explained by an example.

EXAMPLE

In this case, Sour Grapes is dealing with rare coconuts. Obviously a valuable and volatile (price wise) commodity.

5 crates are purchased June 1, 1984 @ $ 80 each = $ 400

10 crates are purchased Oct. 1, 1984 @ $ 90 each = $ 900

10 crates are purchased Dec. 1, 1984 @ $100 each = $1000

Total inventory on hand Dec. 1, 1984 = $2300

On January 5, 1985, 10 crates are sold. Using FIFO, the inventory valuation would be:

5 crates @ $80 and 5 crates @ $90 = $850

Ending inventory (5 @ $90, 10 @ $100) = $1450

LIFO (Last In-First Out)

This is the converse of FIFO. We will use the same example as before.

EXAMPLE

5 crates of coconuts purchased June 1, 1984 @ $ 80 = $ 400

10 crates of coconuts purchased Oct. 1, 1984 @ $ 90 = $ 900

10 crates of coconuts purchased Dec. 1, 1984 @ $100 = $1000

Total inventory on hand Dec. 1, 1984 = $2300

Sale of 10 crates on January 5, 1985. Using LIFO, the valuation would be:

10 crates @ $100 = $1000

Ending inventory (10 @ $90, 5 @ $80) = $1300

As can be seen, the inventory valuation can be substantially affected by the method used. Under times of high inflation, the LIFO method can result in higher costs of goods sold than the FIFO method. This in turn results in lower after-tax profits.

When sales outpace inventory replacement, then LIFO undervalues the inventory that is passed through (or sold to customers) because it was probably purchased for less than replacement costs, and the firm registers higher profit. These are sometimes called "shadow" profits, or "inventory" profits.

3

Finance

Financial analysts and managers are born-again accountants with MBA degrees and personal computers. As business disciplines go, finance typically involves more discipline than others. More specifically, it requires more analysis and strategic planning than accounting. Accountants determine how much there is; financiers determine how much more there could be.

If you believe Shakespeare's Polonius when he said, "Neither a borrower nor a lender be," then you can skip this section of the book. Most of the financial transactions in business involve borrowing and lending in one way or the other. For example, a large corporation "borrows" money from its stockholders, banks, etc., and "loans" it to its plants, subsidiaries, marketing department, etc. The key is to make enough on the loans to satisfy the lenders.

So there you have it: all you ever needed to know about finance in two paragraphs. For the sake of completeness, though, the rest of this chapter has some supplemental material on the following topics:

> Financial ratios
>
> Break-even analysis
>
> Sources and uses statements

Present value/future value analysis
Capital budgeting considerations
Operating leverage/financial leverage formulas
Cost of capital calculations and evaluations
Bond information

Financial Ratios

Financial analysis often begins with evaluating the ratios. Ratio analysis provides a concise overview of a firm's financial position. Financial ratios are commonly divided into four groups: liquidity ratios, leverage ratios, activity ratios, and profitability ratios.

Most of the information for the ratios is taken from the income statement or the balance sheet. For purposes of example we will refer to the balance sheet and income statement on Sour Grapes, Inc. shown in Figures 3-1 and 3-2.

Liquidity Ratios

Liquidity ratios indicate how liquid a firm is; that is, they depict how well a firm is able to meet its current obligations. There are two liquidity ratios in common use: the *current ratio* and the *quick ratio*.

$$\text{Current Ratio} = \frac{\text{Current Assets}}{\text{Current Liabilities}}$$

Current assets usually consist of cash, marketable securities, accounts receivable, and inventories. Current liabilities typically include accounts payable, short-term notes payable, and accrued wages.

In the case of Sour Grapes, Inc., its current ratio is

$$\frac{311,250}{124,500} = 2.5$$

This means that this firm could meet its short-term obligations 2.5 times.

The quick ratio is sometimes called the acid test, because many consider it the true measure of how liquid a firm is. It does not include inventory among the assets, because inventories are usually the least liquid of the current assets, and the most difficult to convert to funds when needed.

$$\text{Quick Ratio} = \frac{\text{Current Assets} - \text{Inventory}}{\text{Current Liabilities}}$$

Applying the acid test to Sour Grapes, Inc. yields

$$\frac{311{,}250 - 133{,}125}{124{,}500} = 1.4$$

In this case, the firm could readily meet its current obligations 1.4 times.

Leverage Ratios

Leverage ratios show the relationship of funds supplied by owners vis-à-vis those supplied by creditors.

The *debt ratio* illustrates how resilient the firm would be if losses were heavy and liquidation necessary. Too high a ratio may concern investors and creditors. The fact that a firm is highly leveraged (high debt ratio) signifies significant risk.

$$\text{Debt Ratio} = \frac{\text{Total Debt}}{\text{Total Assets}} \text{ or } \frac{\text{Total Liabilities}}{\text{Total Assets}}$$

Total assets include current assets and long-term assets (plant, equipment, etc.). Total debt includes current liabilities, bonds, and any long-term bank debt.

The debt ratio for Sour Grapes, Inc. is

$$\frac{124{,}500 + 75{,}000 + 195{,}000}{771{,}250} = .51 \text{ or } 51\%$$

The result shows that slightly over half of the firm's financial structure consists of short- and long-term debt.

The *times interest earned* calculation tells how many times over a firm can "cover" its interest charges. Note that the numerator in the equation is the EBIT figure or gross income.

$$\text{Times Interest Earned} = \frac{\text{Profit Before Taxes} + \text{Interest Charges}}{\text{Interest Charges}}$$

Figure 3-1. BALANCE SHEET.
SOUR GRAPES, INC.
BALANCE SHEET
PERIOD ENDING DEC. 31, 1984

Assets

Current Assets	
Cash	$ 18,750
Marketable securities	65,625
Accounts receivable	93,750
Inventories	133,125
Total current assets	311,250
Gross Plant & Equipment	610,000
Depreciation	150,000
Net Plant & Equipment	460,000
Total Assets	$771,250

Liabilities and Owner's Equity

Current Liabilities	
Accounts Payable	$ 32,625
Notes Payable	41,250
Accrued Wages	50,625
Total current liabilities	124,500
Mortgage Bonds	195,000
Debentures	75,000
Common Stock	225,000
Retained Earnings	151,750
Total Owner's Equity	376,750
Total Liabilities and Owner's Equity	$771,250

For our example company, the times interest earned is

$$\frac{118,550 + 4,500 + 3,000}{3,000 + 4,500} = 16.8$$

Therefore our Sour Grapes friend could cover the interest charges several times over.

Activity Ratios

Activity ratios are measures of resource utilization.

Inventory turnover is a good measure of how sales are moving. If turnover is low, it can portend high inventory carrying costs.

$$\text{Inventory Turnover} = \frac{\text{Total Sales}}{\text{Inventory (at selling price)}}$$

$$= \frac{1,125,000}{133,125} = 8.5$$

The example calculation shows that Sour Grapes turns its inventory over almost 8½ times a year.

The *average collection period* measures the time frame between the sale and the receipt of revenue. It is an important consideration in evaluating cash flow requirements.

$$\frac{\text{Average Collection}}{\text{Period}} = \frac{\text{Accounts Receivable}}{\text{Sales per Day}} = \frac{\text{Accounts Receivable}}{\text{Total Sales} \div 360}$$

$$= \frac{93,750}{1,125,000 \div 360} = \frac{93,750}{3,125} = 30 \text{ days}$$

Sour Grapes takes (on average) 30 days to collect on its outstanding accounts.

The *fixed asset turnover* measures the utilization of the fixed capital structure. Net fixed assets include plant and equipment minus accumulated depreciation.

$$\text{Fixed Asset Turnover} = \frac{\text{Sales}}{\text{Net Fixed Assets}}$$

$$= \frac{1,125,000}{460,000} = 2.4$$

The fixed asset turnover can vary, depending on the depreciation method used. If the firm uses accelerated depreciation methods, the ratio could be abnormally high and could deceptively decrease in later years due to reduced depreciation.

Total asset turnover differs from the fixed asset turnover only in that it gives a picture of utilization of total financial structure.

$$\text{Total Asset Turnover} = \frac{\text{Sales}}{\text{Total Assets}}$$
$$= \frac{1,125,000}{771,250} = 1.5$$

Profitability Ratios

Profitability ratios measure how strong the bottom line really is in relation to the elements which have generated it.

The *profit margin on sales* is an important measure because profits are used for reinvestment and distributed as dividends. If this ratio is too low, the future growth and strength of the firm is questionable. (In the equation, net income is after-tax income.)

$$\frac{\text{Profit margin}}{\text{on Sales}} = \frac{\text{Net Income}}{\text{Sales}} = \frac{75,872}{1,125,000} = 6.7\%$$

Sour Grapes had a 6.7% profit return on total sales. That may be a high or low number depending on the industry average. The overall average for U.S. firms is less than 5%.

Return on total sales is helpful in evaluating the effectiveness of the asset base. A low ratio may indicate the operation is too large or inefficient to support the income that it is generating. Time to trim the sails.

$$\frac{\text{Return on}}{\text{Total Assets}} = \frac{\text{Net Income}}{\text{Total Assets}} = \frac{75,872}{771,250} = 9.8\%$$

Again, this number needs to be evaluated in terms of industry standards and past trends.

Also known as return on equity, *return on owner's equity* (ROE) is a valuable measure for attracting new capital or maintaining the existing base. The calculation depicts the return the investor is getting (or can expect) on his money. This is the reason businesses exist—to give a "reasonable return" to their stockholders.

$$\text{ROE} = \frac{\text{Net Income}}{\text{Owner's Equity}} = \frac{75,872}{225,000 + 151,750} = 20.1\%$$

Figure 3-2. INCOME STATEMENT.

SOUR GRAPES, INC.
INCOME STATEMENT
PERIOD ENDING DEC. 31, 1984

Sales	$1,125,000
Cost of Goods Sold	967,500
Gross Profit	157,500
Selling, General & Administrative	17,200
Lease Payment	10,500
Gross Operating Income	129,800
Depreciation	3,750
Net Operating Income	126,050
Interest on notes payable	3,000
Interest on debentures	4,500
Profit Before Taxes	118,550
Tax (36%)	42,678
Net Income	$ 75,872

Sour Grapes has given a healthy return to its owners. Not many people would scoff at a 20% return on their investment.

Ratio Analysis

Ratio analysis is not the be-all and end-all of financial analysis. The ratios can be misleading if they are the only profile by which the firm's financial portrait is assessed. For example, a firm may have a relatively low current ratio and a high inventory turnover ratio. This may indicate astute inventory management, while other firms in the industry have higher current ratios due to poor inventory management.

Another case in point is the firm that has a lower collection period than other firms in the industry. While the initial indication is positive, the firm's credit policies may be so tight or out of line with competitors that potential sales are being lost. In the 50's and 60's one major American retailer maintained such a conservative credit position that it lost irretrievable market share before it modified its credit policy.

Nonetheless, ratios are easily performed and provide ready indicators of general conditions. Ratio analysis is usually more profitable when comparing firms within the same industry or similar industries. A profit margin that stands out in one industry may be mediocre in another industry. Industry standards are good benchmarks.

Some good sources of information for calculating industry and individual firm ratios are *Dun & Bradstreet, Standard & Poors,* and company annual reports.

Figure 3-3 summarizes all the ratios presented in the preceding pages.

Figure 3-3. FINANCIAL RATIOS

Liquidity Ratios

$$\text{Current} = \frac{\text{Current Assets}}{\text{Current Liabilities}}$$

$$\text{Quick (Acid Test)} = \frac{\text{Current Assets} - \text{Inventory}}{\text{Current Liabilities}}$$

Leverage Ratios

$$\text{Debt} = \frac{\text{Total Debt}}{\text{Total Assets}}$$

$$\text{Times Interest Earned} = \frac{\text{Profit before Taxes \& Interest Charges}}{\text{Interest Charges}}$$

Activity Ratios

$$\text{Inventory Turnover} = \frac{\text{Total Sales}}{\text{Inventory (at selling price)}}$$

$$\text{Average Collection Period} = \frac{\text{Accounts Receivable}}{\text{Total Sales}}$$

$$\text{Fixed Asset Turnover} = \frac{\text{Sales}}{\text{Net Fixed Assets}}$$

$$\text{Total Asset Turnover} = \frac{\text{Sales}}{\text{Total Assets}}$$

Profitability Ratios

$$\text{Profit Margin on Sales} = \frac{\text{Net Income}}{\text{Sales}}$$

$$\text{Return on Total Assets} = \frac{\text{Net Income}}{\text{Total Assets}}$$

$$\text{Return on Owner's Equity} = \frac{\text{Net Income}}{\text{Owner's Equity}}$$

Break-even Analysis

A break-even (BE) analysis determines at what point a firm's revenue just covers its costs; revenues exceeding the break-even point represent profit. Performing a break-even analysis is especially applicable when launching new products or services. Reality replaces euphoria when a firm realizes it needs to sell X number of units *just* to break even.

There are several ways to calculate the break-even point. Three are illustrated here, but first some definitions:

P = price per unit ($10 in the example)
N = number of units sold
F = fixed costs total ($200,000 in the example)
V = variable costs per unit ($6 in the example)
S = sales (revenue) in dollars
π = desired profit level ($50,000 in the example)

Break-even Point in Units Sold

$$N = \frac{F}{P-V}$$
$$= \frac{200,000}{10 - 6} = 50,000 \text{ units}$$

The firm must sell 50,000 units to cover its costs. This is depicted graphically in Figure 3-4.

Break-even Point in Dollars

$$S = \frac{F}{1 - \dfrac{V}{P}}$$
$$= \frac{200,000}{1 - \dfrac{6}{10}} = \frac{200,000}{0.4} = \$500,000$$

The firm needs $500,000 in sales to break even. Obviously, the 50,000 units calculated with the first formula $\times$ $10 = $500,000. The one for-

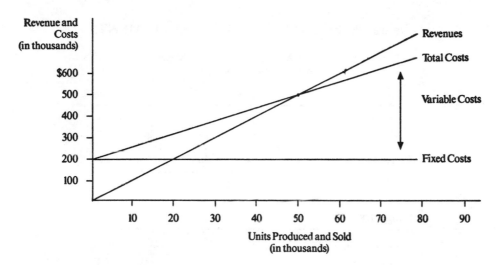

Figure 3-4. Break-even point.

mula serves as a good check for the other in a more complex calculation. Figure 3-4 shows the break-even point in dollars and in units.

Break-even Given a Desired Profit Level

$$N = \frac{F + \pi}{P - V}$$

$$= \frac{200,000 + 50,000}{\$10 - \$6} = 62,500 \text{ units}$$

This says that for the firm to generate a profit of $50K on this particular venture, it must sell 62.5K units.

Sources and Uses of Funds

A sources and uses statement shows where funds came from and how they were used and depicts the interrelationships among uses and sources. A sources and uses statement is most helpful in showing trends and demonstrating what is happening to the various components on the balance sheet year to year. It is also helpful in projecting for future plans for the company.

Figure 3-5. SOURCES AND USES STATEMENT.

SOURCES AND USES STATEMENT
SOUR GRAPES, INC.

Assets	1984	1985	Source	Use
Cash	10	15		5
Accounts Receivable	20	15	5	
Fixed Assets	30	40		10
Total	60	70		
Liabilities				
Accounts Payable	10	20	10	
Notes Payable	15	5		10
Common Stock	25	30	5	
Retained Earnings	10	15	5	
Total	60	70		
Balance			25	25

How to decide what is a source and what is a use is listed below:

Source of Funds:
> Decrease in assets
> Increase in liabilities

Use of Funds:
> Increase in assets
> Decrease in liabilities

A very simple example may help. Figure 3-5 shows a sources and uses statement for Sour Grapes, Inc. The first entry (cash) shows an increase from 1984 to 1985. This increase in an asset is entered in the Use column. Accounts receivable shows a decrease, so this is entered in the Source column, and so on. Note that the totals of the two columns should balance.

Present and Future Value

As any business person knows, time is money. The two formulas presented in this section determine the present or future value of an amount of money. A certain amount of money invested today at a certain rate of return will be worth so much at some point in the future. That is its future value. On the other hand, a promised future payment is equivalent to some quantity of today's dollars invested for a given period and interest rate. That is the present value of the future payment.

The present value and future value analyses are extremely important in evaluating investment proposals. Because the financial impact of a decision made today may not be fully realized for several years, there needs to be a vehicle for equating everything to "now" for the sake of evaluating the costs or benefits of alternative courses of action. Present value and future value analysis is a quantitative means for doing that.

The factors used in the formulas are

FV = future value

PV = present value

r = interest rate

n = number of periods (years, months, etc.)

Future Value

$$FV = PV(1 + r)^n$$

EXAMPLE

A person is considering investing $1,000 at 12% interest for 3 years. What will it be worth at the end of that time?

$$FV = 1000(1 + .12)^3 = \$1404.93$$

In 3 years the investment would be worth $1404.93.

Present Value

$$PV = FV \frac{1}{(1 + r)^n}$$

EXAMPLE

You are expecting to receive $1,000 in 3 years and your capitalization rate is 12%. What is the present value of that future payment?

$$PV = 1000 \frac{1}{(1 + .12)^3} = \$711.78$$

Therefore the future payment is equivalent to $711.78 in your hands today.

Annuities

An annuity is a series of payments. The amount is fixed and the number of years is specified. In these formulas, A is the amount of each payment, and other terms are as defined above.

Future Value of an Annuity

$$FV_A = A \frac{(1 + r)^n - 1}{r}$$

EXAMPLE

What is the future value of $100 annual payment for 7 years invested at 12%?

$$FV_A = 100 \frac{(1 + .12)^7 - 1}{.12} = \$1,008.90$$

In other words, if a person invests $100 annually and can earn 12% interest on the money, then at the end of the seventh year, the value of that investment is $1,008.90.

Present Value of an Annuity

$$PV_A = A \frac{1 - \dfrac{1}{(1 + r)^n}}{r}$$

EXAMPLE

You are offered a choice of getting $460 today or $100 annually for 7 years. Either amount will be invested at 12%. Which should you choose?

$$PV_A = 100 \; \frac{1 - \dfrac{1}{(1 + .12)^7}}{.12} = \$456.38$$

Therefore, you will be ahead approximately $4 by taking the $460 today.

Mortgage Payments

The most familiar form of annuity is our beloved mortgage payment. To show how this fits into the annuity formula, we'll use a simple example:

EXAMPLE

PV (value of the loan) = $120,000
r (annual percentage rate of loan) = 12%
n (number of years for loan) = 30
A (annual payment) = ?

$$PV_A = A \; \frac{1 - \dfrac{1}{(1 + r)^n}}{r}$$

$$\$120,000 = A \; \frac{1 - \dfrac{1}{(1 + .12)^{30}}}{.12}$$

$$A = \$14,897 \text{ per year}$$

To determine the monthly payment, use the same equation, but divide the interest rate by 12 and multiply the number of years by 12:

$$120,000 = A \; \frac{1 - \dfrac{1}{(1 + .01)^{360}}}{.01}$$

$$A = \$1,234.33 \text{ per month}$$

So, the mortgage payment would be $1,234.33 per month or $14,897 per year. Since banks calculate annuities in monthly terms, the $1,234.33 monthly payment would apply.

Gradually Increasing Payments

To take this type of analysis one step further, assume the annual payment is increasing at an established rate (which will often happen with an investment). The present and future values will be calculated as follows, using g to represent the rate of growth of the payment:

Future Value of an Increasing Annuity

$$FV = \left[\frac{(1 + r)^n - (1 + g)^n}{r - g}\right] A \quad \text{for } r \neq g$$

EXAMPLE

A (initial payment) = $100
r (interest rate) = 12%
g (growth rate) = 10% 10%
n (number of years) = 25

$$FV = \left[\frac{(1 + .12)^{25} - (1 + .1)^{25}}{.12 - .10}\right] \$100$$
$$= \$30,826.47$$

We start investing $100 a year. Each year we increase the investment by 10%, and we earn 12% interest on our money. At the end of 25 years we have $30,826 in the account.

Present Value of an Increasing Annuity

$$PV = \left[\frac{1 - \left(\frac{1 + g}{1 + r}\right)^n}{r - g}\right] A \quad \text{for } r \neq g$$

EXAMPLE

A = $100
r = 12%

54   THE MBA TOOLKIT

$g = 10\%$

$n = 25$ years

$$PV = \left[\frac{1 - \left(\frac{1 + .1}{1 + .12} \right)^{25}}{.12 - .10} \right] \$100$$

$$= \$1,813$$

This calculation shows that the investment that yields $30,826 in 30 years is only worth $1,813 in today's dollars. Although that seems a bit shocking, the 12% interest rate and 10% growth rate are what makes the large sum seem so insignificant in today's terms.

Though this example points out the usefulness of present and future value analyses, you may still be thinking, so what? So now we'll run through a practical PV/FV analysis that packs a little more punch.

EXAMPLE

A man 36 years old is interested in planning for retirement. He has $120,000 net worth, half of which is available for retirement investment. He is currently earning $45,000, an amount growing at 10% annually. Inflation is expected at a 6% level for the future. He would like to have the equivalent of $25,000 in today's terms (net of social security) for each year after his retirement. What percentage of income should this man be saving each year? Assume the man will live to age 85, so he needs 20 years of $25,000 a year.

To restate:

- $60,000 available for retirement (half his net worth)
- 29 years from now, retirement payments should start
- $25,000 desired (in present dollars) for 20 years

1. First we calculate how much $25,000 will be worth in 29 years:

   $FV = \$25,000$ @ 6% inflation in 29 years

   $= 25,000(1 + .06)^{29}$

   $= \$135,460$

   Therefore, the annuity amount he will need at retirement to yield $25,000 in present terms is $135,460.

2. Given that he needs an annuity of $135,460 to have $25,000 in present terms, and he needs it for 20 years (age 65 to 85), we can calculate the

total amount he will need to invest today. We use the formula for calculating the present value of a future annuity with a growth (inflation) rate $g = 6\%$ and the interest rate $= 10\%$:

$$PV = A \left[\frac{1 - \left(\frac{1 + g}{1 + r}\right)^n}{r - g} \right]$$

$$= 135,460 \left[\frac{1 - \left(\frac{1.06}{1.1}\right)^{20}}{.04} \right]$$

$$= 135,460 \times 13.082 = \$1,772,087$$

So in 29 years this poor bounder will need a total of $1,772,087 to enable him to have $25,000 (in today's terms) per year for 20 years.

3. He now has $60,000 to invest at 10% for 29 years. We'll see how much that will be worth by using future value analysis.

$$FV = 60,000(1 + .10)^{29} = \$951,786$$

In other words, if he takes his $60 thousand and slaps it into an investment that yields him 10% annually, he'll have $952,000 in 29 years. Subtracting $951,786 from $1,772,087 = $820,301 or the additional amount he needs to generate by saving now.

4. So, now we calculate how much he needs to start saving each year to have the additional $820,301:

$$FV = \left[\frac{(1 + r)^n - (1 + g)^n}{r - g} \right] A$$

$$= \left[\frac{(1.1)^{29} - (1.06)^{29}}{(1.1 - 1.06)} \right] A$$

$$= \left(\frac{10.44}{.04} \right) A$$

$$= (261.12)A$$

The 261.12 is called the "annuity factor." Solving for A:

$$A = \frac{\$820,301}{261.12} = \$3142 \text{ a year or } 7\% \text{ of his } \$45,000 \text{ income}$$

The bottom line is that in order for this fellow to have a comfortable retirement nest egg of $25,000 a year (in today's terms) for 20 years, he needs to invest the $60,000 of his net worth at 10%. Plus he needs to put away 7% of his income (which is growing at 10% annually) each year.

The above example, although a bit complex, shows the potential of PV/FV analysis. In these times of high inflation and growth expectations, any analysis without some type of PV/FV considerations is fundamentally flawed.

Capital Budgeting

Capital budgeting is the process by which a firm evaluates expenditures against predicted revenue to establish investment policy and planning. In other words, capital budgeting is the jargon used for analysis of investment proposals. Three methods of capital budgeting are shown below: the payback method, net present value, and internal rate of return.

Payback Method

The payback method determines the number of years (or time periods) it takes to recover the original investment.

EXAMPLE

Original Investment: $10,000.

Year	Project A Cash Flow		Project B Cash Flow	
	Annual	Cumulative	Annual	Cumulative
1	$1,000	$ 1,000	$ 500	$ 500
2	1,500	2,500	1,000	1,500
3	2,000	4,500	1,500	3,000
4	2,500	7,000	2,000	5,000
5	3,000	10,000	2,500	7,500
6	2,000	12,000	3,000	10,500
7	1,500	13,500	4,000	14,500
8	1,500	15,000	5,000	19,500
Payback Period:	5 years		6 years	

At the end of year 5, Project A has reached the payback of $10,000 while B reaches the point somewhere just prior to the end of year 6. If the firm follows a strict payback policy, then it would choose A, due to its shorter payback period.

This is a simplistic example of the payback method, but it does highlight the two major flaws of this method: (1) The failure to account for cash flow amounts after the payback period has been reached, and (2) the failure to account for the time value of money in analyzing investments. Despite its flaws, many businesses still use this method.

Net Present Value

The net present value method of capital budgeting has more salience in both the classroom and the boardroom. In this analysis, the future payments to be derived from the investment are discounted back to today's value.

$$NPV = \left[\frac{R_1}{(1 + k)^1} + \frac{R_2}{(1 + k)^2} + \cdots \frac{R_n}{(1 + k)^n} \right] - C$$

where

R = annual cash flow
k = marginal cost of capital
C = initial outlay
NPV = Net Present Value

Now we'll look at an example where the NPV method is used to evaluate two investment proposals.

EXAMPLE

As CEO of Sour Grapes, Inc., you are faced with two very attractive investment proposals. Project A is a kumquat juice stand in a mall in San Luis Obispo. Project B is an automatic pineapple dispenser to be located on the campus of a Polynesian business school. Both projects require $10,000 investment.

Another method often used to compute the present values is to invert the marginal cost multiplier (or what is called the present value factor). Thus $1/(1 + .1)^1 = .91$. The cash flows can then be depicted in tabular form as shown in the accompanying tables.

PROJECT A: JUICE STAND

Year	Net Cash Flow	10% PV Factor	PV of Cash Flow
1	$ 2,000	.91	$ 1,820
2	3,000	.83	2,490
3	3,000	.75	2,250
4	4,000	.68	2,720
5	4,000	.62	2,480
6	4,000	.56	2,240
Total Cash	$20,000		
PV of Cash Flows			$14,000
Minus Initial Cost			− 10,000
NPV			=$ 4,000

PROJECT B: PINEAPPLE DISPENSER

Year	Net Cash Flow	10% PV Factor	PV of Cash Flow
1	$ 500	.91	$ 455
2	1,000	.83	830
3	3,000	.75	2,250
4	5,000	.68	3,400
5	5,500	.62	3,410
6	6,000	.56	3,360
Total Cash	$21,000		
PV of Cash Flows			$13,705
Minus Initial Cost			−10,000
NPV			$ 3,705

As the analysis shows, the kumquat juice stand yields the highest NPV even though the pineapple dispenser has a higher accumulated cash flow.

Internal Rate of Return

The internal rate of return (IRR) is that interest rate that equates the present value of future cash flows with the initial cash outlay.

The easiest way (and the *only* way in our opinion) to calculate this measure is to first punch the initial cost outlay in your HP or TI calculator. You can then knock out the cash flows, hit the IRR button and *whamo!*— "one small step for man." In case you are the masochistic type, or you have the kind of boss who shuddered when slide rules and wire radios were replaced, here is the formula for IRR.

$$\frac{R_1}{(1 + r)^1} + \frac{R_2}{(1 + r)^2} + \cdots + \frac{R_n}{(1 + r)^n} - C = 0$$

or

$$\sum_{n=1} \frac{R_n}{(1 + r)^n} - C = 0$$

where

R = future cash flow
C = original investment
n = number of time periods
r = rate

EXAMPLE

Your firm has decided to invest in a machine that manufactures fluorescent orange ping-pong balls. The machine will cost $15,000, but will derive the following cash flows:

ORIGINAL INVESTMENT: $15,000.

Year	Cash Flow	Year	Cash Flow
1	$ 2,500	5	$ 3,000
2	3,000	6	3,000
3	3,000	7	3,500
4	2,500	8	4,000

Plugging these numbers into the formula, we have:

$$\frac{2500}{(1 + r)^1} + \frac{3000}{(1 + r)^2} + \frac{3000}{(1 + r)^3} + \frac{2500}{(1 + r)^4} + \cdots - \$15,000 = 0$$

Solving for r, the IRR = 11.6%

The IRR is a great analytic tool. It is especially helpful in determining if investment proposals meet the hurdle rate (minimum rate of return) established by company policy.

Cost of Capital

This catchy alliteration is a phrase you will hear more often than your own name in business. Cost of capital is the interest charge a firm pays for the utilization of money. The cost of capital is also referred to as the "weighted average cost of capital" (WACC). Since most of the externally obtained capital can be classified into equity capital, and debt, the cost of capital weights each component proportionally in calculating the overall cost, or the WACC.

The following sections explore some of the basic and more complex measures used to calculate the cost of capital.

Basic Cost of Capital (WACC)

The basic after tax cost of capital formula is:

$$WACC = (1 - t)i\theta + (1 - \theta)k$$

where
$t =$ tax rate
$i =$ cost of debt (before taxes)
$\theta =$ debt ratio
$k =$ cost of equity

In simpler terms, the WACC takes the debt portion of the equation and accounts for tax ramifications. Debt is tax deductible (just like the interest portion of a home mortgage) and is thus reduced by the tax variable. The formula then adds the equity portion to the total cost.

EXAMPLE
A firm's capital structure consists of:

$.40 =$ debt (θ),
$.60 =$ equity $(1 - \theta)$
$.50 =$ tax rate (t)
$.10 =$ debt cost (i) (bonds for example)
$.15 =$ cost of equity (k) (market return)

This firm's after-tax cost of capital can be calculated as follows:

$$(1 - .5)(.1 \times .4) + (1 - .4).15 = .11 \text{ or } 11\%$$

So when we take the weighted average of this firm's cost of money, we see that this firm pays 11% for its money. Not too bad.

As stated earlier, the reason for multiplying the debt cost by $(1 - \text{tax rate})$ is that debt payments are tax deductible. This is the reason why debt financing is so attractive, albeit a contributor to a firm's risk.

Cost of Equity Capital (k or k_e)

The most important and the most imprecise portion of the cost of capital equation is the equity cost. Times existed when the business student or analyst could plug in 15% for a k figure. But with the kind of fluctuations that we've seen in the money and capital markets recently, a more detailed evaluation is necessary.

Gordon's Model

Gordon's model* is an oft-used approach for deriving the cost of a firm's equity. The formula is:

$$k_e = \frac{D_o(1 + g)}{P_o} + g$$

where

D_o = dividends at period zero (now)
P_o = price of the stock at period zero
g = growth rate of the dividends (the growth rate in earnings per share can also be used)

EXAMPLE

Dividends = 4.39
Growth in dividends = .022
Current stock price = $36.5

$$k_e = \frac{4.39(1.022)}{36.5} + .022 = .145 \text{ or } 14.5\%$$

---

* Gordon, M., "The Savings, Investment and Valuation of a Corporation," *Review of Economics and Statistics,* February 1962, pp. 37–51.

This model is somewhat simplistic because it assumes a constant growth rate in dividends, which is rare. There are also some noticeable conflicts between earnings growth and dividend growth associated with the model. Nevertheless, it is a good basic approach.

Earnings/Price Calculation
An even easier method for calculating k_e is to invert the price/earnings ratio. This is a rather quick and dirty approach, but it can serve for rough approximations.

EXAMPLE

Current earnings per share (net income ÷ no. of outstanding common shares) = $4.9

Current stock price = $36.5

k_e = 4.9/36.5 = .134 or 13.4%

Capital Asset Pricing Model (CAPM)
The CAPM is another way to calculate k_e. It requires a knowledge of current financial and market conditions. The formula is:

$$\text{CAPM} = k_e = R_f + \beta (R_m - R_f)$$

where

R_f = risk-free rate
R_m = market rate
β = the firm's beta coefficient

Risk-free rate: Several rates can be used, but a common one is the rate for Government Treasury Bonds.

Market rate: Again many options are possible, but one way to calculate the market rate of return is to use the Ibbotson and Sinquefield historical return over 25 years and add the inflation rate. Ibbotson and Sinquefield* calculated the real return on stocks over the period from 1926 to 1982 to be 8.5%. For the inflation rate, take Moody's AA Corporate Bond Yield for this week and subtract the 4.4% historical *real interest* yield on corporate bonds (again according to the Ibbotson and Sinquefield data),

---

* Ibbotson, Roger G., and Sinquefield, Rex A., *Stocks, Bonds, Bills and Inflation: The Past and the Future,* 1982 ed., Financial Analyst Research Foundation, Charlottesville, VA.

and you have a usable inflation measure. Add the inflation rate to Ibbotson and Sinquefield's .085 to get R_m.

For example, say Moody's AA Corporate Bonds Yield for the week ending June 31 is 10.5%. Subtracting the 4.4% *real* interest yield gives an *inflation rate* of 6.1%. Therefore

$$R_m = 8.5\% \text{ real yield} + 6.1\% \text{ inflation factor}$$
$$= 14.6\%$$

Or you can just take Ibbotson and Sinquefield's .085 and add the current inflation number quoted in the papers. (Or you can just throw everything to the wind and use 15%.)

Beta Coefficient: The beta coefficient, β, is a measure of the covariance of a firm's stock with the market. In other words, it indicates how an individual firm's stock moves relative to what the market is doing. When we say "market", we are referring to the stock market. Two gauges that are often used as representative of the "market" are the Dow Jones Industrials and the Standard and Poor's 500.

The "Dow" is comprised of 30 large industrial firms (e.g., General Motors, IBM) whose market movement is taken and averaged each business day. This is the number quoted as the Dow Jones Industrial Average, which falls or rises so many points each day. These are all blue chip firms regarded as quite consistent and conservative (in terms of risk) market performers.

The S&P 500 takes in more firms and is considered by some to be more representative of market swings than the Dow, because of its broader base and increased diversity.

Beta represents how a firm's market valuation can be expected to move, vis à vis such gauges as the Dow or S&P 500. For example, if a firm has a beta of 1.5, that firm's stock would be expected to both rise (and fall) at a rate of 1.5 times the market. Obviously, the stock is more volatile than the market in general, and hence more risky. More risk means that the firm must then generate a greater return for the stockholders. The firm's cost of equity (k_e) will thus be higher than the market in general.

The fact that it incorporates market volatility and risk in the beta is one of the great analytical strengths of the CAPM. The model factors the market rate by a risk/return multiplier (beta) for the individual firm.

The firm's beta is calculated through a complex analysis. Basically, however, the measure is largely determined by its portfolio of assets and/or investments. This "portfolio" takes into account the risk of each individual asset or investment as well as the diversification between these elements. If the portfolio is widely diversified in such a fashion that the risk of losses in one investment (or division) is offset by potential gains in another segment, then the beta is more likely to be close to 1.0, signifying very little variation from the overall market.

EXAMPLE

Going back to our CAPM equation, we can now plug in all the variables. For our example, we will use a risk-free rate (R_f) of 8.5%, using a hypothetical T-bill rate. We will assume that the beta for our firm is 1.5, and market rate (R_m) = 14.6%. So, plugging in the variables, we have:

$$CAPM = k_e = .085 + 1.5(.146 - .085) = .1765 \text{ or } 17.7\%$$

Therefore, even though the market return is 14.6%, this firm (because of its high beta, or higher perceived risk) requires a return of 17.7% to attract investor's funds.

There are some weak points to the CAPM as a measure for evaluating the cost of equity. One of the major faults is the reliance on the beta coefficient. As the equation demonstrates, the beta is a large determinant of the firm's k_e, but market covariance is not the only factor in determining a firm's equity cost. Other aspects, such as firm size, liquidity, ongoing profits, the industry within which it operates, and general market trends, may prove even more valuable in evaluating a firm's position for required return, yet they may not be fully reflected in the beta.

Therefore one needs to exercise caution in using the CAPM. The other factors listed above must be taken into consideration and incorporated into the overall equation.

The astute financial analyst will use several methods and formulas to piece together an entire picture. Concentrated focus on any single measurement can be misleading and even inaccurate.

Cost of Debt

One important distinction in evaluating the cost of debt is the difference between *market value* and *book value*. *Book value* is an inaccurate measure because it measures historical costs; nonetheless it is commonly used in business. To find the book value cost of debt, find the firm's debt structure listed in Moody's or an annual report. Take each component of debt and multiply its interest cost times the percentage weight.

EXAMPLE

Debt Instrument	$ Value	% Total Debt
Sf deb 9s due 2000 (9%)*	$ 100,000	10
8% Mortgage bonds	500,000	50
6% Pollution bonds	400,000	40
Total Debt	$1,000,000	100

$$\text{Book Value Cost of Debt} = .1(.09) + .5(.08) + .4(.06)$$
$$= .073$$

*Sinking fund debentures bearing 9% interest; face value due in the year 2000.

Market value cost of debt is more indicative of actual debt cost because it measures what the debt would cost on the market today and, therefore, the cost to refinance that debt. To find this equation, the same percentage of total debt figures are used as above, but these percentages are multiplied by the current market rates for each debt instrument instead of by the book value rates.

EXAMPLE

Debt Instrument	% Total Debt	Current Market Rate
Sf deb (A-rated corporate bonds)	.10	.12
Mortgage bonds	.50	.105
Pollution bonds	.40	.0825

$$\text{Market Value Cost of Debt} = .1(.12) + .5(.105) + .4(.0825)$$
$$= .0975$$

As these examples show, under inflationary times the book value cost of debt can be unrealistically low. The market value method is also called the "marginal cost of debt" because it measures what one dollar more of debt would cost.

WACC usually utilizes the *marginal* cost of debt, because a firm is interested in knowing what rate it would pay to either maintain the current debt levels or increase them.

Bonds

In the wild and wonderful world of bonds, there are a few key areas to note: current yield, yield to maturity, bond valuation, and convertibility.

Current Yield

$$\text{Current Yield} = \frac{\text{Interest Payment}}{\text{Market Price at Bond}}$$

$$= \frac{\text{Interest}}{\text{Price}}$$

EXAMPLE

A series of 9s for 2000 (which means 9% bonds maturing in year 2000) is currently selling for $950. Note: A bond's par or face value is always $1000.

$$\text{Current Yield} = \frac{9\% \times 1000}{950} = \frac{90}{950} = 9.47\%$$

Yield to Maturity

The pre-tax yield to maturity (YTM) is basically the IRR of a bond, and it is an approximate formula for generating the bond's rate of return. See the section on IRR on page 60.

$$\text{YTM} = \frac{C + (1000 - V)/n}{\dfrac{1000 + V}{2}}$$

where

$C =$ coupon rate (the interest rate payment on the bond)
$V =$ value of the bond (selling price)
$n =$ year to maturity

EXAMPLE

A series of 8s for 1995 selling in 1984 for $900.

$$\frac{80 + (1000 - 900)/11}{\dfrac{1000 + 900}{2}} = 9.38\%$$

Bond Valuation

The formula for bond valuation is

$$V = \frac{I}{(1 + r)} + \frac{I}{(1 + r)^2} + \cdots \frac{I}{(1 + r)^n} + \frac{P}{(1 + r)^n}$$

where

I = interest rate of bond (coupon rate)
r = discount rate, or rate used to equate future cash flows to the present
p = price at which bond is sold, or maturity value
n = number of time periods

Examination of the formula shows that there are two components of bond value evaluation:

1. The present value of all future interest payments.
2. The present value of the maturity value or face value of the bond, i.e., the price at which the bond will be sold.

Convertibility

One item that is discussed a great deal in reference to bonds is their convertibility to common shares. Some relevant terms follow:

$$\text{Conversion Price} = \frac{\text{Par Value of Bond}}{\text{No. of Shares Received upon Conversion}}$$

$$\text{Conversion Value} = (\text{No. of Shares Received on Conversion}) \times (\text{Market Value per Share of Stock})$$

$$\text{Conversion Parity Price} = \frac{\text{Market Price of Convertible Bond}}{\text{No. of Shares Received upon Conversion}}$$

4

Marketing

Marketing marks where business retreats a bit from the strict discipline of the quantitative and enters the flexibility of the qualitative. If accounting is a rule book, then marketing is a science fiction novel—a creative perspective of the future with enough facts blended in to give the story credibility.

Modern marketing developed upon the realization that a product that people wanted generally sold better than one they didn't. Marketing research emerged as an effective tool to gauge a product's potential in the marketplace.

But marketers soon realized that only so many needs existed. Undaunted, marketers undertook a new approach: creating needs for those products we didn't need or want before. There was a time when people thought they only needed plain soap to be clean; now people buy hand soaps, deodorant soaps, skin cream non-soaps, liquid body soaps, liquid hand soaps, plus dish detergents, clothes detergents, fabric softeners, floor soaps, shampoos for dandruff, shampoos for bounce, cream rinses for body, deodorants for smelling nice, deodorants for not smelling at all. Just because people wanted to be clean.

As a result, marketing has come full circle, from asking "Can we make it and sell it?" to asking "What does the customer want?" back to "Can we sell it?" again.

In fact, marketing synthesizes many of the quantitative methodologies of other business disciplines, notably finance and statistics. For all the marketing planning and strategies that may be developed for a venture, marketers nonetheless realize that they do not exist in a corporate vacuum. They must concern themselves with the company's profit/loss posture. As a result, they need to weigh opportunities to determine which venture maximizes the target customers' needs and the corporate return on investment.

This chapter presents brief discussions of issues that should be considered under the following aspects of marketing:

Market share

Segmentation

Product life cycle

Distribution

Strategic planning

Pricing

It also provides these marketing-related formulas and processes:

Break-even analysis

Capital budgeting methods

Marginal cost and marginal revenue

Competitive bidding evaluation

Relative sales performance

Sales force size

For further reference, we suggest a valuable yet out-of-print publication from the American Marketing Association's Committee of Definitions, entitled *Marketing Definitions: A Glossary of Marketing Terms*. The small publication is on file with the AMA library in Chicago.

Market Share

Definition: A company's sales divided by its industry's sales.

Growth and Decline

More important than knowing the market share alone is knowing its dynamic aspects (directional trend over recent and longer-term history) and how the share compares to competition. An endless list of factors will determine the direction in market share: all aspects of the marketing mix controlled by you, those same elements controlled by your competitors, and the largely uncontrollable, external factors such as societal attitudes and current events. What follows are questions you should address as you investigate the elements of the mix (pricing, distribution, advertising/promotion, and product).

Pricing

Market share combined with the position of your product on the product life cycle both affect the cost of manufacturing and the price you can ask. The learning curve and economies of scale phenomena—should the product be in small, early production stages—will probably keep your price above a level at which you can experience growth in share. And at higher production levels, you can enjoy the spoils of more efficient production and cheaper per unit costs, putting your price at or below competition.

High prices usually mean a decrease in share; likewise low prices usually mean an increase in share. But what effect would a decrease in price have on the financial stability of the product? Would an increase in price improve the profitability despite a decrease in share? How would competitors strategically respond to such actions?

Distribution

What channels of distribution currently handle your product? Why? Are those the best, in terms of cost and effectiveness? What other channels could be opened economically that would increase market share? Are there any channels of distribution that are providing little help to your market share?

Advertising and Promotion

When times are tight, often the first area to feel the budgetary grinder is the advertising budget. In other words, budget slicers reason, "Gosh, we aren't selling enough of our product. We'll just have to tell fewer people about it." But advertising and promotional programs *do* tend to be misdirected, carrying The Message to a larger-than-necessary audience. Thus, these questions should be asked: Are you reaching the right audience with your promotional efforts? Does your advertising efficiently hit your targets? If you have identified new target markets to expand share, where are they and how can you communicate to them?

Product

The product itself has the most obvious effect on market share. Grossly oversimplified, if it is a "good" product, share goes up; if it is a "bad" product, share is low. But your product is not sold in a vacuum—the dynamics of the marketplace and of your overall strategies can kill a "good" product, and even save a "bad" one. Where your product is on the cycle of introduction-growth-maturity-decline will give you direction in determining how effective your strategies may be and how the market might be expected to act. The growth/share matrix, a four-celled box cross-tabulating high- and low-growth with high- and low-share, offers varying strategies for each cell. See discussions of "Product Life Cycle" (page 75) and "Strategic Planning" (page 83).

Competition

Your competitors must be identified not only in the most specific, literal terms, but also in the most general, broad terms. Not fully identifying competition can lead to myopic market planning. How do these changes in perspective affect an identification of market share? If you contend that the product is innovative, are there any products that may compete? Do those products give you opportunities to differentiate your offering so as to maximize share? What strategies have competitors taken that have resulted in their products' direction of share? Are those strategies deserving of a competitive response? Have their actions netted a perceptual shift in the industry segmentation and positioning?

Brand Loyalty

Although high market share does not necessarily mean high brand loyalty, if a firm can maintain market share prominence, the chances are reasonably good that a solid core group of brand-loyal customers will emerge. What faction of brand-loyal consumers does your product now enjoy? What makes them loyal? How solidly does your product fulfill the need that makes them loyal? Can you build on that strength to add to loyalty? If you made product adjustments, how would your brand-loyal consumers react? Assuming they react negatively, will you net out a gain or a loss in the short term by losing some old, loyal consumers and gaining new, uncommitted buyers? In the long term? How much of your promotional budget can be trimmed without trimming that loyal base? Or do your promotional and advertising programs provide those buyers a needed reassurance? Would a cost cut that would lead to a lower product price give you, on balance, a market share increase in the short term? In the long term?

Segmentation

Definition: Breaking up the marketplace into groups (defined by demographics, needs, wants, tastes, and attitudes), in order to target a product or service efficiently at those segments who desire it most.

Pros and Cons

The entire concept of segmentation unfolds around the notion that buyers are different—not exactly a profound observation. The purposes of segmentation are two-fold:

1. Initially, to generate purchase of the product.
2. Ultimately, to increase consumer satisfaction, so you generate loyalty to your product and enjoy repeat purchasing behavior.

In most cases, clear-cut market segments can be identified. But whether segmentation will provide a useful perspective for more efficient marketing of a product needs to be investigated. Segmentation, despite its promise to increase efficiency, also promises to increase marketing costs as product variations are created for different segments and as research is conducted to identify, isolate, and monitor appropriate segments. Will segmentation tell you anything you don't already know? For instance, panty hose manufacturers don't need to know that their chief consumers are women and bank robbers. But at the same time, segmentation has helped those same manufacturers target specific shades, sizes and styles to segments of the women's market. Bank robbers are less particular.

By undertaking segmentation, what do you hope to learn? Are you trying to identify market segments where you can get the best response for your efforts, or to answer specific hypotheses about communicating or improving your product line? Or are you merely shaking the trees hoping something falls out?

Bases for Segmentation

Consumers can be grouped using two primary methods, one much simpler and less expensive than the other. The first, and simpler, is *demographic segmentation,* or grouping by easily identifiable attributes such as age, sex, income, occupation, race, region, zip code, education, or household size. Consumers will, on most of these issues, volunteer such "classification" information freely in a marketing research interview or questionnaire. And a simple cross-tabulation of these attributes by preference for your product will yield a pretty simple, inexpensive batch of data.

The second is *psychographic segmentation,* a method that incorporates an endless list of processes and issues for grouping. Psychographics measure consumers' interests, values, life styles, activities, and opinions, and group the consumers based on those attributes. To so classify consumers requires in-depth questioning; their responses are grouped and segmented usually via statistical processes of factor analysis and cluster analysis. The difficulty in gathering and analyzing psychographic data means time, and time means money. And money means few companies attempt such segmentation.

Brand Loyalty and Heavy Users

Segmentation can identify the heaviest user group of your product. Like the economist Pareto's principle, 80% of your product may sell to 20% of its market. To identify and target marketing efforts to this group is to keep the bread-and-butter segment of the market in secure hands: it is a group you cannot afford to lose. Who are they demographically? Psychographically? What makes them loyal? How should your marketing plans be tailored to reach and hold them?

Product Benefit Segmentation

Conducting marketing research not only can identify the segments that make up the marketplace, but can also determine product needs for each segment. From that information, you can determine where your product successfully fulfills consumers' needs, and where other consumers' needs go unfulfilled. Can your product be expanded—or can a new product be developed—to reach those unsatisfied consumer needs?

Product Life Cycle

Definition: The theory that the sales behavior of products pass through four stages: introduction, growth, maturity, and decline.

It is often debated whether products have life cycles or not. Some products, of course, seem to have lives of their own. But the product life cycle, in its most widely accepted state, has the four stages mentioned in the definition: introduction, growth, maturity, and decline. Each offers special challenges for the marketer.

William M. Luther summarizes the product life cycle as shown in Table 4-1.

Table 4-1. MARKETING TACTICS DURING THE PRODUCT LIFE CYCLE.

Strategy	Introduction	Growth	Maturity	Decline
Market Share	Increase	Increase	Maintain	Maintain
Vertical integration	No	Yes*	Yes*	No
Market segmentation	No	Yes*	Yes*	No
Product line extension	No	Yes*	Yes*	No
Pricing	High	Competitive	Decrease	Low
Distribution	Build	Build	Maintain	Maintain
Cost efficiency	No	No	Yes	Yes
Annual product modifications	No	Yes*	Yes*	Maybe
Promotional expenditures	High	Highest	Low	None

*During late growth-early maturity.

Source: Luther, William M., *The Marketing Plan.* New York: AMACOM, 1982.

Introduction

Here, the new product has recently been developed and is now being offered to the unwitting public. Four variations on the "new product" theme are:

1. Pure innovation, or a new concept (for instance, robotics).
2. New process (electric toothbrush).
3. New to the company (retail stores offering financial services).
4. New model, or "improved" (most any brand of laundry detergent).

By the time a product hits the shelves, roughly six product development stages have been exhausted:

1. *Idea generation.* Ideas can come from internal research and development, consumers via marketing research, brainstorm sessions, sales force, top management, the Dead Sea Scrolls, virtually anywhere.

2. *Screening.* Ideas are sifted internally (managerial judgment) and/ or externally (marketing research).

3. *Economic analysis.* Finance, marketing, and operations will review market size, sales potential, cost structure, capital investment, strategic planning, break-even analysis, manufacturing processes, episodes of Wall Street Week, and anything else that can provide some economic color.

4. *Development.* The actual engineering and production development process turns the concept into a bona fide manufactured product.

5. *Test marketing.* It's wise to test the waters with your toe before you bathe. Investigate how successfully your product fulfills the needs of the market segments you are targeting. Many marketers consider this step optional, if not unnecessary. But those are the same marketers who seem to enjoy taking a bath.

6. *Actual public introduction.* Till the land, plant the seeds, and pray for rain.

During the early stages of the product's introduction, costs are high, market share struggling, and margin low. Advertising costs to launch the product and build awareness are a major proportional drain. Plus the inefficiency of early production costs, and the bill due and payable from R&D, all combine to create an enormous cash exodus. Have you been assured 100% support from all levels of management at the outset, when the product was merely a twinkle in its creator's eye?

Growth

In the growth stage, sales level of the product begins to establish itself. The public is aware of its virtues (and its flaws). Market share is built as distribution of the product expands. Ad expenses continue high as competition intensifies. Prices begin to fall, but margins are healthier due to learning curve, economies of scale, and reduction or cessation in development costs.

Prices are highly volatile in the growth stage, what with attempting to knock out the intense competition and solidify share of market. What would price cutting do to your share? Would it damage competition and build a larger share for your product? If so, would you still be sufficiently profitable? Or can your competition go fifteen rounds in a price fight, and ultimately take the title? What would increasing your advertising budget do to price competitiveness? To market share? What would trimming it do? How can you differentiate your product from competition to generate greater share? What distribution outlets is your competition using that you are not, and why? Are there new channels of distribution not yet used by your competition that are worth exploitation?

Maturity

The majority of products fall within the maturity stage. Your product's price and competitive prices have stabilized, and each competitive entry has fairly well solidified its market share or has disappeared from the marketplace altogether. Now your company moves to distinguish your product as greatly as possible from the fray of shake-out survivors. You have a few strategies available to you:

1. *Can you penetrate new demographic or psychographic segments?* The former might mean marketing your product in Europe, or targeting your efforts to appeal to a new age segment. The latter may require advertising so as to strike a new, broader range of consumer opinions or beliefs.

2. *What can be done to differentiate your product?* Give your product additional features ("now cleans *and* softens!"), or add a new twist, like selling motor oil in plastic, recloseable bottles.

3. *How can you recycle it?* Creative problem solving techniques may uncover a new, unexpected application for your product. The most famous and oft-cited example is baking soda as a refrigerator deodorant.

And Merlin Olson tells us that sending flowers is every bit as macho as Rosey Grier doing needlepoint.

Decline

All good things come to an end, even favorite toothpastes and frozen pizzas. Mercifully, all bad things come to an end, as well, and a bit quicker. The beginning of the end initiates this fourth stage, and funeral services usually conclude it. There are, however, a few death-bed strategies that may help pump some oomph into your product.

1. *Reentry.* In this scenario, you relaunch your product with some fanfare, hoping that the consumers you once had will return, and that some new consumers will be attracted. It's a tough assignment to take, and few succeed with it. It's expensive, and rarely are the returns worth the investment. But if your timing is right—perhaps both in getting into the market and in getting out—and if there is enough brand loyalty or nostalgia, you might generate a worthwhile return.

2. *Phase-out.* Darwin was a marketer. Your product is left in the marketplace to die a natural death (from either lack of consumer interest or replacement by superior new products). Do you want to extend life to the dying product by conducting just enough advertising and sales effort to maintain consumer awareness and to prolong consumer interest? Or would you rather let it die sooner, by cutting all marketing expenditures and reaping highest possible margins?

3. *Elimination, or product euthanasia.* Usually elimination is the easiest policy and the most cost-effective and least damaging to long-term reputations. But it is the most painful for the sentimental marketer. If you're having a tough time pulling the trigger, go reread "Old Yeller" for strength.

If your product is entering the "decline" stage, what plans do you have for new products that can replace the market share and profit that is abandoning the old one?

Resurrection, the Fifth Stage

Resurrection may be known by other names, or not at all, depending on whose books you read. This fifth stage is the rebirth of a product in a revised or reformed fashion, that had long ago met its demise. Examples:

• A famous weekly magazine, once recognized for its newsworthy photo essays, after several reclusive years returns as a features-in-photos monthly yet with its well-known look intact.

• A toy company reintroduces some of its early wooden toys, and sells them as "classics" editions with exorbitant prices.

• A personal products manufacturer revives the old-fashioned shaving cup, brush and lather, with advertising that communicates with one foot in the future and one foot firmly entrenched in nostalgia.

Why move backwards in product development? Why not? The past can provide, but does not guarantee, fertile ideas for the present and future. It's commonly recognized that trends come and go—but rarely do marketers see that that cycle can, under the right circumstances, continue. How can you control the timing of a declining product to allow for an adequate sabbatical and reprieve in the marketplace?

Distribution

Definition: The system that takes the product from the manufacturer to the customer.

Channels of Distribution

The "place" in the four marketing P's (price, place, product, and promotion) refers to the distribution channels, or marketing channels. The five basic elements for constructing your channel of distribution are:

1. Manufacturer
2. Broker
3. Wholesaler or jobber
4. Retailer
5. Consumer

You, as manufacturer, have a rather loose, autonomous, yet synergistic relationship with the wholesaler and retailer, as you all deal among yourselves to sell your product to the benefit of all parties, even the customer.

With these five key players, you can build any combination of channels appropriate to the distribution of your product. The most basic combinations are:

1. Manufacturer–Customer
2. Manufacturer–Retailer–Customer
3. Manufacturer–Wholesaler–Customer
4. Manufacturer–Wholesaler–Retailer–Customer
5. Manufacturer–Broker–Wholesaler–Retailer–Customer

Determining which strategy will serve you best depends upon an analysis of your marketing mix, as you decide which strategy yields the most efficient distribution of your product. A short channel may not necessarily result in least cost to you and most attractive cost to your customer, because efficiency stems from time factors, distance factors, the range of products you make, and the volume in which you manufacture them.

Extent of Distribution

As the channel and target audience are determined, you'll want also to judge how pervasive your distribution needs to be in order to reach the audience efficiently. You might categorize the extent to which you distribute your product into three areas:

1. *Intensive:* where distribution involves most or all outlets in a channel. Gum and razor blades will turn up at virtually every convenience store, supermarket, and drug store. Low-priced, high-frequency items typically are distributed intensively.

2. *Selective:* where distribution involves only certain outlets in a channel. Shopping goods, such as major appliances, furnishings, and brand-name men's and women's clothing, are ordinarily sold with selective distribution.

3. *Exclusive:* where distribution involves only one outlet in a specific territory, usually because of special facilities or sales/service training required by the nature of the product. New automobiles are marketed through exclusive distribution, where the territory is defined on a neighborhood scale.

Market, Product, and Channel Operations

These three broad areas will greatly affect your distribution decision. The following questions and observations relate to those areas.

The Market: Who are your buyers, and where are they? Where will they expect to find your product? What is the historically accepted channel of distribution for your product or its genre? What are your competitors doing—and does it make sense? How can you reach your customers: are they clustered in one or a few locations or are they fairly well dispersed through the population? How frequently will your customers purchase your product? If purchase is frequent and/or in small volumes per purchase (e.g., grocery items), you will want to sell through middlemen. Large volume and/or infrequent purchases might be handled sufficiently by you, the manufacturer.

The Product: Does your product stand alone, or is it part of a larger product line? Middlemen may be just right for a lone product, or for products in a wide line—but less appropriate if you have a deep product line. What is the physical makeup of the product? Is it large or bulky and require any sort of special handling or inventory demands? Does it have a short shelf life because of perishability? Because of fads or fashions? How much will your product cost per unit? The higher the price, the more appropriate selective distribution becomes. Is your product technical or innovative? Does its technical complexity or its innovativeness mean you will need to deal with middlemen in order to communicate your product and educate your customer most efficiently?

Does your product have a base of brand-loyal consumers? If so, distribution will be easier to attain in an intensive strategy, as a variety of channels clamor to have a piece of your action. On what scale will your product be promoted? Will you implement a "push" strategy, where your sales representatives and promotion programs encourage channel members to sell your product through to the customer? Or a "pull" strategy, where promotional efforts prod the customer to demand your product, thereby pulling it through the distribution channel?

Distribution Channel Operations: Do you offer service contracts or warranties with your product? If so, who is going to handle them for you? Or will you service your customers yourself, as manufacturer? In your promotional efforts, will you be the only member of the distribution channel promoting your product? Would it be cost-effective to offer other channel members cooperative advertising allowances, in which you share promotional costs and messages with them? Would carrying your product create a financial burden on channel members? If yes, can you afford to assist them in the financing necessary to place your product in their inventories?

Wholesale vs. Retail

It's been noted above that making use of the direct manufacturer–customer channel of distribution is most sensible when customers are few, orders are infrequent, and order sizes are great. Fact is, when you're dealing with consumers-at-large, consumers are large in numbers but small in orders. Trying to reach consumers by taking your product directly to them, or by coaxing them to travel to your manufacturing facility, is as unrealistic as farmers driving to the nearest Sears outlet and driving home in a new combine. Middlemen earn their keep by efficiently taking your goods to the masses.

Therefore, you must decide between taking your products to the wholesale or retail market. What is your line assortment? That is, what are the width and depth of your line? If you have a wide line (e.g., a broad range of home appliances), taking your products to retail may be wise, whereas a narrow line would not be worth the effort. Deep lines (e.g., several models and variations of a particular appliance) also invite manufacturer-to-retail distribution, though in a more selective fashion, as you educate the consumer as to where he will find your products. Do you offer with your product line complementary services such as assembly, installation, or repair? If you worked through wholesalers, who would perform these tasks? By working through wholesalers, you may achieve vastly greater distribution for your product than possible through contacting retail outlets directly, and at a far more efficient cost.

Vertical vs. Horizontal

Merchandising your product can be handled in traditional channels, as those described above, where you deal with wholesalers, jobbers, and retailers to sell your product in a manner beneficial to all.

In a vertically integrated system, you maintain direct control through ownership over some or all of the other elements in the distribution process. Sherwin-Williams paint and Goodyear tires are all distributed, for instance, through company-owned retail outlets. Fast-food franchises demonstrate a contractual form of vertical integration.

In horizontally integrated systems, companies join together to maximize combined strengths and minimize individual weaknesses, thereby developing a distribution synergy. For example, MGM and United Artists studios joined to take advantage of the former's distribution strengths and the latter's production strengths. Kraft, recognized for its prowess in distributing refrigerator foods, teamed with Pillsbury to market refrigerated dough products manufactured and advertised by Pillsbury.

Strategic Planning

Definition: The evaluation of the corporate mission in terms of how day-to-day operations and activities can satisfy that mission.

Four Strategic Questions

Four questions basic to strategic planning are:

1. *Where is the company going?* As planner, you need to know the underpinnings of the economy, and how the economic picture relates to the operations of the company. You must know what your company's mission and objectives are. Further, you must study trend analyses of your company and products, as well as your competitors. These pieces will provide the boundaries within which your plans can materialize, and beyond which your plans may, financially and economically, fail.

2. *How can it improve in its efforts to accomplish its objectives?* You will need to determine how to reach the company's objectives, where it is succeeding and where it is failing in meeting them. In tandem with other company departments, you will set plans and goals that direct the company toward the satisfaction of its objectives and periodically measure how well those goals are being satisfied.

3. *What opportunities are available to meet those objectives?* As question 2 above looks inward to determine how well the company's present plans are progressing toward meeting its objectives, this question looks outward to make new plans for fulfilling these objectives. Are we satisfying our target markets? Are there new concepts that will reach our markets more thoroughly?

4. *How should those opportunities be implemented?* The planner stud-

ies the company's resources—in finance, production, marketing—and matches them with the new plans for fulfilling corporate objectives.

Growth/Share Analysis

Developed by the Boston Consulting Group, growth/share analysis highlights the need to establish and maintain market share, a vital element in building the financial and marketing power of the company. This analysis is often represented in a quadrant diagram, as shown in Figure 4-1.

Following are brief descriptions and objectives for each cell in the growth/share matrix.

1. *Star:* High market growth and high share. Continue to invest heavily in the building of market share, at the expense of reported earnings.

2. *Question:* High market growth, low share. Increase market share significantly, redefine the product's market segment, or cut your losses and get out.

Market Share

	High	Low
Market Growth		
High	Star	Question
Low	Cash Cow	Dog

Figure 4–1. Growth/share analysis, developed by Boston Consulting Group.

3. *Dog:* Low market growth, low share. Milk the product—optimize your cash position, or kill the product and withdraw from the market to stem present or future losses.

4. *Cash Cow:* Low market growth, high share. Nirvana. Maintain efficiency and market share, funnel cash into the development of related products or new markets.

As the general continental drift of all products is toward the southeast corner—the dog house—product line strategy must be carefully considered and implemented to optimize the company's desired objectives and overall market position.

The growth/share matrix can be a valuable tool in the analysis of your company's portfolio of products or services, as it can describe the current status for each product, and, when tracked over time, can illustrate the direction each product is taking. In your portfolio evaluation, the matrix will alert you to when you have too few in the high market growth quadrants, so you can take the necessary R&D steps. And it will also warn you when your stable has few if any cash cows. This is valuable information to have, as those products provide crucial cash flow.

Much discussion has surfaced lately around the validity and/or intent of the matrix as a planning tool. Arguments have been made that the purpose is more for identification than implementation. Determine for yourself the applicability to your strategy planning and analysis.

Pricing

Definition: An element of the marketing mix that states how much customers will pay for goods or services, based on market conditions, expectations and manipulations.

Methods for Determining Pricing

Beyond such time-honored techniques as dartboards and dice (and such technologically superior methods as random number generators), you have several considerations as you determine your pricing strategy. Items 1 through 6 below are quantifiable strategies, and items 7 through 9 are more qualitative in nature.

1. *Relevant range pricing:* This method contends that a type of product or service will usually command a price within a specific range. Light

oil-packed tuna, for instance, may have a relevant retail range of $.60 and $.80 per 6½-ounce can.

2. *Competitive pricing:* Pricing decisions often entail an investigation of what the other guy is doing. Often labelled "me too" pricing, it merely matches the price at which established competitive products are listed.

3. *Undercutting:* To undercut is to price your product slightly under what the existing and accepted prices are for competitive products.

4. *Demand-oriented pricing:* The price of a product correlates with the demand for the product, or truly what the market will bear. Demand-oriented pricing is probably best reflected in produce, meats, and commodity-based products.

5. *Cost-markup pricing:* First costs are calculated, then a sufficient markup percentage is tacked on to determine the appropriate price.

6. *Profit-based pricing:* Somewhat similar to cost-markup pricing, it adds to the cost of the product the margin required by the company to meet any operating income or return-on-investment objectives.

7. *Penetration pricing:* Not dissimilar to undercutting, penetration pricing is a short-term strategy to maximize market penetration and share, by cutting profit markup to a bare minimum. When a consumer base is established and some brand loyalty develops, price is raised slowly to a more acceptable profit level.

8. *Predatory pricing.* A marketer's version of terrorism. Also like undercutting, predatory pricing undercuts competition severely, with the intent to drive them out of the marketplace altogether. By the way, it's illegal.

9. *Skimming:* If predatory pricing marches to the valleys, skimming heads for the hills. Skimming says to charge the highest possible (though not necessarily conscionable) price, with the objectives of getting the product into the market, maximizing its return on investment quickly, and then either dropping the price or pulling the product out of the market altogether.

Retail Pricing Strategies

In retail pricing, you should make note of these five common strategies, occasionally known as K-Mart's Greatest Hits:

1. *Price lining:* A strategy where assorted products, usually shopping goods, are sold at only a handful of particular price points. For example,

men's suits, of a wide variety of sizes, fabrics, and cuts, may be priced only at price points of $199, $259, and $319.

2. *Customary pricing:* When pricing is determined by custom or by history. Classic examples are nickel candy bars and one-cent bubble gum, not to mention penny-for-your-thoughts. But now after a decade of high inflation, candy bars are $.40 to $.50, gum is a nickel apiece, and John Naisbett will charge you $15,000 per year for a subscription to his thoughts.

3. *Odd pricing:* Where a price falls not at a round number, but at a value ending in an odd or unexpected number. Instead of selling for amounts of even dollars, you may price everything at an $.88 or $.99 interval. Some marketers contend that doing so is a psychological advantage, encouraging purchase. They may call it psychological pricing, but we call it odd.

4. *Multiple-unit pricing:* When several units of a product are tied together to encourage multiple purchase. Cat food cans may sell for 3/$1.00, for example.

5. *Loss leader pricing:* When a few reasonably popular items in a retail store are advertised at an unreasonably low price. The intent is to generate store traffic and boost storewide sales.

No one strategy for pricing, either those listed above or any others, may be appropriate alone. Companies usually combine several pricing strategies to good effect.

Pricing can be used as an aggressive element of the marketing mix. In using predatory pricing, for instance, you seek to drive competition out of the market with your aggressive undercutting. Or pricing can be used as a method to strengthen the company's financial position, as in skimming, where you reap the greatest possible profit in the shortest time.

Whatever the strategy, pricing is often misused because it is so easily manipulated. Firms that utilize price reductions to modify the marketing mix and fail to complement the product line with other changes in the mix generally end up frustrated and confused. A thorough understanding of the market, the customer, competition, and perceived value is a prerequisite to effective pricing decisions.

Break-even Analysis

Break-even analysis was presented in Chapter 3, but we repeat the formulas here because it is such a necessary part of product pricing. Both price and break-even point are likely to be affected by advertising/promotion, distribution, and other marketing expenditures.

P = price per unit

N = number of units sold

F = fixed costs, total

V = variable costs per unit

S = sales (revenue) in dollars

π = desired profit level

Break-even Point in Units Sold:

$$N = \frac{F}{P - V}$$

Break-even Point in Dollars:

$$S = \frac{F}{1 - \dfrac{V}{P}}$$

Break-even Point (given a desired profit level):

$$N = \frac{F + \pi}{P - V}$$

Capital Budgeting Methods

Marketers are commonly accused, notably by corporate financial analysts, of aiming to build market share without concern for a product's basic ability to return its investment. Thus, capital budgeting methods, such as payback period and net present value, should be integral to market planning. These techniques are explained and illustrated in Chapter 3, pages 57–59.

Marginal Cost and Marginal Revenue

When you produce and sell one additional unit of your product, your cost and revenue should both increase. Those incremental increases are termed marginal cost and marginal revenue.

Marginal Cost

$$M_c = C_n - C_o$$

where

M_c = marginal cost
C_o = total cost at old production level
    = total fixed costs + total variable costs (at old production level)
C_n = total cost at new production level
    = total fixed costs + total variable costs (at new production level)

Marginal Revenue

$$M = R_n - R_o$$

where

M_r = marginal revenue
R_o = total revenue at old sales level and/or old price
    = old unit sales × old price
R_n = total revenue at new sales level and/or new price
    = new unit sales × new price

Competitive Bidding Evaluation

In bidding for business, marketing-related or otherwise, you study how much it will cost you to conduct the job. But knowing the cost of the job isn't necessarily enough to decide how much your bid should be. In a bidding evaluation, you identify:

1. Your cost of fulfilling the assignment.
2. A range of bids you could offer your client.
3. For each of those bids, a probability that it will be accepted.

The range of possible bids should stretch from the price level so low that the probability of the bid being accepted is 1.0, or certain, to a price level so high that the probability of acceptance is nil, or 0.0.

EXAMPLE

1. Determine the cost *to you* to conduct the business for which you are bidding. Assume it will cost $100,000.

(1)	(2)	(3)	(4)	(5)
Your Cost	Bid	Probability of Acceptance	Profit (2) − (1)	Expected Profit (3) × (4)
$100,000	$ 95,000	1.00	($5,000)	($5,000)
100,000	100,000	.90	0	0
100,000	104,000	.80	4,000	3,200
100,000	108,500	.70	8,500	5,950
100,000	115,000	.60	15,000	9,000
100,000	120,000	.50	20,000	10,000
100,000	122,000	.40	22,000	8,800
100,000	124,000	.30	24,000	7,200
100,000	127,000	.20	27,000	5,400
100,000	129,500	.10	29,500	2,950
100,000	135,000	.00	35,000	0

2. Pick a range of bids you might submit to your client, from a low where probability of acceptance is 1.0, to a high where probability is 0.0.

3. Assign probabilities for each bid you list.

4. Subtract your cost from each possible bid, to determine the net profit or loss for each bid.

5. Multiply each profit (loss) value by its corresponding probability, to find an expected profit or loss.

6. Where the expected profit is at its maximum is where your profit and your likelihood of bid acceptance are optimally combined. Go bid for the job at $120,000.

Relative Sales Performance

A tool for judging sales performance among your sales force is to determine each territory or salesperson's relative sales performance. At first blush, a territory responsible for $3 million in sales is a star, compared to another territory pulling in a mere $1.5 million. But what if the former territory is Los Angeles, and the latter is Kansas City—and your product is suntan lotion? Relative sales performance calculations compare actual sales performance to the corresponding sales potential of that territory or person.

$$\text{Relative Sales Performance} = \frac{\text{\% of Total Sales}}{\text{\% of Total Potential}}$$

EXAMPLE

In the last reporting period, your six territories sold $615,000 in a market that you deem to have a potential of $2,225,000 in a comparable period. The six territories' actual sales figures and their respective market potentials are shown in columns 2 and 3 in the accompanying table. How, relatively speaking, are the six territories performing?

(1) Territory	(2) Actual Sales	(3) Market Potential	(4) % Actual Sales	(5) % Market Potential	(6) Relative Sales Performance
1	$120,000	$500,000	19.5%	22.5%	.87
2	80,000	250,000	13.0	11.2	1.16
3	95,000	290,000	15.4	13.0	1.18
4	107,000	475,000	17.4	21.3	.82
5	99,000	280,000	16.1	12.6	1.28
6	114,000	430,000	18.5	19.3	.96
Total:	$615,000	$2,225,000			

1. For each territory, calculate the percentage of actual sales to total sales, and the market potential to total potential. (Columns 4 and 5.)
2. Calculate a relative sales performance (RSP) value for each territory, by dividing the percentage of actual sales by the percentage of market potential. The resulting figures (column 6) show which territories exceed the company-wide average (those whose RSP is greater than 1.00), and which territories fall below the average (where RSP is less than 1.00).

Your calculations show that territories 5 and 4 are, respectively, the strongest and poorest performing territories, based on relative sales performance. Territory 6 performs closest to average.

Sales Force Size

To determine the size of a sales force necessary to handle a given workload, follow these steps, as adapted from Benson P. Shapiro, *Sales Program Management: Foundation and Implementation,* (McGraw-Hill, 1977).

1. Identify the number of sales accounts your sales force must visit in a coming period (for example, a year).

2. Place those accounts into groups according to the extent of service each requires. An active account or a large account will require more frequent and thorough attention than prospective or small accounts, for instance.

3. For each of your account groups, determine how often sales calls must be made over the time period.

4. Multiply the number of calls times the number of accounts for each account group, then sum the products. Your product is the number of doorbells your sales force will ring over the period studied.

5. "Ballpark" how many sales calls one salesperson can make. Any calculation is only as good as its assumptions.

6. Divide the number of calls to be made (step 4) by the number of calls per person (step 5). Your dividend is how many salespersons you'll need to make your period's projected sales calls.

EXAMPLE

1. Sales accounts to be visited = 120.

2. Identify the number of accounts to be serviced by size/activity classifications (I being the smallest accounts, IV the largest):

ACCOUNT SIZE

Account Activity	I	II	III	IV	Total
Active	10	15	5	5	35
Semi-active	15	25	10	5	55
Prospects	20	5	5	0	30
	45	45	20	10	120

3. Determine the number of sales calls per company, by size/activity classifications:

ACCOUNT SIZE

Account Activity	I	II	III	IV	Total
Active	4	8	10	15	37
Semi-active	3	4	6	12	25
Prospects	2	2	2	4	10
	9	14	18	31	72

4. Multiply the number of total sales calls by size/activity classifications (e.g. Active, size I: 10 companies $\times$ 4 calls/company = 40 sales calls):

ACCOUNT SIZE

Account Activity:	I	II	III	IV	Total
Active	40	120	50	75	285
Semi-active	45	100	60	60	265
Prospects	40	10	10	0	60
	125	230	120	135	610

5. Estimated calls per salesperson per year = 22 (in real life, you will want to adjust for duration of sales calls, drive time, and other possible variables across your variety of sales accounts).

6. 610 sales calls ÷ 22 calls/salesperson = 27.72. Therefore, you will need 28 salespersons to cover your workload requirements.

5

Statistics

Procrastination lives in America.

In business schools across the country, one requirement is more often postponed to the last possible semester than any other: statistics. Actually, there are plenty of good reasons why statistics is such a dreaded subject of study:

1. No one really understands it. No one.
2. Some people have an annoyingly better control of the stuff than the rest of us. So they think that they can push us around with their numbers and Greek letters and levels of statistical significance.
3. They're right.
4. Statisticians make up words like "platykurtic" and "homoscedasticity," just to make sure no one knows what's going on.
5. Because of statistical methods, we have such hallmarks of accuracy as actuarial tables and EPA mileage estimates.

Nevertheless, the business person inevitably runs head-on into statistics in one form or another. This chapter will help you survive. It contains formulas and theories in these areas:

Frequency distribution
Types of graphs and charts

Means, modes, medians, and range

Frequency curve

Standard deviation and variance

Probability and Bayes' Theorem

Factorials

Combinations

Binomial distribution

Poisson distribution

Normal distribution and area under the curve (z value)

Central limit theorem

Standard error of the mean

Confidence levels

Types of data

Tests for statistical significance (chi-square, z test, Friedman test, and t-test)

Decision trees

If it all depresses you, just keep in mind that you only need to suffer through a few problems and analyses. Some people do this for a living.

Frequency Distribution

A frequency distribution organizes the unorganized: related but presently unmanageable data can be combined and sifted into a comprehensible table that shows the number of occurrences of each statistic in the data.

EXAMPLE

1. You've interviewed buyers of your consumer-goods product in order to find out how old your customers are. On a sample of 50, you garnered the results shown below. This is your raw data.

29	22	27	21	20	25	24	23	23	24
19	26	31	32	37	27	28	26	27	27
24	22	26	39	31	21	18	31	20	26
41	33	19	26	28	30	23	34	35	25
36	30	25	22	24	36	25	25	30	28

2. Build an array, or tally sheet, to organize the data. First find your high and low responses, list them and all numbers in between, and tick off each number from your survey.

Age	Tally	Age	Tally	Age	Tally
18	/	26	/////	34	/
19	//	27	////	35	/
20	//	28	///	36	//
21	//	29	/	37	/
22	///	30	///	38	
23	///	31	///	39	/
24	////	32	/	40	
25	/////	33	/	41	/

3. Create intervals (even ones if possible) in which to compile your data. Write down the number of occurrences in each interval (the frequency distribution, and calculate, if desired, the relative frequency (percentage of sample).

Age Interval	Frequency Distribution	Relative Frequency (% of Sample)
18–21	7	14 %
22–25	15	30
26–29	13	26
30–33	8	16
34–37	5	10
38–41	2	4
Total	50	100%

Types of Graphs and Charts

Histogram: A bar chart with vertical bars representing a frequency distribution (Figure 5-1).

Bar chart: A histogram with horizontal histos (Figure 5-2).

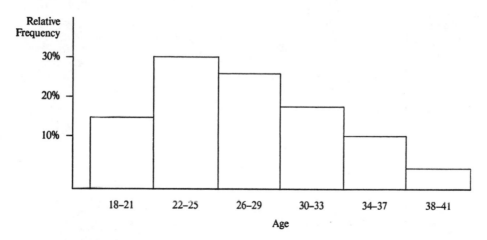

Figure 5–1. Histogram.

Frequency polygon: Turns a histogram into a line graph (Figure 5-3).

Ogives: Cumulative frequency distribution, shown as a line graph (Figure 5-4). Also, a word you will never see again.

Pie charts: A circle divided into wedges; the circle represents 100% (Figure 5-5).

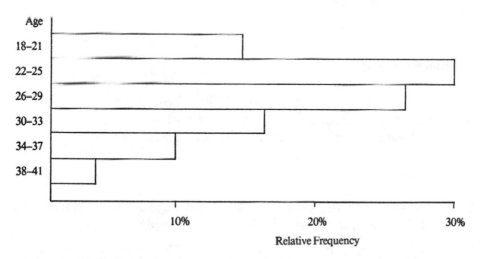

Figure 5–2. Bar chart.

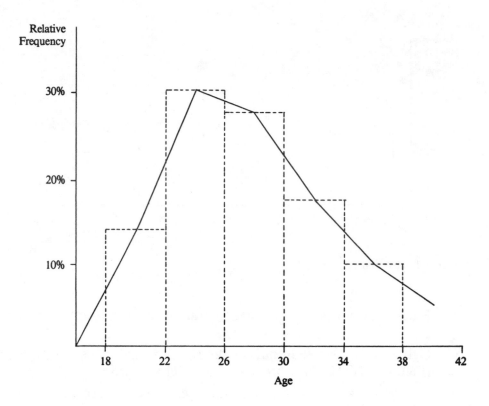

_____ Frequency Polygon

--------- Corresponding Histogram

Figure 5–3. Frequency polygon.

Arithmetic Mean

No one calls it the arithmetic mean. "Mean" or "average" are the more common terms, although they are less descriptive. The mean is the sum of a set of values divided by the number of values in the set:

$$\text{Mean} = \frac{X_1 + X_2 + X_3 + \cdots + X_n}{n}$$

Using the age frequency distribution data on page 95, the mean age is the sum of all the ages in the set divided by the sample number:

$$\text{Mean} = \frac{29 + 19 + 24 + 41 + \cdots + 28}{50} + \frac{1,351}{50} = 27.02 \text{ years}$$

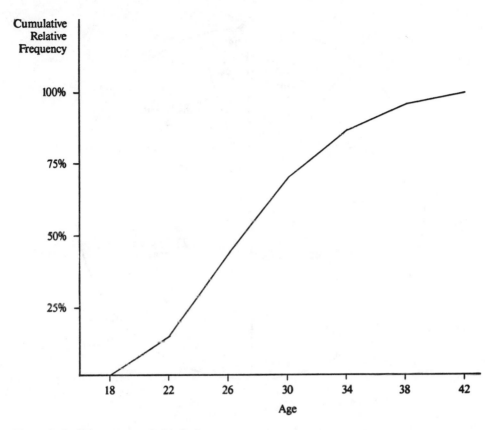

Figure 5–4. Ogive, or cumulative frequency.

If you've built an array of your data (like the tally sheet on page 96) there's a more efficient way to calculate the mean. Multiply a value by the number of times it appears in your set, add up the products, and divide by the total number of values:

$$\text{Mean} = \frac{\Sigma K(X)}{n}$$

where

X = value

K = frequency of a value in the set (how often a given number shows up)

n = number of values in the set

Figure 5–5. Pie chart.

Using same age data as before, the calculation would look like this:

$$\text{Mean} = \frac{18(1) + 19(2) + 20(2) + 21(2) + \cdots 41(1)}{50}$$

$$= \frac{1351}{50} = 27.02 \text{ years}$$

Weighted Means

Weighted means are averages that are derived by giving extra importance, or "weight," to certain values, and giving less weight to others.

Chapter 1 contains information on weighted moving averages, and it serves as a valid tool for illustrating a weighted mean. If you were forecasting sales for a nonseasonal, noncyclical product, and you had noticed a gradual sales trend upward or downward for the past several months, you would want to assign extra importance, or weight, to the more recent months' sales performances.

If, however, you were a swimming pool manufacturer wanting to forecast sales for September, which previous month's sales would you find most beneficial in your forecasting—August just ended, or September last year? Probably the previous September, because it would be a better guide for the seasonal sales of your product. Weights let you take this into account.

$$\text{Weighted Mean} = \frac{\Sigma w(X)}{n_w}$$

where

$X =$ value
$w =$ weight you assign to the value
$n_w =$ total of all *weights*

EXAMPLE

You are deciding between two copiers for purchase. You have first identified what features are important to you, and you have rated each of those features on a scale of 1 to 10 (10 = very important, 1 = not important at all).

After much research, you have rated each of the two copiers on each feature, again using a 1-to-10 scale (10 = excellent, 1 = very poor). Your results look like this:

(Weights) Ratings	Feature	Copier A	Copier B
10	Clear, readable copies	9	7
8	Warranty	7	8
8	Availability of service calls	7	5
7	Reliability	9	9
6	Availability of supplies	10	10
6	Speed per copy	7	7
5	Ease of operation	6	8
4	Collating	1	5
2	2-sided copying	6	6
1	Portability	7	4
57		69	69

Totaling the points, you find copiers A and B have equal numbers of ratings points (69). Which do you buy?

1. Multiply the copiers' ratings by the weights, and sum the products.

Weight(w)	Copier A	A(w)	Copier B	B(w)
10	9	90	7	70
8	7	56	8	64
8	7	56	5	40
7	9	63	9	63
6	10	60	10	60
6	7	42	7	42
5	6	30	8	40
4	1	4	5	20
2	6	12	6	12
1	7	7	4	4
57		420		415

2. To convert the copiers' respective scores to a weighted mean in the 1–10 (excellent to poor) scale, divide each sum by the total of your weights:

Copier A: $\dfrac{420}{57} = 7.4$

Copier B: $\dfrac{415}{57} = 7.3$

It's close, but buy Copier A.

Median, Mode, and Range

Median is the middle value in a series of rank-ordered values. Of a class of 15 schoolboys lined up by height, boy number 8 is of median height. If you have 10 boys, median height is the midpoint, or average, between the heights of boys 5 and 6. If n is the number of values in a data set, the data point representing the median value is

$$\text{Median} = \frac{n}{2} + \frac{1}{2}$$

EXAMPLE

Using the age frequency distribution data on page 96, the median age is found as follows:

1. Calculate which data point represents your median value (n = 50):

$$\text{Median} = \frac{50}{2} + \frac{1}{2} = 25.5$$

2. Since n is an even number, you've ended up with a median between two data points (points 25 and 26). Find the value of points 25 and 26 from your array:

   Value 25 = 26 years
   Value 26 = 26 years

3. Both values equal 26; therefore, the median age equals 26 years. If they were different, the median age would be the average of the two values.

Mode is determined through observation. It is the value that crops up more often than any other. If more of the schoolboys are 5'7" than any other single measurement, then 5'7" is the mode height. Two values that turn up equally often, yet more often than any other values, give you two modes. They call that bi-modal.

EXAMPLE

1. On your array, find the value or values that appear more often than the others. From the age array:

Age	Tally
25	/////
26	/////

2. Since the most frequent numbers turn up equally, there is a bi-modal condition, with modes at 25 and 26 years.

Range is the largest value for your variable minus the smallest value. In the age frequency distribution data, the range is 41 − 18, or 23. Some people insist that the range include both high and low points, making the formula: high − low +1. The answer to the above would then be 24.

Frequency Curves

The age data in the preceding pages was organized into segments and graphically represented as segments, as in Figures 5-1 through 5-6. Other data will be continuous, and will be graphed with a curved line, called a *frequency curve.* Normal distribution yields a bell-shaped curve, which has for years provided teachers with an excuse to give very few As. The frequency curve is a graphic way of describing the probable occurrence of an event, based on data in a normal distribution. Data points are plotted along the horizontal axis; the area beneath the curve represents the total probability of all possible events and is equal to 1.0. The probable occurrence of values less than or greater than any particular value can be determined using z values. For further discussion of this subject, turn to page 119.

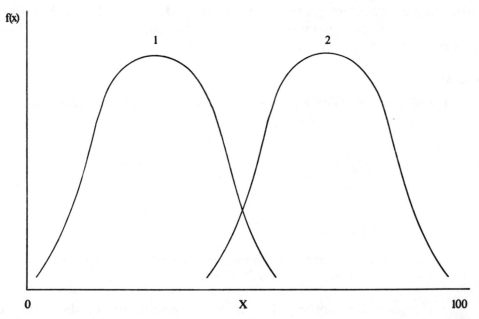

Figure 5–6. Average.

Average, kurtosis, skewness, and dispersion are terms that describe the bends and bulges taken on by a given distribution.

Average (Figure 5-6): Curve 1 has a low, or "small" average; curve 2 has a high or "large" average.

Kurtosis (Figure 5-7) refers to the shape of the curve near the mean. Curve 3 is leptokurtic (peaked kurtosis); curve 4 is mesokurtgic (normal); and curve 5 platykurtic (flat).

Skewness (Figure 5-8) describes the lack of symmetry around the mean. Curve 6 is positively skewed (it leans to the left) and curve 7 is negatively skewed.

Dispersion (Figure 5-9) refers to the amount of scatter of the data around the mean. Dispersion on curve 8 is narrow, and wide on curve 9.

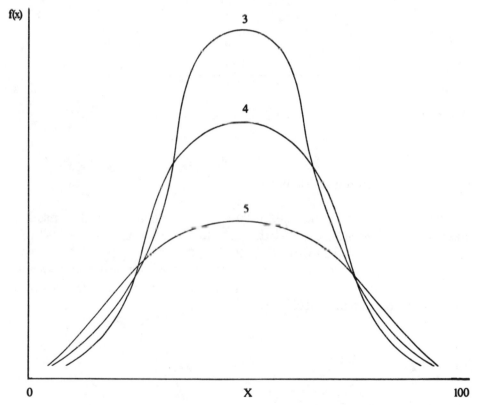

Figure 5-7. Kurtosis.

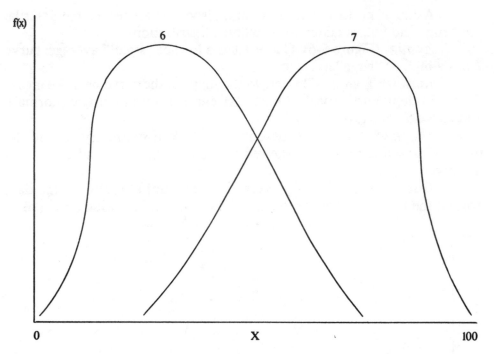

Figure 5–8. Skewness.

Standard Deviation and Variance

Standard deviation is the square root of the variance, and is used as a measure of dispersion around the mean. Variance is the average of the squares of the deviation from the mean. Got that?

We'll show two ways to calculate standard deviation and variance. The first method has a more manageable formula, but the second is actually simpler in practice. Take your pick.

Method 1

$$s_x = \sqrt{\frac{\sum_{i=1}^{n} (X_i - \overline{X})^2}{n - 1}}$$

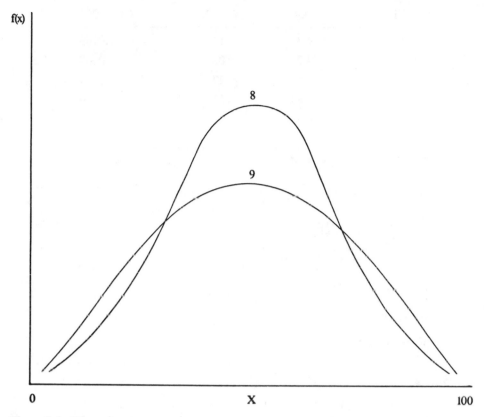

Figure 5-9. Dispersion.

$$s_x^2 = \frac{\displaystyle\sum_{i=1}^{n} (X_i - \overline{X})^2}{n - 1}$$

where

s_x^2 = variance of X
s_x = standard deviation of X
X_i = value of a variable
$\overline{X}$ = mean value of a variable
n = number of values, or sample size
i = number of incidences

EXAMPLE

1. Calculate $\overline{X}$, the individual deviations from $\overline{X}$, the squares of the individual deviations from $\overline{X}$, and the sum of the squares.

i	X_i	$X_i - \overline{X}$	$(X_i - \overline{X})^2$
1	4.3	.13	.0169
2	4.2	.03	.0009
3	3.9	−.27	.0729
4	4.4	.23	.0529
5	4.2	.03	.0009
6	4.0	−.17	.0289
	$\overline{X} = 4.17$		$\Sigma(X_i - \overline{X})^2 = .1734$

2. Calculate s^2 and s.

$$s_X^2 = \frac{\sum_{i=1}^{6} (X_i - \overline{X})^2}{n - 1}$$

$$s_X^2 = \frac{.1734}{5}$$

$$s_X^2 = .035$$

$$s_X = \sqrt{.035} = .186$$

Method 2

$$s_X^2 = \frac{\Sigma X_i^2 - \dfrac{(\Sigma X_i)^2}{n}}{n - 1}$$

EXAMPLE (USING SAME DATA)

1. Calculate ΣX and ΣX^2.

X_i	X_i^2
4.3	18.49
4.2	17.64
3.9	15.21
4.4	19.36
4.2	17.64
4.0	16.00
$\Sigma X_i = 25$	$\Sigma X_i^2 = 104.34$

2. Calculate s^2 and s.

$$s_X^2 = \frac{\Sigma X_i^2 - \frac{(\Sigma X_i)^2}{n}}{n-1}$$

$$s_X^2 = \frac{104.34 - \frac{25^2}{6}}{5}$$

$$s_X^2 = .035$$

$$s_X = .186$$

Probability

Probability is the likelihood of an event's occurrence, on a 0 to 1 scale. At a probability of 1, an event will happen; at 0, the event doesn't have a snowball's chance in Phoenix. Between 0 and 1, percentages express the likelihood that something will or will not happen.

Simple probability is as described above. P(A) represents the probability that event A will occur. P($\sim$A), conversely, is the probability that event A will not occur. *Joint probability* is the likelihood that more than one specified event will happen together. Represented as P(A,B), it reads as the "probability of events A and B." *Conditional probability* reflects the likelihood that event B will occur given that event A occurs, written as P(B|A). *Marginal probability* is an alternate perspective on simple probability, as you will see below.

For example, where only two events are possible:

	P(A)	P($\sim$A)	Total
P(B)	.18	.34	.52
P($\sim$B)	.40	.08	.48
Total	.58	.42	1.00

Simple Probability:

$$P(A) = .58$$
$$P(\sim A) = .42$$

$$P(B) = .52$$
$$P(\sim B) = .48$$

Joint Probability:

$$P(A,B) = .18 = P(A)P(B|A)$$
$$P(A,\sim B) = .40$$

Conditional Probability:

$$P(B|A) = \frac{P(B,A)}{P(A)} = \frac{.18}{.58} = .31$$

$$P(A|B) = \frac{P(B,A)}{P(B)} = \frac{.18}{.52} = .34$$

Marginal Probability:

$$P(B) = P(B,A) + P(B,\sim A)$$
$$= .18 + .34$$
$$= .52$$

Bayes' Theorem

Say at Sour Grapes, Inc., you have been using two delivery services regularly. With Speedo Deliveries, on-time delivery has occurred 87% of the time, whereas Quickie Services has delivered your products on time 71% of the time. Shipping has followed a schedule of giving two out of three delivery assignments to Speedo.

You know your initial event probabilities:

$$P(Speedo) = .67$$
$$P(Quickie) = .33$$

And you know your posterior probabilities:

$$P(On\text{-}time|Speedo) = .87$$
$$P(Late|Speedo) = .13$$
$$P(On\text{-}time|Quickie) = .71$$
$$P(Late|Quickie) = .29$$

But, you wonder as you hang up the phone with an irate customer who hasn't yet received his case of Frozen Guava-On-A-Stick Desserts, what is the probability that Quickie was assigned the delivery?

One of the questions of the ages, until crafty Bayes solved it in the 1600's. His theorem would solve it as follows:

$$P(Quickie|Late)$$

$$= \frac{P(Quickie)P(Late|Quickie)}{P(Speedo)P(Late|Speedo) + P(Quickie)P(Late|Quickie)}$$

$$= \frac{(.33)(.29)}{(.67)(.13) + (.33)(.29)}$$

$$= \frac{.0957}{.0871 + .0957}$$

$$= .524$$

Therefore, given that the delivery is late, chances are .524 that Quickie was assigned to make the delivery. It's very close, but check your Quickie files first.

Stated for your use, Bayes' Theorem is:

$$P(J|K) = \frac{P(J)P(K|J)}{P(J)P(K|J) + P(J)P(K|J)}$$

In English, the likelihood that event J will happen once K happens is equal to the chance that both J and K will happen, divided by the chance that K will happen.

Probability Terminology

Other terms associated with probability are these (see Figure 5-10):

Mututally exclusive: Two or more events that cannot possibly occur at the same time, e.g., "attending USC" and "rooting for UCLA."

$$P(X \text{ or } Y) = P(X) + P(Y)$$

Nonmutually exclusive: Two or more events that may or may not occur at the same time, e.g., "attending USC" and "voting Republican."

$$P(X \text{ or } Y) = P(X) + P(Y) - P(X,Y)$$

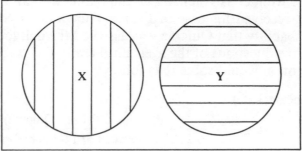

a. Mutually exclusive.

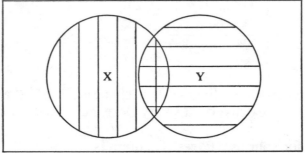

b. Nonmutually exclusive.

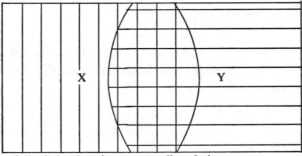

c. Collectively exhaustive, nonmutually exclusive.

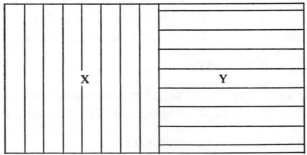

d. Collectively exhaustive, mutually exclusive.

Figure 5–10. Probability terminology.

You need to subtract $P(X,Y)$; otherwise you're double counting that probability.

Collectively exhaustive: Two or more events that, together, have a probability of 1.0. That is, one of those events must occur. The events may or may not be mutually exclusive as well.

$P(X \text{ or } Y) = 1$

Multiplying dependent and independent probabilities:

Dependent: $P(X,Y) = P(X)P(Y/X)$

or

$P(X,Y) = P(Y)P(X/Y)$

Independent: $P(X,Y) = P(X)P(Y)$

Factorials, Combinations, and Binomial Probability

Factorials

Factorials are pretty straightforward, and not very exciting, despite the exclamation mark.

$$N! = 1 \times 2 \times 3 \times 4 \times \ldots n$$
$$0! = 1 \text{ (take our word for it)}$$
$$1! = 1$$
$$2! = 1 \times 2 = 2$$
$$3! = 1 \times 2 \times 3 = 6$$
$$4! = 1 \times 2 \times 3 \times 4 = 24$$
$$5! = 1 \times 2 \times 3 \times 4 \times 5 = 120$$
$$6! = 1 \times 2 \times 3 \times 4 \times 5 \times 6 = 720$$
$$7! = 1 \times 2 \times 3 \times 4 \times 5 \times 6 \times 7 = 5,040$$
$$8! = 1 \times 2 \times 3 \times 4 \times 5 \times 6 \times 7 \times 8 = 40,320$$
$$9! = 1 \times 2 \times 3 \times 4 \times 5 \times 6 \times 7 \times 8 \times 9 = 362,880$$
$$10! = 1 \times 2 \times 3 \times 4 \times 5 \times 6 \times 7 \times 8 \times 9 \times 10 = 3,628,800$$

Combinations

The number of possible sequences in which r number of successes can happen in n attempts is called a *combination*.

$$_nC_r = \frac{n!}{r!(n-r)!}$$

where

$_nC_r$ = number of combinations
n = number of attempts
r = number of successes

Combinations are an integral part of binomial probability, and the example in the section below serves to illustrate both.

Binomial Probability

The probability of r successes in n number of attempts equals the probability of *one* combination of r successes in n attempts, multiplied by the number of possible combinations.

$$P(r) = [p^r(1-p)^{n-r}]_nC_r$$

where

$_nC_r$ = the number of combinations possible for r successes in n attempts
r = number of successes
n = number of attempts
p = probability of success in one attempt
$1 - p$ = probability of non-success in one attempt
$[p^r(1-p)^{n-r}]$ = probability of *one* combination of r successes in n attempts
$P(r)$ = probability of r number of successes

Binomial probability is relevant only when just two outcomes—on/off, yes/no, success/failure, buy/don't buy—are being investigated.

Below, we'll show you two ways to calculate binomial probability. The first, determining the solution through your own calculations, helps you understand the mechanics of binomial probability, but it is terribly cumbersome if n gets too large. The second method employs Tables E and F in the Appendix, and is substantially simpler.

EXAMPLE 1

Question: What is the probability that a baseball batter with a batting average of .341 will get *exactly* three hits in five at-bats (assuming no walks)?

Solution: Calculate for P(3):

$$P(r) = [p^r(1 - p)^{n-r}]_nC_r$$

$$P(3) = [.341^3(1 - .341)^2]\frac{5!}{3!2!}$$

$$= [.0397(.4343)]\frac{5 \times 4 \times 3 \times 2 \times 1}{3 \times 2 \times 1 \times 2 \times 1}$$

$$= (.0172)10$$

$$= .172$$

Answer: The probability that the .341 batter will get exactly three hits in five at-bats is .172, or less than onc-in-five.

Question: What is the probability that he will have *3 or more* hits in 5 at-bats?

Solution: Calculate P(3), P(4), and P(5), and sum the three values.

$$P(3,4,5) = P(3) + P(4) + P(5)$$

$$P(3) = .172 \text{ (as calculated above)}$$

$$P(4) = [(.341)^4(.659)^1]\frac{5!}{4!1!}$$

$$= (.0089)5$$

$$= .045$$

$$P(5) = [(.341)^5(.659)^0]\frac{5!}{5!0!}$$

$$= (.0046)^1$$

$$= .0005$$

$$P(3,4,5) = .172 + .045 + .005$$

$$= .222$$

EXAMPLE 2

At Sour Grapes, Inc., your manager of Accounts Receivable reports that 12% of your company's receivables historically are not collected within the first 60 days. This month, you have taken on 20 new entries as receivables. What is the probability that exactly 17 will be collected within the initial 60 days?

1. Identify values for p, n, and r.

$p = .12 =$ probability of account *not* being collected within 60 days
$n = 20$
$r = (20 - 17) = 3$ accounts not to be collected within 60 days

2. In Table E, Binomial Distribution of Individual Terms, find:

$P(r = 3, n = 20, p = .12) = .224$

What is the probability that fewer than 16 will be collected?

1. Identify values for p, n, and r.

$p = .12$
$n = 20$
$r \geq 5 (20 - 15)$
$r \geq 5$

2. Use Table F, Binomial Distribution of Cumulative Terms, find

$p(r \geq 5, n = 20, p = .12) = .083$

Poisson Distribution

A Poisson distribution is used to determine the probability of an event occurring in a large number of independent repeated trials. It bases the likelihood of X events occurring per series of trials on the number of events that have occurred per series in the past.

$$P(r) = \frac{e^{-m}m^r}{r!}$$

where

$e =$ base of natural logarithms $= 2.71828$
$m =$ *mean* number of successes per unit measured
$r =$ number of successes actually experienced
$P(r) =$ probability that *r* number of successes will occur, given *m mean* number of successes per unit measured.

As with binomial distribution, we will show you how to calculate by hand (in Example 1) and how to use Tables G and H in the Appendix (in Example 2).

EXAMPLE 1

What is the likelihood of the quality control team finding 5, 6, 7, and 8 flaws in the paint job of a new car, given that an average of 6 flaws are ordinarily uncovered?

$$P(5) = \frac{e^{-m}m^r}{r!}$$

$$= \frac{e^{-6}6^5}{5!}$$

$$= \frac{(.00248)(7776)}{120}$$

$$= .161$$

$$P(6) = \frac{e^{-6}6^6}{6!}$$

$$= \frac{(.00248)(46656)}{720}$$

$$= .161$$

$$P(7) = \frac{e^{-6}6^7}{7!}$$

$$= \frac{(.00248)(279936)}{5040}$$

$$= .138$$

$$P(8) = \frac{e^{-6}6^8}{8!}$$

$$= \frac{(.00248)(1679616)}{40320}$$

$$= .103$$

If you were calculating a series of Poisson probabilities, such as those above, here is a short-cut: note that from $P(r)$ to $P(r + 1)$, the numerator of the calculation is multiplied by m, and the denominator is multiplied by r. Therefore,

$$P(r + 1) = \frac{P(r)m}{r}$$

Thus, using the data above:

$$P(5) = .161 \text{ (as calculated above)}$$

$$P(6) = .161 \, (6/6)$$
$$= .161$$
$$P(7) = .161 \, (6/7)$$
$$= .138$$
$$P(8) = .138 \, (6/8)$$
$$= .103$$

EXAMPLE 2

Using the same data as in Example 1, m = 6 and r = 5, 6, 7, and 8. Turning to Table G, Poisson Distribution of Individual Terms (note that Tables G and H use X instead of r):

$$P(r = 5, m = 6) = .161$$
$$P(r = 6, m = 6) = .161$$
$$P(r = 7, m = 6) = .138$$
$$P(r = 8, m = 6) = .103$$

Building upon the same data, what is the probability that *5 or more* flaws are found? Turning to Table H, Poisson Distribution of Cumulative Terms:

$$P(r \geq 5, m = 6) = .715$$

Normal Distribution and Area Under the Curve

The formula for the famous bell-curve, or normal distribution, is:

$$y = \frac{1}{\sqrt{2\pi\sigma}} e^{-1/2 \frac{(x - \mu)2}{\sigma 2}}$$

where

μ = mean, and the expected value of x
σ^2 = variance
σ = standard deviation
e = 2.71828
π = 3.14159

(The symbols μ and σ are used when describing the entire population; $\overline{X}$ and S, their respective equivalents, are used when describing a sample of that population.) Fortunately, you will probably never have to

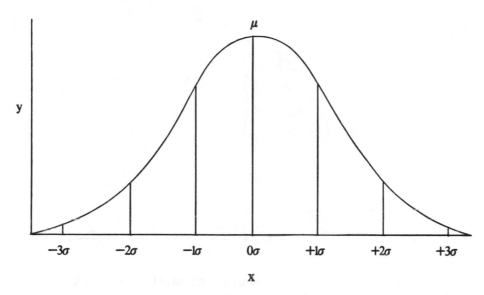

Figure 5–11. Normal distribution curve.

use the formula. The curve is shown in Figure 5-11, along with the areas representing ± 1, ± 2, and ± 3 standard deviations:

$$\mu = 0$$
$$\pm 1\sigma = 68.27\% \text{ of the area under the curve}$$
$$\pm 2\sigma = 95.45\% \text{ of the area under the curve}$$
$$\pm 3\sigma = 99.73\% \text{ of the area under the curve}$$

The Z Value

The "standard normal deviate," or "z value," is crucial to the calculation of probabilities and statistical significance levels. It represents the number of standard deviations applicable to a particular piece of data.

$$z = \frac{x - \overline{X}}{s}$$

where

x = point along the x axis
$\overline{X}$ = mean
s = standard deviation

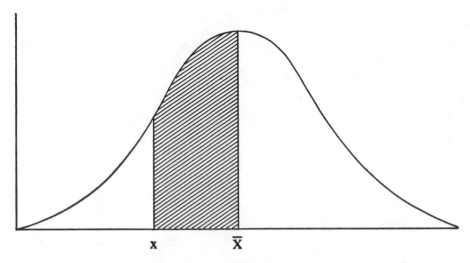

Figure 5–12. Z values are used to find the area under the curve between x and $\bar{X}$, based on a total area under the curve of 1.0.

Looking up your z value in Table A of the Appendix, ignoring + or − signs, will reveal the proportion of the area between x and $\bar{X}$ under the normal distribution curve. The z values are based on the definition that the total area beneath the curve equals 1.0. See Figure 5-12.

EXAMPLE

A random-sample national consumer survey (sample (n) = 1,000 consumers) measuring taste ratings of Sour Grapes' new fruit drink Redd Razz (using a 100-point scale, with 100 = excellent tasting and 0 = terrible tasting) yielded a mean score of 76, and a standard deviation of 10.8. Assume the data were normally distributed.

a. What proportion of the consumers' ratings should be between 59 and 76?

$$z_{59-76} = \frac{59 - 76}{10.8} = -1.57$$

Area = .4418 (from Table A)

The result shows that, given a normal distribution, approximately 44% of the respondents are expected to rate the product between 59 and 76. Note that you should ignore any minus signs appearing in front of the Z values.

b. What proportion of the ratings should be between 65 and 82? For this

120 THE MBA TOOLKIT

question, you must find the area between 65 and 76, then 76 and 82, and sum the two areas.

$$z_{65-76} = \frac{65 - 76}{10.8} = -1.02$$

$$\text{Area}_a = .3461$$

$$z_{76-82} = \frac{82 - 76}{10.8} = .56$$

$$\text{Area}_b = .2123$$

$$\text{Area}_{a+b} = .3461 + .2123 = .5584 \text{ or } 55.84\%$$

c. What proportion should be under 66? By definition, the mean evenly splits the total area of 1.0 under the curve. Therefore, the area on either side of the mean is 0.5. Knowing that, just calculate the area between 66 and your mean, 76, then subtract from 0.5 to find the area south of 66.

$$z_{66-76} = \frac{66 - 76}{10.8} = -.93$$

$$\text{Area}_a = .3238$$

$$\text{Area}_b = .5 - .3238 = .1762$$

d. What proportion should be between 80 and 89? First, calculate the area between 76 and 89, then subtract from it the area between 76 and 80.

$$z_{76-89} = \frac{89 - 76}{10.8} = 1.20$$

$$\text{Area}_a = .3849$$

$$z_{76-80} = \frac{80 - 76}{10.8} = .37$$

$$\text{Area}_b = .1443$$

$$\text{Area}_{a-b} = .3849 - .1443 = .2406$$

Central Limit Theorem

The central limit theorem states that, as a random sample from a population increases, the distribution of the values or means gathered in the sample are increasingly likely to resemble the normal distribution frequency. That is, the larger the random sample, the closer the distribution will resemble the bell curve.

Standard Error of the Mean and Confidence Levels

The standard error of the mean ($s_{\bar{x}}$) gives you a feeling of how accurate your sampling was. It tells you how much your sampling mean may vary from the population mean. The formula is:

$$s_{\bar{x}} = \frac{s}{\sqrt{n}}$$

where

$s_{\bar{x}}$ = standard error of the mean
s = standard deviation
n = sample size

Calculations of confidence levels help the decision maker sleep nights. A 95% confidence level, in simplest terms, says that chances are 95 in 100 that your sample reflects the total population. Ranges of confidence levels are calculated by multiplying standard error of the mean ($s_{\bar{x}}$) and a z value.

1. Determine what confidence level you will use. The level you've chosen represents, in effect, the area under the normal distribution curve within which the true population mean is allowed to fall.
2. Find the z value in Table A that matches your confidence level. Below are commonly used confidence levels and corresponding z values, in a two-tailed test:

Confidence Level	z
90%	1.645
95%	1.96
99%	2.58

3. Multiply your z value by the standard error. The result is the range around the sample mean, within your chosen confidence level.

EXAMPLE

Recall the taste test data on page 120 in which the mean score $(\overline{X})$ was 76 and the standard deviation (s) was 10.8. If the sample size (n) was 50, 200, and 1000, calculate the respective standard errors of the mean:

$$n = 50: \quad s_{\overline{x}} = \frac{10.8}{\sqrt{50}} = 1.53$$

$$n = 200: \quad s_{\overline{x}} = \frac{10.8}{\sqrt{200}} = .76$$

$$n = 1000: \quad s_{\overline{x}} = \frac{10.8}{\sqrt{1000}} = .34$$

Using a confidence level of 95% (z = 1.96), you could rest assured that, 95 samples out of 100, your mean would fall within these ranges:

$$n = 50: \quad 76 \pm (1.96)(1.53) = 76 \pm 3.00$$
$$n = 200: \quad 76 \pm (1.96)(.76) = 76 \pm 1.49$$
$$n = 1000: \quad 76 \pm (1.96)(.34) = 76 \pm .67$$

Types of Data

Nominal: Numbers used to represent names or words, such as name or marital status. Can be dichotomous (two outcomes possible, e.g., yes/no, male/female) or multichotomous (more than two outcomes possible, e.g., race, brand of TV set owned). Preference between or among items can be treated statistically as nominal, if it is first translated into "preferred/not preferred" status.

Ordinal: Data with an order, such as ranking college football teams or the top 500 corporations.

Inverval/Ratio: Together, called "metric" data. The order of the data is significant, as is the space between each datum. Ratio data have a 0 point, such as distance; a 0 point means you can make statements such as "point A is twice as far away as point B." Interval data, like temperature, have no 0 per se; you cannot, for instance, say 60° is twice as warm as 30°.

Tests for Statistical Significance

Below are formulas for six of the most commonly employed statistical significance tests: chi-square (x^2), z test (proportions), Friedman test, simple t-test, independent groups t-test (equal variances), and independent groups t-test (unequal variances).

In using these significance tests, you are trying to prove or disprove an assumption about your sample data and how they relate to the population from which you have taken your data. The assumption is termed the *null hypothesis*. Whether the null hypothesis is true or not, and whether on the basis of your data you accept or reject it, it can yield two types of errors, which statisticians have cleverly labeled Type I and Type II errors.

If the null hypothesis is true, but on the basis of your data you reject it, then you have committed a Type I error. If the null hypothesis is false but you accept it, then you've got a Type II error.

Type I: Your null hypothesis says there is no difference between your new fruit drink Redd Razz and your older product Raspberry Rush. From a preference test with consumers, your statistician said Redd Razz was the preferred drink, at a 95% confidence level. That means there is a 5% chance Redd Razz *isn't* preferred. As a good businessperson, you reject the null hypothesis and introduce Redd Razz. But what if the 5% chance were correct? What if it isn't the preferred drink? You have committed the Type I error, by rejecting the null hypothesis even though it was actually true.

Type II: In another research study, your statistician says that in the preference between your grape and papaya fruit rolls, preference for the grape yields only a 30% confidence level—that is, chances are 3 in 10 that grape is actually the preferred flavor. Null hypothesis said there is no difference. You do the smart thing and market both flavors, thereby accepting the null hypothesis. But . . . in a few months, retailers carrying your product are taking a bath on the papaya rolls, and you're in a sticky situation. You have experienced the Type II error, by accepting the null hypothesis although it was actually false.

Chi-Square (X^2)

The chi-square test should be used for nominal data only, and when inspecting one group or several independent groups of data.

$$X^2 = \Sigma \frac{(O - E)^2}{E}$$

where

X^2 = chi-square
O = observed frequencies
E = expected frequencies

EXAMPLE

A survey of 200 mothers of children (106 mothers of boys, 94 mothers of girls) was taken to ask which type of pedalled ride-on vehicle their children enjoyed most. These were the results:

REPORTED PREFERENCES

	Mothers of Boys	Mothers of Girls	Total
Tricycle (metal)	19	28	47
Big-wheel (plastic)	87	66	153
	106	94	200

Was there a significant difference in stated preferences between mothers of boys and mothers of girls?

1. For easy visualization, map out the data onto a row/column grid with totals, as above.
2. Calculate the expected frequencies for each box in the grid, by multiplying the corresponding row (across) and column (down) totals and dividing by your total sample (in this example, 200). You may want to build another grid to house your expected frequencies, as below:

Let B = mothers of boys
G = mothers of girls
T = prefer tricycles

P = prefer plastic, big-wheeled ride-ons

E = expected frequency

$$E_{TB} = \frac{(106)(47)}{200} = 24.91$$

$$E_{TG} = \frac{(94)(47)}{200} = 22.09$$

$$E_{PB} = \frac{(106)(153)}{200} = 81.09$$

$$E_{PG} = \frac{(94)(153)}{200} = 71.91$$

EXPECTED PREFERENCES

	Mothers of Boys	Mothers of Girls	Total
Tricycle (metal)	24.91	22.09	47*
Big-wheel (plastic)	81.09	71.91	153*
Total	106*	94*	200

*Notice the totals are maintained.

3. Using the expected frequencies you have found, calculate the chi-square, using:

$$X^2 = \Sigma \frac{(O - E)^2}{E}$$

$$X^2 = \frac{(19 - 24.91)^2}{24.91} + \frac{(28 - 22.09)^2}{22.09} + \frac{(87 - 81.09)^2}{81.09}$$

$$+ \frac{(66 - 71.91)^2}{71.91}$$

$$= 3.90$$

4. Check X^2 tables, at (rows − 1)(columns − 1) degrees of freedom (in this case, degrees of freedom = 1) and at your desired level of confidence (for this example, use .95). Chi-square values are found in Table B in the Appendix.

$X^2(@ .95, \text{d.f.} = 1) = 3.84$

5. Compare your X^2 with the X^2 in the table. If yours is larger, then the difference in your data is statistically significant (here, at the .95 confidence level).

$3.90 > 3.84$

∴Significant at .95 level.

Z Test Using Proportions

Determining significance of data versus a norm, or between two groups, can be done with proportions or percentages. There are two tests for this significance using z values:

1. z test (described on page 119)
2. z test for two proportions, a mathematically legal extension of z calculations.

Z Test (Expected vs. Observed Proportions)

$$z = \frac{P_o - P_e}{S_{Po}}$$

where

P_o = observed proportion (of sample)
P_e = expected proportion, or norm

$$S_{Po} = \sqrt{\frac{(P_e)(1 - P_e)}{n}}$$

n = sample size

EXAMPLE

$P_o = .52$
$P_e = .60$
$n = 200$

1. $S_{Po} = \sqrt{\dfrac{(.60)(.40)}{200}}$

$S_{Po} = \sqrt{.0012}$

$S_{Po} = .0346$

2. $z = \dfrac{.52 - .6}{.0346} = -2.31$

3. Ignoring $+$ or $-$ signs, compare your z value with that in Table A in the Appendix. At 95% confidence (assume a two-tailed test), $z = 1.96$.

$2.31 > 1.96$

$\therefore$ Difference between the sample and norm proportions is significant at 95% confidence level.

Z Test for Two Proportions

$$Z = \dfrac{P_1 - P_2}{S_{P_1 - P_2}}$$

where

$P_1 =$ proportion of sample 1
$P_2 =$ proportion of sample 2

$$S_{P_1-P_2} = \sqrt{\overline{P}(1 - \overline{P})\left(\dfrac{1}{n_1} + \dfrac{1}{n_2}\right)}$$

$\overline{P} =$ weighted proportion $= \dfrac{(P_1)(n_1) + (P_2)(n_2)}{n_1 + n_2}$

$n_1 =$ size of sample 1
$n_2 =$ size of sample 2

EXAMPLE

$P_1 = .52$
$P_2 = .60$
$n_1 = 130$
$n_2 = 180$

1. $\overline{P} = \dfrac{(.52)130 + (.60)180}{130 + 180}$

$= \dfrac{67.6 + 108}{310}$

$= .566$

2. $S_{P_1-P_2} = \sqrt{(.566)(.434)\left(\dfrac{1}{130} + \dfrac{1}{180}\right)}$

$\qquad = \sqrt{.0032543}$

$\qquad = .057$

3. $z = \dfrac{P_1 - P_2}{S_{P_1 - P_2}}$

$\qquad = \dfrac{-.08}{.057}$

$\qquad = -1.40$

4. Again, ignore + or − signs. Compare your z with Table A. At 95% confidence level in a two-tailed test, $Z = 1.96$.

$1.40 < 1.96$

∴ Difference between the two proportions is *not* significant at the 95% confidence level.

Friedman Test

Use the Friedman Test if you are looking for differences within rank-orders.

$$F = \left[\left(\dfrac{12}{nk(k + 1)}\right)(\Sigma R_k^2)\right] - 3n(k + 1)$$

where

$\qquad F =$ Friedman statistic
$\qquad n =$ sample size
$\qquad k =$ number of rankings
$\qquad R_k =$ total of the rankings

EXAMPLE

Three new soft drinks were taste-tested with these rankings resulting from a consumer survey ($n = 350$):

	1st	2nd	3rd
Soft drink P	124	117	109
Soft drink L	118	124	108
Soft drink T	108	109	133

Did any statistically significant differences emerge from the data?

1. Calculate the sum of the rankings for each subject ranked, by multiplying each rank by the number of people assigning the soft drink that rank, and then summing the product.

Soft drink P: $(124)1 + (117)2 + (109)3 = 685$
Soft drink L: $(118)1 + (124)2 + (108)3 = 690$
Soft drink T: $(108)1 + (109)2 + (133)3 = 725$

2. Calculate the Friedman statistic:

$$F = \left[\left(\frac{12}{nk(k+1)} \right) (\Sigma R_k^2) \right] - 3(n)(k+1)$$

Let

$n = 350$
$k = 3$
R_k = total of the rankings times frequencies

$$F = \left[\left(\frac{12}{(350)(3)(4)} \right) (685^2 + 690^2 + 725^2) \right] - 3(350)(4)$$
$$= [(.0028571)(1470950)] - 4200$$
$$= 2.65$$

3. Check the X^2 tables for .95 confidence level, 2 degrees of freedom (3 ranks − 1), then compare your X^2 to determine significance:

$X^2(.95, d.f. = 2) = 5.99$
$2.65 < 5.99$

∴ Not significant at .95 confidence level.

Simple t-Test

The t-test, based on the non-normal t distribution, can be used to compare an observed set of values to an existing norm, when your values are interval or ratio data. The formula is:

$$t = \frac{\overline{X} - \mu}{s/\sqrt{n}}$$

where

$\overline{X}$ = observed mean
μ = existing norm mean
s = observed standard deviation
n = sample size

Note that the denominator equals the standard error of your observed sample. So if you know the standard error ($s_{\overline{X}}$), save yourself a step or two and plug it in for your denominator.

EXAMPLE

Your botanists on staff at Sour Grapes, Inc. have claimed that the average seed count on their newly developed What-a-Melon strain of watermelon will not exceed 100. So you and your staff slice up 25 new-strain watermelons and count up. Your tallies show a mean seed count of 97, with a standard deviation of 8.8. Can you substantiate your botanists' claim, using a 95% confidence level?

1. $t = \dfrac{\overline{X} - \mu}{s/\sqrt{n}}$

$= \dfrac{97 - 100}{8.8/\sqrt{25}}$

$= -1.70$

2. Search in the t-tables (Table C) for a one-tailed t-value at 95% confidence level (the equivalent of a two-tailed t-value at 90%) with $25 - 1 = 24$ degrees of freedom:

$t(.90, d.f. = 24) = 1.71$

$|-1.70| < 1.71$

$\therefore$ Not significant at 95% confidence level.

Hard luck. At 95% confidence, you cannot say the average What-a-melon will not have 100 seeds or less. But at 94%. . . .

Independent Groups t-Test

When you wish to compare two groups of metric data, use the independent groups t-test. But first, you must decide which version to use: version 1, for equal variances, or version 2, for unequal variances. To make that decision, run this quick determining test: the F-test for equal variances. First calculate F with this equation:

$$F = \frac{S_L^2}{S_s^2}$$

where

$S_L^2 = $ larger variance
$S_s^2 = $ smaller variance

Then look up a corresponding F value in Table D for $(n_s - 1)$ degrees of freedom at your chosen confidence level. If your F value is greater than the F from Table D, then the variances are unequal.

Equal Variances t-Test

If your variances are equal, these two formulas should be employed:

$$s_p^2 = \frac{s_1^2(n_1 - 1) + s_2^2(n_2 - 1)}{n_1 + n_2 - 2}$$

$$t = \frac{\overline{X}_1 - \overline{X}_2}{\sqrt{s_p^2 \left(\frac{1}{n_1} + \frac{1}{n_2}\right)}}$$

where

$s = $ standard deviation
$s^2 = $ variance
$s_p^2 = $ "pooled" variance, or combined variance of the two groups of data
$\overline{X} = $ mean
$n = $ sample size
$t = $ t-statistic

Unequal Variances t-Test

For two samples with unequal variances, these are the necessary t-test formulas:

$$t = \frac{\overline{X}_1 - \overline{X}_2}{\sqrt{\dfrac{s_1^2}{n_1} + \dfrac{s_2^2}{n_2}}}$$

$$\text{d.f.} = \frac{1}{\dfrac{\left(\dfrac{s_1^2/n_1}{\dfrac{s_1^2}{n_1} + \dfrac{s_2^2}{n_2}}\right)^2}{n_1 - 1} + \dfrac{\left(1 - \dfrac{s_1^2/n_1}{\dfrac{s_1^2}{n_1} + \dfrac{s_2^2}{n_2}}\right)^2}{n_2 - 1}}$$

EXAMPLE

In the survey conducted to determine preference between Redd Razz and Raspberry Rush, you learned that Redd Razz was preferred. But someone in advertising wants to know if the two drinks appeal to consumers of differing mean income levels, using a 95% confidence level.

These are your data:

RESPONDENTS' PREFERENCE

	Redd Razz	Raspberry Rush
Mean income ($\overline{X}$)	$27,900	$22,200
Standard deviation (s)	8,200	7,900
Variance (s^2)	67,240,000	62,410,000
Sample size (n)	188	160

1. Are the variances equal or unequal?

$$F = \frac{67,240,000}{62,410,000} = 1.04$$

2. Use the tables to interpolate an F value at 95% confidence and a two-tailed test. (You will be "ballparking" between the values 120 and ∞.)

$$F(.95, \text{d.f.} = 187, 159) \cong 1.30$$
$$1.04 < 1.30$$

$\therefore$ Variances are equal: use equal variances t-test.

3. Calculate these formulas:

$$s_p^2 = \frac{s_1^2(n_1 - 1) + s_1^2(n_2 - 1)}{n_1 + n_2 - 2}$$

$$t = \frac{\overline{X}_1 - \overline{X}_2}{\sqrt{s_p^2\left(\dfrac{1}{n_1} + \dfrac{1}{n_2}\right)}}$$

$$s_p^2 = \frac{67,240,000(187) + 62,410,000(159)}{346} = 65,020,434$$

$$t = \frac{27,900 - 22,200}{\sqrt{65,020,434\left(\dfrac{1}{188} + \dfrac{1}{160}\right)}} = 6.57$$

4. Find the t-value in Table C:

t(.05, d.f. $\cong$ 346) = 1.96

6.57 > 1.96

∴Income levels are significantly higher for Redd Razz.

EXAMPLE 2

For the sake of demonstration, adjust your standard deviations and variances in the data (so we can demonstrate the t-test for unequal variances) as below:

RESPONDENTS' PREFERENCES

	Redd Razz	Raspberry Rush
Mean income ($\overline{X}$)	$27,900	$22,200
Standard deviation (s)	8,200	7,100
Variance (s^2)	67,240,000	50,410,000
Sample size (n)	188	160

1. $F = \dfrac{67,240,000}{50,410,000} = 1.33$

2. $F(.95, \text{d.f.} = 187, 159) \cong 1.30$

$$1.33 > 1.30$$

$\therefore$Variances are unequal: use unequal variances t-test.

3. Calculate these formulas:

$$t = \frac{\overline{X}_1 - \overline{X}_2}{\sqrt{\dfrac{s_1^2}{n_1} + \dfrac{s_2^2}{n_2}}}$$

$$\text{d.f.} = \frac{1}{\dfrac{\left(\dfrac{s_1^2/n_1}{\dfrac{s_1^2}{n_1} + \dfrac{s_2^2}{n_2}}\right)^2}{n_1 - 1} + \dfrac{\left(1 - \dfrac{s_1^2/n_1}{\dfrac{s_1^2}{n_1} + \dfrac{s_2^2}{n_2}}\right)^2}{n_2 - 1}}$$

$$t = \frac{27,900 - 22,200}{\sqrt{\dfrac{67,240,000}{188} + \dfrac{50,410,000}{160}}} = 6.95$$

$$\text{d.f.} = \frac{1}{\dfrac{\left(\dfrac{67,240,000/188}{\dfrac{67,240,000}{188} + \dfrac{50,410,000}{160}}\right)^2}{187} + \dfrac{\left(1 - \dfrac{67,240,000/188}{\dfrac{67,240,000}{188} + \dfrac{50,410,000}{160}}\right)^2}{159}}$$

$$= \frac{1}{\dfrac{.283}{187} + \dfrac{.219}{159}} = 345.89 \cong 346$$

4. Find the corresponding t-value in Table C:

$$t = (.95, \text{d.f.} = 346) = 1.96$$

$$6.59 > 1.96$$

$\therefore$The decision remains: Those who prefer Redd Razz have significantly higher incomes.

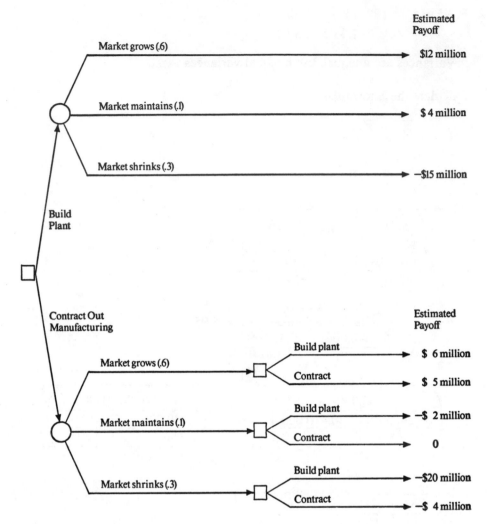

Figure 5–13. New Products, Inc. decision tree.

Decision Trees

If there were a key to decision trees, it would be to work forward in time when drawing them, and to work backward in time when analyzing them. The symbols used in the example decision tree (Figure 5-13) are:

$\square$ = decision point

$\bigcirc$ = event

(p) = probability of event

Payoffs appear at the end of lines.

EXAMPLE

New Products, Inc. markets a currently successful, innovative product, presently manufactured by another company on contract. New Products is debating whether to build a plant so it can take advantage of certain economies of scale. The trouble is that they are uncertain of the product's future. New Products has assigned these probabilities to possible market directions:

(.6) = The market will continue to grow.

(.1) = The market will maintain its current level.

(.3) = The market will shrink.

New Products has also determined payoffs accordings to how the market behaves. Additionally, it has looked into the possible payoffs if they waited 6 more months to see what the market does before deciding whether or not to build.

The resulting decision tree, and the company's estimated payoffs, are shown in Figure 5-13.

1. Start at the outermost (furthest right) branches first. Assume the company decides to manufacture under contract for now. If the market maintains or shrinks, payoffs are better if the company continues to have its product manufactured under contract. Therefore cross out "build plant" options if the market doesn't grow, and cross out the contract option if the market does grow.

2. You now have payoffs for all possible events. Under the "build plant" decision only, multiply each probability by its corresponding payoff, and sum the products. The resulting value is the probable payoff if you decide today to build the plant: $3.1 million.

$$.6 \times 12 \quad = \quad 7.2 \text{ million}$$
$$.1 \times 4 \quad = \quad .4 \text{ million}$$
$$.3 \times -15 = \underline{-4.5 \text{ million}}$$
$$\$3.1 \text{ million}$$

3. Repeat step 2 for the "contract out" decision. The result is a probable payoff of 2.4 million.

$$.6 \times 6 \;\;=\;\; 3.6 \text{ million}$$
$$.1 \times 0 \;\;=\;\; 0$$
$$.3 \times -4 = \underline{-1.2 \text{ million}}$$
$$\$2.4 \text{ million}$$

4. Review the two probable payoffs. In this scenario, New Products, Inc. would do well to build now, rather than continuing to contract out their manufacturing needs because the "build" option yields a payoff higher than the option to contract out ($3.1 million versus $2.4 million).

Statistical Tables

Table A. Z-VALUES: PERCENT AREA UNDER NORMAL CURVE

Z	%	Z	%	Z	%	Z	%
0.00	00.00	0.76	27.64	1.52	43.52	2.28	48.87
0.02	00.80	0.78	28.23	1.54	43.82	2.30	48.93
0.04	01.60	0.80	28.81	1.56	44.06	2.32	48.98
0.06	02.39	0.82	29.39	1.58	44.29	2.34	49.04
0.08	03.19	0.84	29.95	1.60	44.52	2.36	49.09
0.10	03.98	0.86	30.51	1.62	44.74	2.38	49.13
0.12	04.78	0.88	31.06	1.64	44.95	2.40	49.18
0.14	05.57	0.90	31.59	1.66	45.15	2.42	49.22
0.16	06.36	0.92	32.12	1.68	45.35	2.44	49.27
0.18	07.14	0.94	32.64	1.70	45.54	2.46	49.31
0.20	07.93	0.96	33.15	1.72	45.73	2.48	49.34
0.22	08.71	0.98	33.65	1.74	45.91	2.50	49.38
0.24	09.48	1.00	34.13	1.76	46.08	2.52	49.41
0.26	10.26	1.02	34.61	1.78	46.25	2.54	49.45
0.28	11.03	1.04	35.08	1.80	46.41	2.56	49.48
0.30	11.79	1.06	35.54	1.82	46.56	2.58	49.51
0.32	12.55	1.08	35.99	1.84	46.71	2.60	49.53
0.34	13.31	1.10	36.43	1.86	46.86	2.62	49.56
0.36	14.06	1.12	36.86	1.88	46.99	2.64	49.59
0.38	14.80	1.14	37.29	1.90	47.13	2.66	49.61
0.40	15.54	1.16	37.70	1.92	47.26	2.68	49.63
0.42	16.28	1.18	38.10	1.94	47.38	2.70	49.65
0.44	17.00	1.20	38.49	1.96	47.50	2.72	49.67
0.46	17.72	1.22	38.88	1.98	47.61	2.74	49.69
0.48	18.44	1.24	39.25	2.00	47.72	2.76	49.71
0.50	19.15	1.26	39.62	2.02	47.83	2.78	49.73
0.52	19.85	1.28	39.97	2.04	47.93	2.80	49.74
0.54	20.54	1.30	40.32	2.06	48.03	2.82	49.76
0.56	21.23	1.32	40.66	2.08	48.12	2.84	49.77
0.58	21.90	1.34	40.99	2.10	48.21	2.86	49.79
0.60	22.57	1.36	41.31	2.12	48.30	2.88	49.80
0.62	23.24	1.38	41.62	2.14	48.38	2.90	49.81
0.64	23.89	1.40	41.92	2.16	48.46	2.92	49.83
0.66	24.54	1.42	42.22	2.18	48.54	2.94	49.84
0.68	25.18	1.44	42.51	2.20	48.61	2.96	49.85
0.70	25.80	1.46	42.79	2.22	48.68	2.98	49.86
0.72	26.42	1.48	43.06	2.24	48.75	3.00	49.86
0.74	27.04	1.50	43.32	2.26	48.81	3.50	49.97

From *Complete Handjbook of Profitable Marketing Research Techniques* by Robert P. Vichas, © 1982 by Order of the Cross Society. Published by Prentice-Hall, Inc., Englewood Cliffs, N.J. 07632.

Table B. CRITICAL VALUES OF CHI-SQUARE

Degrees of Freedom	CONFIDENCE LEVEL			
	80%	90%	95%	99%
1	1.64	2.71	3.84	6.64
2	3.22	4.61	5.99	9.21
3	4.64	6.25	7.82	11.35
4	5.99	7.78	9.49	13.28
5	7.29	9.24	11.07	15.09
6	8.56	10.58	12.59	16.81
7	9.80	12.01	14.07	18.48
8	11.01	13.44	15.51	20.09
9	12.16	14.71	16.92	21.67
10	13.42	15.98	18.31	23.21
11	14.64	17.31	19.68	24.73
12	15.76	18.49	21.03	26.22
13	16.95	19.82	22.36	27.71
14	18.20	21.09	23.69	29.12
15	19.32	22.34	25.00	30.64
16	20.47	23.45	26.30	32.01
17	21.61	24.83	27.59	38.41
18	22.78	25.97	28.87	34.81
19	23.94	27.20	30.14	36.20
20	24.96	28.39	31.41	37.57
21	26.18	29.55	32.67	38.89
22	27.34	30.82	33.92	40.31
23	28.44	32.03	35.17	41.59
24	29.56	33.19	36.42	43.00
25	30.69	34.44	37.65	44.29
26	31.82	35.61	38.89	45.64
27	32.89	36.70	40.11	46.97
28	34.03	37.88	41.34	48.31
29	35.11	39.10	42.56	49.60
30	36.25	40.34	43.77	50.89

Table C. t-VALUES

Degrees of Freedom	CONFIDENCE LEVEL			
	80%	90%	95%	99%
1	3.08	6.31	12.71	63.66
2	1.89	2.92	4.30	9.92
3	1.64	2.35	3.18	5.84
4	1.53	2.13	2.78	4.60
5	1.48	2.02	2.57	4.03
6	1.44	1.94	2.45	3.71
7	1.42	1.90	2.36	3.50
8	1.41	1.86	2.31	3.36
9	1.38	1.83	2.26	3.25
10	1.37	1.81	2.23	3.17
11	1.36	1.80	2.20	3.11
12	1.35	1.78	2.18	3.06
13	1.37	1.77	2.16	3.01
14	1.34	1.76	2.14	2.98
15	1.34	1.75	2.13	2.95
16	1.33	1.75	2.12	2.92
17	1.33	1.74	2.11	2.90
18	1.33	1.74	2.10	2.88
19	1.32	1.73	2.09	2.86
20	1.32	1.73	2.08	2.84
21	1.32	1.72	2.07	2.83
22	1.32	1.72	2.07	2.82
23	1.31	1.72	2.06	2.81
24	1.31	1.71	2.06	2.80
25	1.31	1.71	2.06	2.79
26	1.31	1.71	2.06	2.78
27	1.31	1.70	2.05	2.77
28	1.31	1.70	2.05	2.76
29	1.31	1.70	2.05	2.75
30	1.31	1.70	2.04	2.75
40	1.30	1.68	2.02	2.70
60	1.29	1.67	2.00	2.66
120	1.28	1.66	1.98	2.62
—	1.28	1.64	1.96	2.58

Tables B and C from the book *Complete Handbook of Profitable Marketing Research Techniques* by Robert P. Vichas, © 1982 by Order of the Cross Society. Published by Prentice-Hall, Inc., Englewood Cliffs, N.J. 07632.

Table D. CRITICAL VALUES OF THE F DISTRIBUTION
95% CONFIDENCE LEVEL (p = .05)

DEGREES OF FREEDOM OF THE NUMERATOR

df	1	2	3	4	5	6	7	8	9	10	15	30	60	120	∞
1	161.40	199.50	215.70	224.60	230.20	234.00	236.80	238.90	240.50	241.90	245.90	250.10	252.20	253.30	254.30
2	18.51	19.00	19.16	19.25	19.30	19.33	19.35	19.37	19.38	19.40	19.43	19.46	19.48	19.49	19.50
3	10.13	9.55	9.28	9.12	9.01	8.94	8.89	8.85	8.81	8.79	8.70	8.62	8.57	8.55	8.53
4	7.71	6.94	6.59	6.39	6.26	6.16	6.09	6.04	6.00	5.96	5.86	5.75	5.69	5.66	5.63
5	6.61	5.79	5.41	5.19	5.05	4.95	4.88	4.82	4.77	4.74	4.62	4.50	4.43	4.40	4.36
6	5.99	5.14	4.76	4.53	4.39	4.28	4.21	4.15	4.10	4.06	3.94	3.81	3.74	3.70	3.67
7	5.59	4.74	4.35	4.12	3.97	3.87	3.79	3.73	3.68	3.64	3.51	3.38	3.30	3.27	3.23
8	5.32	4.46	4.07	3.84	3.69	3.58	3.50	3.44	3.39	3.35	3.22	3.08	3.01	2.97	2.93
9	5.12	4.26	3.86	3.63	3.48	3.37	3.29	3.23	3.18	3.14	3.01	2.86	2.79	2.75	2.71
10	4.96	4.10	3.71	3.48	3.33	3.22	3.14	3.07	3.02	2.98	2.85	2.70	2.62	2.58	2.54
11	4.84	3.98	3.59	3.36	3.20	3.09	3.01	2.95	2.90	2.85	2.72	2.57	2.49	2.45	2.40
12	4.75	3.89	3.49	3.26	3.11	3.00	2.91	2.85	2.80	2.75	2.62	2.47	2.38	2.34	2.30
13	4.67	3.81	3.41	3.18	3.03	2.92	2.83	2.77	2.71	2.67	2.53	2.38	2.30	2.25	2.21
14	4.60	3.74	3.34	3.11	2.96	2.85	2.76	2.70	2.65	2.60	2.46	2.31	2.22	2.18	2.13
15	4.54	3.68	3.29	3.06	2.90	2.79	2.71	2.64	2.59	2.54	2.40	2.25	2.16	2.11	2.07
16	4.49	3.63	3.24	3.01	2.85	2.74	2.66	2.59	2.54	2.49	2.35	2.19	2.11	2.06	2.01
17	4.45	3.59	3.20	2.96	2.81	2.70	2.61	2.55	2.49	2.45	2.31	2.15	2.06	2.01	1.96
18	4.41	3.55	3.16	2.93	2.77	2.66	2.58	2.51	2.46	2.41	2.27	2.11	2.02	1.97	1.92
19	4.38	3.52	3.13	2.90	2.74	2.63	2.54	2.48	2.42	2.38	2.23	2.07	1.98	1.93	1.88
20	4.35	3.49	3.10	2.87	2.71	2.60	2.51	2.45	2.39	2.35	2.20	2.04	1.95	1.90	1.84
21	4.32	3.47	3.07	2.84	2.68	2.57	2.49	2.42	2.37	2.32	2.18	2.01	1.92	1.87	1.81
22	4.30	3.44	3.05	2.82	2.66	2.55	2.46	2.40	2.34	2.30	2.15	1.98	1.89	1.84	1.78
23	4.28	3.42	3.03	2.80	2.64	2.53	2.44	2.37	2.32	2.27	2.13	1.96	1.86	1.81	1.76
24	4.26	3.40	3.01	2.78	2.62	2.51	2.42	2.36	2.30	2.25	2.11	1.94	1.84	1.79	1.73
25	4.24	3.39	2.99	2.76	2.60	2.49	2.40	2.34	2.28	2.24	2.09	1.92	1.82	1.77	1.71
26	4.23	3.37	2.98	2.74	2.59	2.47	2.39	2.32	2.27	2.22	2.07	1.90	1.80	1.75	1.69
27	4.21	3.35	2.96	2.73	2.57	2.46	2.37	2.31	2.25	2.20	2.06	1.88	1.79	1.73	1.67
28	4.20	3.34	2.95	2.71	2.56	2.45	2.36	2.29	2.24	2.19	2.04	1.87	1.77	1.71	1.65
29	4.18	3.33	2.93	2.70	2.55	2.43	2.35	2.28	2.22	2.18	2.03	1.85	1.75	1.70	1.64
30	4.17	3.32	2.92	2.69	2.53	2.42	2.33	2.27	2.21	2.16	2.01	1.84	1.74	1.68	1.62
40	4.08	3.23	2.84	2.61	2.45	2.34	2.25	2.18	2.12	2.08	1.92	1.74	1.64	1.58	1.51
60	4.00	3.15	2.76	2.53	2.37	2.25	2.17	2.10	2.04	1.99	1.84	1.65	1.53	1.47	1.39
120	3.92	3.07	2.68	2.45	2.29	2.17	2.09	2.02	1.96	1.91	1.75	1.55	1.43	1.35	1.25
∞	3.84	3.00	2.60	2.37	2.21	2.10	2.01	1.94	1.88	1.83	1.67	1.46	1.32	1.22	1.00

DEGREES OF FREEDOM OF THE DENOMINATOR

Table D (continued) 99% CONFIDENCE LEVEL (p = .01)

DEGREES OF FREEDOM OF THE NUMERATOR

DEGREES OF FREEDOM OF THE DENOMINATOR	1	2	3	4	5	6	7	8	9	10	15	30	60	120	∞
1	4052.00	4999.50	5403.00	5625.00	5764.00	5859.00	5928.00	5982.00	6022.00	6056.00	6157.00	6261.00	6313.00	6339.00	6366.00
2	98.50	99.00	99.17	99.25	99.30	99.33	99.36	99.37	99.39	99.40	99.43	99.47	99.48	99.49	99.50
3	34.12	30.82	29.46	28.71	28.24	27.91	27.67	27.49	27.35	27.23	26.87	26.50	26.32	26.22	26.13
4	21.20	18.00	16.69	15.98	15.52	15.21	14.98	14.80	14.66	14.55	14.20	13.84	13.65	13.56	13.46
5	16.26	13.27	12.06	11.39	10.97	10.67	10.46	10.29	10.16	10.05	9.72	9.38	9.20	9.11	9.02
6	13.75	10.92	9.78	9.15	8.75	8.47	8.26	8.10	7.98	7.87	7.56	7.23	7.06	6.97	6.88
7	12.25	9.55	8.45	7.85	7.46	7.19	6.99	6.84	6.72	6.62	6.31	5.99	5.82	5.74	5.65
8	11.26	8.65	7.59	7.01	6.63	6.37	6.18	6.03	5.91	5.81	5.52	5.20	5.03	4.95	4.86
9	10.56	8.02	6.99	6.42	6.06	5.80	5.61	5.47	5.35	5.26	4.96	4.65	4.48	4.40	4.31
10	10.04	7.56	6.55	5.99	5.64	5.39	5.20	5.06	4.94	4.85	4.56	4.25	4.08	4.00	3.91
11	9.65	7.21	6.22	5.67	5.32	5.07	4.89	4.74	4.63	4.54	4.25	3.94	3.78	3.69	3.60
12	9.33	6.93	5.95	5.41	5.06	4.82	4.64	4.50	4.39	4.30	4.01	3.70	3.54	3.45	3.36
13	9.07	6.70	5.74	5.21	4.86	4.62	4.44	4.30	4.19	4.10	3.82	3.51	3.34	3.25	3.17
14	8.86	6.51	5.56	5.04	4.69	4.46	4.28	4.14	4.03	3.94	3.66	3.35	3.18	3.09	3.00
15	8.68	6.36	5.42	4.89	4.56	4.32	4.14	4.00	3.89	3.80	3.52	3.21	3.05	2.96	2.87
16	8.53	6.23	5.29	4.77	4.44	4.20	4.03	3.89	3.78	3.69	3.41	3.10	2.93	2.84	2.75
17	8.40	6.11	5.18	4.67	4.34	4.10	3.93	3.79	3.68	3.59	3.31	3.00	2.83	2.75	2.65
18	8.29	6.01	5.09	4.58	4.25	4.01	3.84	3.71	3.60	3.51	3.23	2.92	2.75	2.66	2.57
19	8.18	5.93	5.01	4.50	4.17	3.94	3.77	3.63	3.52	3.43	3.15	2.84	2.67	2.58	2.49
20	8.10	5.85	4.94	4.43	4.10	3.87	3.70	3.56	3.46	3.37	3.09	2.78	2.61	2.52	2.42
21	8.02	5.78	4.87	4.37	4.04	3.81	3.64	3.51	3.40	3.31	3.03	2.72	2.55	2.46	2.36
22	7.95	5.72	4.82	4.31	3.99	3.76	3.59	3.45	3.35	3.26	2.98	2.67	2.50	2.40	2.31
23	7.88	5.66	4.76	4.26	3.94	3.71	3.54	3.41	3.30	3.21	2.93	2.62	2.45	2.35	2.26
24	7.82	5.61	4.72	4.22	3.90	3.67	3.50	3.36	3.26	3.17	2.89	2.58	2.40	2.31	2.21
25	7.77	5.57	4.68	4.18	3.85	3.63	3.46	3.32	3.22	3.13	2.85	2.54	2.36	2.27	2.17
26	7.72	5.53	4.64	4.14	3.82	3.59	3.42	3.29	3.18	3.09	2.81	2.50	2.33	2.23	2.13
27	7.68	5.49	4.60	4.11	3.78	3.56	3.39	3.26	3.15	3.06	2.78	2.47	2.29	2.20	2.10
28	7.64	5.45	4.57	4.07	3.75	3.53	3.36	3.23	3.12	3.03	2.75	2.44	2.26	2.17	2.06
29	7.60	5.42	4.54	4.04	3.73	3.50	3.33	3.20	3.09	3.00	2.73	2.41	2.23	2.14	2.03
30	7.56	5.39	4.51	4.02	3.70	3.47	3.30	3.17	3.07	2.98	2.70	2.39	2.21	2.11	2.01
40	7.31	5.18	4.31	3.83	3.51	3.29	3.12	2.99	2.89	2.80	2.52	2.20	2.02	1.92	1.80
60	7.08	4.98	4.13	3.65	3.34	3.12	2.95	2.82	2.72	2.63	2.35	2.03	1.84	1.73	1.60
120	6.85	4.79	3.95	3.48	3.17	2.96	2.79	2.66	2.56	2.47	2.19	1.86	1.66	1.53	1.38
∞	6.63	4.61	3.78	3.32	3.02	2.80	2.64	2.51	2.41	2.32	2.04	1.70	1.47	1.32	1.00

From the book *Complete Handbook of Profitable Marketing Research Techniques* by Robert P. Vichas, © 1982 by Order of the Cross Society. Published by Prentice-Hall, Inc., Englewood Cliffs, N.J. 07632.

Table E. BINOMIAL DISTRIBUTION OF INDIVIDUAL TERMS

$$P(r) = {}_nC_r p^r q^{n-r}$$

n	r	.01	.02	.04	.05	.06	.08	.10	.12	.14	.15	p .16	.18	.20	.22	.24	.25	.30	.35	.40	.45	.50	r
2	0	980	960	922	902	884	846	810	774	740	722	706	672	640	608	578	562	490	422	360	302	250	0
	1	020	039	077	095	113	147	180	211	241	255	269	295	320	343	365	375	420	455	480	495	500	1
	2	0+	0+	002	002	004	006	010	014	020	022	026	032	040	048	058	062	090	122	160	202	250	2
3	0	970	941	885	857	831	779	729	681	636	614	593	551	512	475	439	422	343	275	216	166	125	0
	1	029	058	111	135	159	203	243	279	311	325	339	363	384	402	416	422	441	444	432	408	375	1
	2	0+	001	005	007	010	018	027	038	051	057	065	080	096	113	131	141	189	239	288	334	375	2
	3	0+	0+	0+	0+	0+	001	001	002	003	003	004	006	008	011	014	016	027	043	064	091	125	3
4	0	961	922	849	815	781	716	656	600	547	522	498	452	410	370	334	316	240	179	130	092	063	0
	1	039	075	142	171	199	249	292	327	356	368	379	397	410	418	421	422	412	384	346	299	250	1
	2	001	002	009	014	019	033	049	067	087	098	108	131	154	177	200	211	265	311	346	368	375	2
	3	0+	0+	0+	0+	001	002	004	006	009	011	014	019	026	033	042	047	076	111	154	200	250	3
	4	0+	0+	0+	0+	0+	0+	0+	0+	0+	001	001	001	002	002	003	004	008	015	026	041	062	4
5	0	951	904	815	774	734	659	590	528	470	444	418	371	328	289	254	237	168	116	078	050	031	0
	1	048	092	170	204	234	287	328	360	383	392	398	407	410	407	400	396	360	312	259	206	156	1
	2	001	004	014	021	030	050	073	098	125	138	152	179	205	230	253	264	309	336	346	337	312	2
	3	0+	0+	001	001	002	004	008	013	020	024	029	039	051	065	080	088	132	181	230	276	312	3
	4	0+	0+	0+	0+	0+	0+	0+	001	002	002	003	004	006	009	013	015	028	049	077	113	156	4
	5	0+	0+	0+	0+	0+	0+	0+	0+	0+	0+	0+	0+	0+	001	001	001	002	005	010	018	031	5
6	0	941	886	783	735	690	606	531	464	405	377	351	304	262	225	193	178	118	075	047	028	016	0
	1	057	108	196	232	264	316	354	380	395	399	401	400	393	381	365	356	303	244	187	136	094	1
	2	001	006	020	031	042	069	098	130	161	176	191	220	246	269	288	297	324	328	311	278	234	2
	3	0+	0+	001	002	004	008	015	024	035	041	049	064	082	101	121	132	185	235	276	303	312	3
	4	0+	0+	0+	0+	0+	001	001	002	004	005	007	011	015	021	029	033	060	095	138	186	234	4
	5	0+	0+	0+	0+	0+	0+	0+	0+	0+	0+	001	001	002	002	004	004	010	020	037	061	094	5
	6	0+	0+	0+	0+	0+	0+	0+	0+	0+	0+	0+	0+	0+	0+	0+	0+	001	002	004	008	016	6
7	0	932	868	751	698	648	558	478	409	348	321	295	249	210	176	146	133	082	049	028	015	008	0
	1	066	124	219	257	290	340	372	390	396	396	393	383	367	347	324	311	247	185	131	087	055	1
	2	002	008	027	041	055	089	124	160	194	210	225	252	275	293	307	311	318	298	261	214	164	2
	3	0+	0+	002	004	006	013	023	036	053	062	071	092	115	138	161	173	227	268	290	292	273	3
	4	0+	0+	0+	0+	0+	001	003	005	009	011	014	020	029	039	051	058	097	144	194	239	273	4
	5	0+	0+	0+	0+	0+	0+	0+	0+	001	001	002	003	004	007	010	012	025	047	077	117	164	5
	6	0+	0+	0+	0+	0+	0+	0+	0+	0+	0+	0+	0+	0+	001	001	001	004	008	017	032	055	6
	7	0+	0+	0+	0+	0+	0+	0+	0+	0+	0+	0+	0+	0+	0+	0+	0+	001	002	004	008		7
8	0	923	851	721	663	610	513	430	360	299	272	248	204	168	137	111	100	058	032	017	008	004	0
	1	075	139	240	279	311	357	383	392	390	385	378	359	336	309	281	267	198	137	090	055	031	1
	2	003	010	035	051	070	109	149	187	222	238	252	276	294	305	311	311	296	259	209	157	109	2
	3	0+	0+	003	005	009	019	033	051	072	084	096	121	147	172	196	208	254	279	279	257	219	3
	4	0+	0+	0+	0+	001	002	005	009	015	018	023	033	046	061	077	087	136	188	232	263	273	4
	5	0+	0+	0+	0+	0+	0+	001	002	003	003	006	009	014	020	023	027	047	081	124	172	219	5
	6	0+	0+	0+	0+	0+	0+	0+	0+	0+	0+	001	001	002	003	004	004	010	022	041	070	109	6
	7	0+	0+	0+	0+	0+	0+	0+	0+	0+	0+	0+	0+	0+	0+	0+	0+	001	003	008	016	031	7
	8	0+	0+	0+	0+	0+	0+	0+	0+	0+	0+	0+	0+	0+	0+	0+	0+	0+	0+	001	002	004	8
9	0	914	834	693	630	573	472	387	316	257	232	208	168	134	107	085	075	040	021	010	005	002	0
	1	083	153	260	299	329	370	387	388	377	368	357	331	302	271	240	225	156	100	060	034	018	1
	2	003	013	043	063	084	129	172	212	245	260	272	291	302	306	304	300	267	216	161	111	070	2
	3	0+	001	004	008	013	026	045	067	093	107	121	149	176	201	224	234	267	272	251	212	164	3
	4	0+	0+	0+	001	001	003	007	014	023	028	035	049	066	085	106	117	172	219	251	260	246	4
	5	0+	0+	0+	0+	0+	0+	001	002	004	005	007	011	017	024	033	039	074	118	167	213	246	5
	6	0+	0+	0+	0+	0+	0+	0+	0+	0+	001	001	002	003	005	007	009	021	042	074	116	164	6
	7	0+	0+	0+	0+	0+	0+	0+	0+	0+	0+	0+	0+	0+	001	001	001	004	010	021	041	070	7
	8	0+	0+	0+	0+	0+	0+	0+	0+	0+	0+	0+	0+	0+	0+	0+	0+	0+	001	004	008	018	8
	9	0+	0+	0+	0+	0+	0+	0+	0+	0+	0+	0+	0+	0+	0+	0+	0+	0+	0+	0+	001	002	9
10	0	904	817	665	599	539	434	349	279	221	197	175	137	107	083	064	056	028	013	006	003	001	0
	1	091	167	277	315	344	378	387	380	360	347	333	302	268	235	203	188	121	072	040	021	010	1
	2	004	015	052	075	099	148	194	233	264	276	286	298	302	298	288	282	233	176	121	076	044	2
	3	0+	001	006	010	017	034	057	085	115	130	145	174	201	224	243	250	267	252	215	166	117	3
	4	0+	0+	0+	001	002	005	011	020	033	040	048	067	088	111	134	146	200	238	251	238	205	4
	5	0+	0+	0+	0+	0+	001	001	003	006	008	011	018	026	037	051	058	103	154	201	234	246	5
	6	0+	0+	0+	0+	0+	0+	0+	0+	001	001	002	003	006	009	013	016	037	069	111	160	205	6
	7	0+	0+	0+	0+	0+	0+	0+	0+	0+	0+	0+	0+	001	001	002	003	009	021	042	075	117	7
	8	0+	0+	0+	0+	0+	0+	0+	0+	0+	0+	0+	0+	0+	0+	0+	0+	001	004	011	023	044	8
	9	0+	0+	0+	0+	0+	0+	0+	0+	0+	0+	0+	0+	0+	0+	0+	0+	0+	001	002	004	010	9

Table E. BINOMIAL DISTRIBUTION OF INDIVIDUAL TERMS (Continued)

$$P(r) = {}_nC_r p^r q^{n-r}$$

n	r	.01	.02	.04	.05	.06	.08	.10	.12	.14	.15	.16	.18	.20	.22	.24	.25	.30	.35	.40	.45	.50	r
10	10	0+	0+	0+	0+	0+	0+	0+	0+	0+	0+	0+	0+	0+	0+	0+	0+	0+	0+	0+	0+	001	10
11	0	895	801	638	569	506	400	314	245	190	167	147	113	086	065	049	042	020	009	004	001	0+	0
	1	099	180	293	329	355	382	384	368	341	325	308	272	236	202	170	155	093	052	027	013	005	1
	2	005	018	061	087	113	166	213	251	277	287	293	299	295	284	268	258	200	140	089	051	027	2
	3	0+	001	008	014	022	043	071	103	135	152	168	197	221	241	254	258	257	225	177	126	081	3
	4	0+	0+	001	001	003	008	016	028	044	054	064	086	111	136	160	172	220	243	236	206	161	4
	5	0+	0+	0+	0+	0+	001	002	005	010	013	017	027	039	054	071	080	132	183	221	236	226	5
	6	0+	0+	0+	0+	0+	0+	0+	001	002	002	003	006	010	015	022	027	057	099	147	193	226	6
	7	0+	0+	0+	0+	0+	0+	0+	0+	0+	0+	0+	001	002	003	005	006	017	038	070	113	161	7
	8	0+	0+	0+	0+	0+	0+	0+	0+	0+	0+	0+	0+	0+	0+	001	001	004	010	023	046	081	8
	9	0+	0+	0+	0+	0+	0+	0+	0+	0+	0+	0+	0+	0+	0+	0+	0+	001	002	005	013	027	9
	10	0+	0+	0+	0+	0+	0+	0+	0+	0+	0+	0+	0+	0+	0+	0+	0+	0+	0+	001	002	005	10
	11	0+	0+	0+	0+	0+	0+	0+	0+	0+	0+	0+	0+	0+	0+	0+	0+	0+	0+	0+	0+	0+	11
12	0	886	785	613	540	476	368	282	216	164	142	123	092	069	051	037	032	014	006	002	001	0+	0
	1	107	192	306	341	365	384	377	353	320	301	282	243	206	172	141	127	071	037	017	008	003	1
	2	006	022	070	099	128	183	230	265	286	292	296	294	283	266	244	232	168	109	064	034	016	2
	3	0+	001	010	017	027	053	085	120	155	172	188	215	236	250	257	258	240	195	142	092	054	3
	4	0+	0+	001	002	004	010	021	037	057	068	080	106	133	159	183	194	231	237	213	170	121	4
	5	0+	0+	0+	0+	0+	001	004	008	015	019	025	037	053	072	092	103	158	204	227	222	193	5
	6	0+	0+	0+	0+	0+	0+	0+	001	003	004	005	010	016	024	034	040	079	128	177	212	226	6
	7	0+	0+	0+	0+	0+	0+	0+	0+	0+	001	001	002	003	006	009	011	029	059	101	149	193	7
	8	0+	0+	0+	0+	0+	0+	0+	0+	0+	0+	0+	001	001	002	002	008	020	042	076	121	8	8
	9	0+	0+	0+	0+	0+	0+	0+	0+	0+	0+	0+	0+	0+	0+	0+	001	005	012	028	054	9
	10	0+	0+	0+	0+	0+	0+	0+	0+	0+	0+	0+	0+	0+	0+	0+	0+	001	002	007	016	10
	11	0+	0+	0+	0+	0+	0+	0+	0+	0+	0+	0+	0+	0+	0+	0+	0+	0+	0+	001	003	11
	12	0+	0+	0+	0+	0+	0+	0+	0+	0+	0+	0+	0+	0+	0+	0+	0+	0+	0+	0+	0+	12
13	0	878	769	588	513	447	338	254	190	141	121	104	076	055	040	028	024	010	004	001	0+	0+	0
	1	115	204	319	351	371	382	367	336	298	277	257	216	179	145	116	103	054	026	011	004	002	1
	2	007	025	080	111	142	199	245	275	291	294	293	285	268	245	220	206	139	084	045	022	010	2
	3	0+	002	012	021	033	064	100	138	174	190	205	229	246	254	254	252	218	165	111	066	035	3
	4	0+	0+	001	003	005	014	028	047	071	084	098	126	154	179	201	210	234	222	184	135	087	4
	5	0+	0+	0+	0+	001	002	006	012	021	027	033	050	069	091	114	126	180	215	221	199	157	5
	6	0+	0+	0+	0+	0+	0+	001	002	004	006	008	015	023	034	048	056	103	155	197	217	209	6
	7	0+	0+	0+	0+	0+	0+	0+	0+	001	001	002	003	006	010	015	019	044	083	131	177	209	7
	8	0+	0+	0+	0+	0+	0+	0+	0+	0+	0+	0+	001	001	002	004	005	014	034	066	109	157	8
	9	0+	0+	0+	0+	0+	0+	0+	0+	0+	0+	0+	0+	0+	0+	001	001	003	010	024	050	087	9
	10	0+	0+	0+	0+	0+	0+	0+	0+	0+	0+	0+	0+	0+	0+	0+	0+	001	002	006	016	035	10
	11	0+	0+	0+	0+	0+	0+	0+	0+	0+	0+	0+	0+	0+	0+	0+	0+	0+	0+	001	004	010	11
	12	0+	0+	0+	0+	0+	0+	0+	0+	0+	0+	0+	0+	0+	0+	0+	0+	0+	0+	0+	002	12	12
	13	0+	0+	0+	0+	0+	0+	0+	0+	0+	0+	0+	0+	0+	0+	0+	0+	0+	0+	0+	0+	13
14	0	869	754	565	488	421	311	229	167	121	103	087	062	044	031	021	018	007	002	001	0+	0+	0
	1	123	215	329	359	376	379	356	319	276	254	232	191	154	122	095	083	041	018	007	003	001	1
	2	008	029	089	123	156	214	257	283	292	291	287	272	250	223	195	180	113	063	032	014	006	2
	3	0+	002	015	026	040	074	114	154	190	206	219	239	250	252	246	240	194	137	085	046	022	3
	4	0+	0+	002	004	007	018	035	058	085	100	115	144	172	195	214	220	229	202	155	104	061	4
	5	0+	0+	0+	0+	001	003	008	016	028	035	044	063	086	110	135	147	196	218	207	170	122	5
	6	0+	0+	0+	0+	0+	0+	001	003	007	009	012	021	032	047	064	073	126	176	207	209	183	6
	7	0+	0+	0+	0+	0+	0+	0+	001	001	002	003	005	009	015	023	028	062	108	157	195	209	7
	8	0+	0+	0+	0+	0+	0+	0+	0+	0+	0+	001	002	004	006	008	023	051	092	140	183	8	8
	9	0+	0+	0+	0+	0+	0+	0+	0+	0+	0+	0+	0+	001	001	002	007	018	041	076	122	9	9
	10	0+	0+	0+	0+	0+	0+	0+	0+	0+	0+	0+	0+	0+	0+	0+	001	005	014	031	061	10
	11	0+	0+	0+	0+	0+	0+	0+	0+	0+	0+	0+	0+	0+	0+	0+	0+	001	003	009	022	11
	12	0+	0+	0+	0+	0+	0+	0+	0+	0+	0+	0+	0+	0+	0+	0+	0+	0+	001	002	006	12
	13	0+	0+	0+	0+	0+	0+	0+	0+	0+	0+	0+	0+	0+	0+	0+	0+	0+	0+	0+	001	13
	14	0+	0+	0+	0+	0+	0+	0+	0+	0+	0+	0+	0+	0+	0+	0+	0+	0+	0+	0+	0+	14
15	0	860	739	542	463	395	286	206	147	104	087	073	051	035	024	016	013	005	002	0+	0+	0+	0
	1	130	226	339	366	378	373	343	301	254	231	209	168	132	102	077	067	031	013	005	002	0+	1
	2	009	032	099	135	169	227	267	287	290	286	279	258	231	201	171	156	092	048	022	009	003	2
	3	0+	003	018	031	047	086	129	170	204	218	230	245	250	246	234	225	170	111	063	032	014	3
	4	0+	0+	002	005	009	022	043	069	100	116	131	162	188	208	221	225	219	179	127	078	042	4

Table E. BINOMIAL DISTRIBUTION OF INDIVIDUAL TERMS (Continued)

$P(r) = {}_nC_r p^r q^{n-r}$

n	r	.01	.02	.04	.05	.06	.08	.10	.12	.14	.15	.16	.18	.20	.22	.24	.25	.30	.35	.40	.45	.50	r
15	5	0+	0+	0+	001	001	004	010	021	036	045	055	078	103	129	154	165	206	212	186	140	092	5
	6	0+	0+	0+	0+	0+	001	002	005	010	013	017	029	043	061	081	092	147	191	207	191	153	6
	7	0+	0+	0+	0+	0+	0+	0+	001	002	003	004	008	014	022	033	039	081	132	177	201	196	7
	8	0+	0+	0+	0+	0+	0+	0+	0+	0+	001	001	002	003	006	010	013	035	071	118	165	196	8
	9	0+	0+	0+	0+	0+	0+	0+	0+	0+	0+	0+	0+	001	001	003	003	012	030	061	105	153	9
	10	0+	0+	0+	0+	0+	0+	0+	0+	0+	0+	0+	0+	0+	0+	0+	001	003	010	024	051	092	10
	11	0+	0+	0+	0+	0+	0+	0+	0+	0+	0+	0+	0+	0+	0+	0+	0+	001	002	007	019	042	11
	12	0+	0+	0+	0+	0+	0+	0+	0+	0+	0+	0+	0+	0+	0+	0+	0+	0+	0+	002	005	014	12
	13	0+	0+	0+	0+	0+	0+	0+	0+	0+	0+	0+	0+	0+	0+	0+	0+	0+	0+	0+	001	003	13
	14	0+	0+	0+	0+	0+	0+	0+	0+	0+	0+	0+	0+	0+	0+	0+	0+	0+	0+	0+	0+	0+	14
	15	0+	0+	0+	0+	0+	0+	0+	0+	0+	0+	0+	0+	0+	0+	0+	0+	0+	0+	0+	0+	0+	15
16	0	851	724	520	440	372	263	185	129	090	074	061	042	028	019	012	010	003	001	0+	0+	0+	0
	1	138	236	347	371	379	366	329	282	233	210	187	147	113	085	063	053	023	009	003	001	0+	1
	2	010	036	108	146	182	239	275	289	285	277	268	242	211	179	148	134	073	035	015	006	002	2
	3	0+	003	021	036	054	097	142	184	216	229	238	248	246	236	218	208	146	089	047	022	009	3
	4	0+	0+	003	006	011	027	051	081	114	131	147	177	200	216	224	225	204	155	101	057	028	4
	5	0+	0+	0+	001	002	006	014	027	045	056	067	093	120	146	170	180	210	201	162	112	067	5
	6	0+	0+	0+	0+	0+	001	003	007	013	018	023	037	055	076	098	110	165	198	198	168	122	6
	7	0+	0+	0+	0+	0+	0+	0+	001	003	005	006	012	020	030	044	052	101	152	189	197	175	7
	8	0+	0+	0+	0+	0+	0+	0+	0+	001	001	001	003	006	010	016	020	049	092	142	181	196	8
	9	0+	0+	0+	0+	0+	0+	0+	0+	0+	0+	0+	001	001	002	004	006	019	044	084	132	175	9
	10	0+	0+	0+	0+	0+	0+	0+	0+	0+	0+	0+	0+	0+	0+	001	001	006	017	039	075	122	10
	11	0+	0+	0+	0+	0+	0+	0+	0+	0+	0+	0+	0+	0+	0+	0+	0+	001	005	014	034	067	11
	12	0+	0+	0+	0+	0+	0+	0+	0+	0+	0+	0+	0+	0+	0+	0+	0+	0+	001	004	011	028	12
	13	0+	0+	0+	0+	0+	0+	0+	0+	0+	0+	0+	0+	0+	0+	0+	0+	0+	0+	001	003	009	13
	14	0+	0+	0+	0+	0+	0+	0+	0+	0+	0+	0+	0+	0+	0+	0+	0+	0+	0+	0+	001	002	14
	15	0+	0+	0+	0+	0+	0+	0+	0+	0+	0+	0+	0+	0+	0+	0+	0+	0+	0+	0+	0+	0+	15
	16	0+	0+	0+	0+	0+	0+	0+	0+	0+	0+	0+	0+	0+	0+	0+	0+	0+	0+	0+	0+	0+	16
17	0	843	709	500	418	349	242	167	114	077	063	052	034	023	015	009	008	002	001	0+	0+	0+	0
	1	145	246	354	374	379	358	315	264	213	189	167	128	096	070	051	043	017	006	002	001	0+	1
	2	012	040	118	158	194	249	280	288	278	267	255	225	191	158	128	114	058	026	010	004	001	2
	3	001	004	025	041	062	108	156	196	226	236	243	246	239	223	202	189	125	070	034	014	005	3
	4	0+	0+	004	008	014	033	060	094	129	146	162	189	209	221	223	221	187	132	080	041	018	4
	5	0+	0+	0+	001	002	007	017	033	054	067	080	108	136	162	183	191	208	185	138	087	047	5
	6	0+	0+	0+	0+	0+	001	004	009	018	024	031	047	068	091	116	128	178	199	184	143	094	6
	7	0+	0+	0+	0+	0+	0+	001	002	005	007	009	016	027	040	057	067	120	168	193	184	148	7
	8	0+	0+	0+	0+	0+	0+	0+	0+	001	001	002	004	008	014	023	028	064	113	161	188	185	8
	9	0+	0+	0+	0+	0+	0+	0+	0+	0+	0+	0+	001	002	004	007	009	028	061	107	154	185	9
	10	0+	0+	0+	0+	0+	0+	0+	0+	0+	0+	0+	0+	0+	001	002	002	009	026	057	101	148	10
	11	0+	0+	0+	0+	0+	0+	0+	0+	0+	0+	0+	0+	0+	0+	0+	001	003	009	024	052	094	11
	12	0+	0+	0+	0+	0+	0+	0+	0+	0+	0+	0+	0+	0+	0+	0+	0+	001	002	008	021	047	12
	13	0+	0+	0+	0+	0+	0+	0+	0+	0+	0+	0+	0+	0+	0+	0+	0+	0+	001	002	007	018	13
	14	0+	0+	0+	0+	0+	0+	0+	0+	0+	0+	0+	0+	0+	0+	0+	0+	0+	0+	0+	002	005	14
	15	0+	0+	0+	0+	0+	0+	0+	0+	0+	0+	0+	0+	0+	0+	0+	0+	0+	0+	0+	0+	001	15
	16	0+	0+	0+	0+	0+	0+	0+	0+	0+	0+	0+	0+	0+	0+	0+	0+	0+	0+	0+	0+	0+	16
	17	0+	0+	0+	0+	0+	0+	0+	0+	0+	0+	0+	0+	0+	0+	0+	0+	0+	0+	0+	0+	0+	17
18	0	835	695	480	397	328	223	150	100	066	054	043	028	018	011	007	006	002	0+	0+	0+	0+	0
	1	152	255	360	376	377	349	300	246	194	170	149	111	081	058	041	034	013	004	001	0+	0+	1
	2	013	044	127	168	205	258	284	285	268	256	241	207	172	139	109	096	046	019	007	002	001	2
	3	001	005	028	047	070	120	168	207	233	241	244	243	230	209	184	170	105	055	025	009	003	3
	4	0+	0+	004	009	017	039	070	106	142	159	175	200	215	221	218	213	168	110	061	029	012	4
	5	0+	0+	001	001	003	009	022	040	065	079	093	123	151	175	193	199	202	166	115	067	033	5
	6	0+	0+	0+	0+	0+	002	005	012	023	030	038	058	082	107	132	144	187	194	166	118	071	6
	7	0+	0+	0+	0+	0+	0+	001	003	006	009	013	022	035	052	071	082	138	179	189	166	121	7
	8	0+	0+	0+	0+	0+	0+	0+	001	001	002	003	007	012	020	031	038	081	133	173	186	167	8
	9	0+	0+	0+	0+	0+	0+	0+	0+	0+	0+	001	002	003	006	011	014	039	079	128	169	185	9
	10	0+	0+	0+	0+	0+	0+	0+	0+	0+	0+	0+	0+	001	002	003	004	015	038	077	125	167	10
	11	0+	0+	0+	0+	0+	0+	0+	0+	0+	0+	0+	0+	0+	0+	001	001	005	015	037	074	121	11
	12	0+	0+	0+	0+	0+	0+	0+	0+	0+	0+	0+	0+	0+	0+	0+	0+	001	005	015	035	071	12
	13	0+	0+	0+	0+	0+	0+	0+	0+	0+	0+	0+	0+	0+	0+	0+	0+	0+	001	004	013	033	13
	14	0+	0+	0+	0+	0+	0+	0+	0+	0+	0+	0+	0+	0+	0+	0+	0+	0+	0+	001	004	012	14
	15	0+	0+	0+	0+	0+	0+	0+	0+	0+	0+	0+	0+	0+	0+	0+	0+	0+	0+	0+	001	003	15
	16	0+	0+	0+	0+	0+	0+	0+	0+	0+	0+	0+	0+	0+	0+	0+	0+	0+	0+	0+	0+	001	16
	17	0+	0+	0+	0+	0+	0+	0+	0+	0+	0+	0+	0+	0+	0+	0+	0+	0+	0+	0+	0+	0+	17
	18	0+	0+	0+	0+	0+	0+	0+	0+	0+	0+	0+	0+	0+	0+	0+	0+	0+	0+	0+	0+	0+	18

Table E. BINOMIAL DISTRIBUTION OF INDIVIDUAL TERMS (Continued)

$$P(r) = {}_nC_r p^r q^{n-r}$$

n	r	.01	.02	.04	.05	.06	.08	.10	.12	.14	.15	.16	.18	.20	.22	.24	.25	.30	.35	.40	.45	.50	r
19	0	826	681	460	377	309	205	135	088	057	046	036	023	014	009	005	004	001	0+	0+	0+	0+	0
	1	159	264	364	377	374	339	285	228	176	153	132	096	068	048	033	027	009	003	001	0+	0+	1
	2	014	049	137	179	215	265	285	280	258	243	226	190	154	121	093	080	036	014	005	001	0+	2
	3	001	006	032	053	078	131	180	217	238	243	244	236	218	194	160	152	087	042	017	006	002	3
	4	0+	0+	005	011	020	045	080	118	155	171	186	207	218	219	210	202	149	091	047	020	007	4
	5	0+	0+	001	002	004	012	027	048	076	091	106	137	164	185	199	202	192	147	093	050	022	5
	6	0+	0+	0+	0+	001	002	007	015	029	037	047	070	095	122	146	157	192	184	145	095	052	6
	7	0+	0+	0+	0+	0+	0+	001	004	009	012	017	029	044	064	086	097	153	184	180	144	096	7
	8	0+	0+	0+	0+	0+	0+	0+	001	002	003	005	009	017	027	041	049	098	149	180	177	144	8
	9	0+	0+	0+	0+	0+	0+	0+	0+	0+	001	001	003	005	009	016	020	051	098	146	177	176	9
	10	0+	0+	0+	0+	0+	0+	0+	0+	0+	0+	0+	001	001	003	005	007	022	053	098	145	176	10
	11	0+	0+	0+	0+	0+	0+	0+	0+	0+	0+	0+	0+	0+	001	001	002	008	023	053	097	144	11
	12	0+	0+	0+	0+	0+	0+	0+	0+	0+	0+	0+	0+	0+	0+	0+	0+	002	008	024	053	096	12
	13	0+	0+	0+	0+	0+	0+	0+	0+	0+	0+	0+	0+	0+	0+	0+	0+	001	002	008	023	052	13
	14	0+	0+	0+	0+	0+	0+	0+	0+	0+	0+	0+	0+	0+	0+	0+	0+	0+	001	002	008	022	14
	15	0+	0+	0+	0+	0+	0+	0+	0+	0+	0+	0+	0+	0+	0+	0+	0+	0+	0+	001	002	007	15
	16	0+	0+	0+	0+	0+	0+	0+	0+	0+	0+	0+	0+	0+	0+	0+	0+	0+	0+	0+	0+	002	16
	17	0+	0+	0+	0+	0+	0+	0+	0+	0+	0+	0+	0+	0+	0+	0+	0+	0+	0+	0+	0+	0+	17
	18	0+	0+	0+	0+	0+	0+	0+	0+	0+	0+	0+	0+	0+	0+	0+	0+	0+	0+	0+	0+	0+	18
	19	0+	0+	0+	0+	0+	0+	0+	0+	0+	0+	0+	0+	0+	0+	0+	0+	0+	0+	0+	0+	0+	19
20	0	818	668	442	358	290	189	122	078	049	039	031	019	012	007	004	003	001	0+	0+	0+	0+	0
	1	165	272	368	377	370	328	270	212	159	137	117	083	058	039	026	021	007	002	0+	0+	0+	1
	2	016	053	146	189	225	271	285	274	247	229	211	173	137	105	078	067	028	010	003	001	0+	2
	3	001	006	036	060	086	141	190	224	241	243	228	205	178	148	134	134	072	032	012	004	001	3
	4	0+	001	006	013	023	052	090	130	167	182	195	213	218	213	199	190	130	074	035	014	005	4
	5	0+	0+	001	002	005	015	032	057	087	103	119	149	175	192	201	202	179	127	075	036	015	5
	6	0+	0+	0+	0+	001	003	009	019	035	045	057	082	109	136	159	169	192	171	124	075	037	6
	7	0+	0+	0+	0+	0+	001	002	005	012	016	022	036	055	076	100	112	164	184	166	122	074	7
	8	0+	0+	0+	0+	0+	0+	0+	001	003	005	007	013	022	035	051	061	114	161	180	162	120	8
	9	0+	0+	0+	0+	0+	0+	0+	0+	001	001	002	004	007	013	022	027	065	116	160	177	160	9
	10	0+	0+	0+	0+	0+	0+	0+	0+	0+	0+	001	002	004	008	010	031	069	117	159	176		10
	11	0+	0+	0+	0+	0+	0+	0+	0+	0+	0+	0+	0+	0+	001	002	003	012	034	071	119	160	11
	12	0+	0+	0+	0+	0+	0+	0+	0+	0+	0+	0+	0+	0+	0+	001	001	004	014	035	073	120	12
	13	0+	0+	0+	0+	0+	0+	0+	0+	0+	0+	0+	0+	0+	0+	0+	0+	001	004	015	037	074	13
	14	0+	0+	0+	0+	0+	0+	0+	0+	0+	0+	0+	0+	0+	0+	0+	0+	0+	001	005	015	037	14
	15	0+	0+	0+	0+	0+	0+	0+	0+	0+	0+	0+	0+	0+	0+	0+	0+	0+	0+	001	005	015	15
	16	0+	0+	0+	0+	0+	0+	0+	0+	0+	0+	0+	0+	0+	0+	0+	0+	0+	0+	0+	001	005	16
	17	0+	0+	0+	0+	0+	0+	0+	0+	0+	0+	0+	0+	0+	0+	0+	0+	0+	0+	0+	0+	001	17
	18	0+	0+	0+	0+	0+	0+	0+	0+	0+	0+	0+	0+	0+	0+	0+	0+	0+	0+	0+	0+	0+	18
	19	0+	0+	0+	0+	0+	0+	0+	0+	0+	0+	0+	0+	0+	0+	0+	0+	0+	0+	0+	0+	0+	19
	20	0+	0+	0+	0+	0+	0+	0+	0+	0+	0+	0+	0+	0+	0+	0+	0+	0+	0+	0+	0+	0+	20
21	0	810	654	424	341	273	174	109	068	042	033	026	015	010	005	003	002	001	0+	0+	0+	0+	0
	1	172	280	371	376	366	317	255	195	144	122	103	071	048	032	021	017	005	001	0+	0+	0+	1
	2	017	057	155	198	233	276	284	267	234	215	196	157	121	091	066	055	022	007	002	0+	0+	2
	3	001	007	041	066	094	152	200	230	242	241	236	218	192	162	132	117	058	024	009	003	001	3
	4	0+	001	008	016	027	059	100	141	177	191	202	215	216	205	187	176	113	059	026	009	003	4
	5	0+	0+	001	003	006	018	038	065	098	115	131	161	183	197	201	199	164	109	059	026	010	5
	6	0+	0+	0+	0+	001	004	011	024	043	054	067	094	122	148	169	177	188	156	105	057	026	6
	7	0+	0+	0+	0+	0+	001	003	007	015	020	027	044	065	089	114	126	172	180	149	101	055	7
	8	0+	0+	0+	0+	0+	0+	001	002	004	006	009	017	029	044	063	074	129	169	174	144	097	8
	9	0+	0+	0+	0+	0+	0+	0+	001	002	002	002	005	010	018	029	036	080	132	168	170	140	9
	10	0+	0+	0+	0+	0+	0+	0+	0+	0+	0+	001	001	003	006	011	014	041	085	134	167	168	10
	11	0+	0+	0+	0+	0+	0+	0+	0+	0+	0+	0+	0+	001	002	003	005	018	046	089	137	168	11
	12	0+	0+	0+	0+	0+	0+	0+	0+	0+	0+	0+	0+	0+	0+	001	001	006	021	050	093	140	12
	13	0+	0+	0+	0+	0+	0+	0+	0+	0+	0+	0+	0+	0+	0+	0+	0+	002	008	023	053	097	13
	14	0+	0+	0+	0+	0+	0+	0+	0+	0+	0+	0+	0+	0+	0+	0+	0+	0+	002	009	025	055	14
	15	0+	0+	0+	0+	0+	0+	0+	0+	0+	0+	0+	0+	0+	0+	0+	0+	0+	001	009	026		15
	16	0+	0+	0+	0+	0+	0+	0+	0+	0+	0+	0+	0+	0+	0+	0+	0+	0+	0+	001	003	010	16
	17	0+	0+	0+	0+	0+	0+	0+	0+	0+	0+	0+	0+	0+	0+	0+	0+	0+	0+	0+	001	003	17
	18	0+	0+	0+	0+	0+	0+	0+	0+	0+	0+	0+	0+	0+	0+	0+	0+	0+	0+	0+	0+	001	18
	19	0+	0+	0+	0+	0+	0+	0+	0+	0+	0+	0+	0+	0+	0+	0+	0+	0+	0+	0+	0+	0+	19
	20	0+	0+	0+	0+	0+	0+	0+	0+	0+	0+	0+	0+	0+	0+	0+	0+	0+	0+	0+	0+	0+	20
	21	0+	0+	0+	0+	0+	0+	0+	0+	0+	0+	0+	0+	0+	0+	0+	0+	0+	0+	0+	0+	0+	21

Table E. BINOMIAL DISTRIBUTION OF INDIVIDUAL TERMS (Continued)

$$P(r) = {}_nC_r p^r q^{n-r}$$

n	r	.01	.02	.04	.05	.06	.08	.10	.12	.14	.15	.16	.18	.20	.22	.24	.25	.30	.35	.40	.45	.50	r
22	0	802	641	407	324	256	160	098	060	036	028	022	013	007	004	002	002	0+	0+	0+	0+	0+	0
	1	178	288	373	375	360	306	241	180	130	109	090	061	041	026	017	013	004	001	0+	0+	0+	1
	2	019	062	163	207	241	279	281	258	222	201	181	141	107	078	055	046	017	005	001	0+	0+	2
	3	001	008	045	073	103	162	208	235	241	237	230	207	178	146	116	102	047	018	006	002	0+	3
	4	0+	001	009	018	031	067	110	152	186	199	208	216	211	196	174	161	096	047	019	006	002	4
	5	0+	0+	001	003	007	021	044	075	109	126	143	170	190	199	197	193	149	091	046	019	006	5
	6	0+	0+	0+	001	001	005	014	029	050	063	077	106	134	159	177	183	181	139	086	043	018	6
	7	0+	0+	0+	0+	0+	001	004	009	019	025	033	053	077	102	128	139	177	171	131	081	041	7
	8	0+	0+	0+	0+	0+	0+	001	002	006	008	012	022	036	054	075	087	142	173	164	125	076	8
	9	0+	0+	0+	0+	0+	0+	0+	0+	001	002	004	007	014	024	037	045	095	145	170	164	119	9
	10	0+	0+	0+	0+	0+	0+	0+	0+	0+	001	001	002	005	009	015	020	053	101	148	169	154	10
	11	0+	0+	0+	0+	0+	0+	0+	0+	0+	0+	0+	001	001	003	005	007	025	060	107	151	168	11
	12	0+	0+	0+	0+	0+	0+	0+	0+	0+	0+	0+	0+	0+	001	002	002	010	029	066	113	154	12
	13	0+	0+	0+	0+	0+	0+	0+	0+	0+	0+	0+	0+	0+	0+	001	001	003	012	034	071	119	13
	14	0+	0+	0+	0+	0+	0+	0+	0+	0+	0+	0+	0+	0+	0+	0+	0+	001	004	014	037	076	14
	15	0+	0+	0+	0+	0+	0+	0+	0+	0+	0+	0+	0+	0+	0+	0+	0+	0+	001	005	016	041	15
	16	0+	0+	0+	0+	0+	0+	0+	0+	0+	0+	0+	0+	0+	0+	0+	0+	0+	0+	001	006	018	16
	17	0+	0+	0+	0+	0+	0+	0+	0+	0+	0+	0+	0+	0+	0+	0+	0+	0+	0+	0+	002	007	17
	18	0+	0+	0+	0+	0+	0+	0+	0+	0+	0+	0+	0+	0+	0+	0+	0+	0+	0+	0+	0+	002	18
	19	0+	0+	0+	0+	0+	0+	0+	0+	0+	0+	0+	0+	0+	0+	0+	0+	0+	0+	0+	0+	0+	19
	20	0+	0+	0+	0+	0+	0+	0+	0+	0+	0+	0+	0+	0+	0+	0+	0+	0+	0+	0+	0+	0+	20
	21	0+	0+	0+	0+	0+	0+	0+	0+	0+	0+	0+	0+	0+	0+	0+	0+	0+	0+	0+	0+	0+	21
	22	0+	0+	0+	0+	0+	0+	0+	0+	0+	0+	0+	0+	0+	0+	0+	0+	0+	0+	0+	0+	0+	22
23	0	794	628	391	307	241	147	089	053	031	024	018	010	006	003	002	001	0+	0+	0+	0+	0+	0
	1	184	295	375	372	354	294	226	166	117	097	079	053	034	021	013	010	003	001	0+	0+	0+	1
	2	020	066	172	215	248	281	277	249	209	188	166	127	093	066	046	038	013	004	001	0+	0+	2
	3	001	009	050	079	111	215	237	238	232	232	222	195	163	131	101	088	038	013	004	004	001	3
	4	0+	001	010	021	035	074	120	162	194	204	211	214	204	185	160	146	082	037	014	004	001	4
	5	0+	0+	002	004	009	025	051	084	120	137	153	179	194	198	192	185	133	076	035	013	004	5
	6	0+	0+	0+	001	002	006	017	034	059	073	087	118	145	168	182	185	171	122	070	032	012	6
	7	0+	0+	0+	0+	0+	001	005	011	023	031	040	063	088	115	139	150	178	160	113	064	029	7
	8	0+	0+	0+	0+	0+	0+	001	003	008	011	015	028	044	065	088	100	153	172	151	105	058	8
	9	0+	0+	0+	0+	0+	0+	0+	001	002	003	005	010	018	030	046	056	109	155	168	143	097	9
	10	0+	0+	0+	0+	0+	0+	0+	0+	0+	001	001	003	006	012	020	026	065	117	157	164	136	10
	11	0+	0+	0+	0+	0+	0+	0+	0+	0+	0+	0+	001	002	004	008	010	033	074	123	159	161	11
	12	0+	0+	0+	0+	0+	0+	0+	0+	0+	0+	0+	0+	001	002	003	014	040	082	130	161		12
	13	0+	0+	0+	0+	0+	0+	0+	0+	0+	0+	0+	0+	0+	001	001	005	018	046	090	136		13
	14	0+	0+	0+	0+	0+	0+	0+	0+	0+	0+	0+	0+	0+	0+	002	007	022	053	097			14
	15	0+	0+	0+	0+	0+	0+	0+	0+	0+	0+	0+	0+	0+	0+	0+	0+	002	009	026	058		15
	16	0+	0+	0+	0+	0+	0+	0+	0+	0+	0+	0+	0+	0+	0+	0+	0+	001	003	011	029		16
	17	0+	0+	0+	0+	0+	0+	0+	0+	0+	0+	0+	0+	0+	0+	0+	0+	0+	001	004	012		17
	18	0+	0+	0+	0+	0+	0+	0+	0+	0+	0+	0+	0+	0+	0+	0+	0+	0+	0+	001	004		18
	19	0+	0+	0+	0+	0+	0+	0+	0+	0+	0+	0+	0+	0+	0+	0+	0+	0+	0+	0+	001		19
	20	0+	0+	0+	0+	0+	0+	0+	0+	0+	0+	0+	0+	0+	0+	0+	0+	0+	0+	0+	0+	0+	20
	21	0+	0+	0+	0+	0+	0+	0+	0+	0+	0+	0+	0+	0+	0+	0+	0+	0+	0+	0+	0+	0+	21
	22	0+	0+	0+	0+	0+	0+	0+	0+	0+	0+	0+	0+	0+	0+	0+	0+	0+	0+	0+	0+	0+	22
	23	0+	0+	0+	0+	0+	0+	0+	0+	0+	0+	0+	0+	0+	0+	0+	0+	0+	0+	0+	0+	0+	23
24	0	786	616	375	292	227	135	080	047	027	020	015	009	005	003	001	001	0+	0+	0+	0+	0+	0
	1	190	302	375	369	347	282	213	152	105	086	070	045	028	017	010	008	002	0+	0+	0+	0+	1
	2	022	071	180	223	255	282	272	239	196	174	153	114	081	056	038	031	010	003	001	0+	0+	2
	3	002	011	055	086	119	180	221	239	234	225	213	183	149	117	088	075	031	010	003	001	0+	3
	4	0+	001	012	024	040	082	129	171	200	209	213	211	196	173	146	132	069	029	010	003	001	4
	5	0+	0+	002	005	010	029	057	093	130	147	162	185	196	195	184	176	118	062	027	009	003	5
	6	0+	0+	0+	001	002	008	020	040	067	082	098	129	155	174	184	185	160	106	056	024	008	6
	7	0+	0+	0+	0+	0+	002	006	014	028	037	048	073	100	126	149	159	176	147	096	050	021	7
	8	0+	0+	0+	0+	0+	0+	001	004	010	014	019	034	053	076	100	112	160	168	136	087	044	8
	9	0+	0+	0+	0+	0+	0+	0+	001	003	004	007	013	024	038	056	067	122	161	161	126	078	9
	10	0+	0+	0+	0+	0+	0+	0+	0+	001	001	002	004	009	016	027	033	079	130	161	155	117	10
	11	0+	0+	0+	0+	0+	0+	0+	0+	0+	0+	001	001	003	006	011	014	043	089	137	161	149	11
	12	0+	0+	0+	0+	0+	0+	0+	0+	0+	0+	0+	001	001	002	004	005	020	052	099	143	161	12
	13	0+	0+	0+	0+	0+	0+	0+	0+	0+	0+	0+	0+	0+	001	001	002	008	026	061	108	149	13
	14	0+	0+	0+	0+	0+	0+	0+	0+	0+	0+	0+	0+	0+	0+	0+	0+	003	011	032	069	117	14

Table E. BINOMIAL DISTRIBUTION OF INDIVIDUAL TERMS (Concluded)

$P(r) = {}_nC_r p^r q^{n-r}$

n	r	.01	.02	.04	.05	.06	.08	.10	.12	.14	.15	^{P}.16	.18	.20	.22	.24	.25	.30	.35	.40	.45	.50	r
24	15	0+	0+	0+	0+	0+	0+	0+	0+	0+	0+	0+	0+	0+	0+	0+	0+	001	004	014	038	078	15
	16	0+	0+	0+	0+	0+	0+	0+	0+	0+	0+	0+	0+	0+	0+	0+	0+	001	005	017	044	16
	17	0+	0+	0+	0+	0+	0+	0+	0+	0+	0+	0+	0+	0+	0+	0+	0+	0+	002	007	021	17
	18	0+	0+	0+	0+	0+	0+	0+	0+	0+	0+	0+	0+	0+	0+	0+	0+	0+	0+	002	008	18
	19	0+	0+	0+	0+	0+	0+	0+	0+	0+	0+	0+	0+	0+	0+	0+	0+	0+	0+	001	003	19
	20	0+	0+	0+	0+	0+	0+	0+	0+	0+	0+	0+	0+	0+	0+	0+	0+	0+	0+	0+	001	20
	21	0+	0+	0+	0+	0+	0+	0+	0+	0+	0+	0+	0+	0+	0+	0+	0+	0+	0+	0+	0+	21
	22	0+	0+	0+	0+	0+	0+	0+	0+	0+	0+	0+	0+	0+	0+	0+	0+	0+	0+	0+	0+	22
	23	0+	0+	0+	0+	0+	0+	0+	0+	0+	0+	0+	0+	0+	0+	0+	0+	0+	0+	0+	0+	23
	24	0+	0+	0+	0+	0+	0+	0+	0+	0+	0+	0+	0+	0+	0+	0+	0+	0+	0+	0+	0+	24
25	0	778	603	360	277	213	124	072	041	023	017	013	007	004	002	001	001	0+	0+	0+	0+	0+	0
	1	196	308	375	365	340	270	199	140	094	076	061	038	024	014	008	006	001	0+	0+	0+	0+	1
	2	024	075	188	231	260	282	266	228	183	161	139	101	071	048	031	025	007	002	0+	0+	0+	2
	3	002	012	060	093	127	188	226	239	229	217	203	170	136	104	076	064	024	008	002	0+	0+	3
	4	0+	001	014	027	045	090	138	179	205	211	213	206	187	161	132	118	057	022	007	002	0+	4
	5	0+	0+	002	006	012	033	065	103	140	156	170	190	196	190	175	165	103	051	020	006	002	5
	6	0+	0+	0+	001	003	010	024	047	076	092	108	139	163	179	184	183	147	091	044	017	005	6
	7	0+	0+	0+	0+	0+	002	007	017	034	044	056	083	111	137	158	165	171	133	080	038	014	7
	8	0+	0+	0+	0+	0+	0+	002	005	012	017	024	041	062	087	112	124	165	161	120	070	032	8
	9	0+	0+	0+	0+	0+	0+	0+	001	004	006	009	017	029	046	067	078	134	163	151	108	061	9
	10	0+	0+	0+	0+	01	01	0+	0+	001	002	003	006	012	021	034	042	092	141	161	142	097	10
	11	0+	0+	0+	0+	0+	0+	0+	0+	0+	0+	001	002	004	008	015	019	054	103	147	158	133	11
	12	0+	0+	0+	0+	0+	0+	01	01	0+	0+	0+	0+	001	003	005	007	027	065	114	151	155	12
	13	0+	0+	0+	0+	0+	0+	0+	0+	0+	0+	0+	0+	0+	001	002	002	011	035	076	124	155	13
	14	0+	0+	0+	0+	0+	0+	0+	0+	0+	0+	0+	0+	0+	0+	001	004	016	043	087	133	14
	15	0+	0+	0+	0+	0+	0+	0+	0+	0+	0+	0+	0+	0+	0+	0+	001	006	021	052	097	15
	16	0+	0+	0+	0+	0+	0+	0+	0+	0+	0+	0+	0+	0+	0+	0+	0+	002	009	027	061	16
	17	0+	0+	0+	0+	0+	0+	0+	0+	0+	0+	0+	0+	0+	0+	0+	0+	001	003	012	032	17
	18	0+	0+	0+	0+	0+	0+	0+	0+	0+	0+	0+	0+	0+	0+	0+	0+	0+	001	004	014	18
	19	0+	0+	0+	0+	0+	0+	0+	0+	0+	0+	0+	0+	0+	0+	0+	0+	0+	0+	001	005	19
	20	0+	0+	0+	0+	0+	0+	0+	0+	0+	0+	0+	0+	0+	0+	0+	0+	0+	0+	0+	002	20
	21	0+	0+	0+	0+	0+	0+	0+	0+	0+	0+	0+	0+	0+	0+	0+	0+	0+	0+	0+	0+	21
	22	0+	0+	0+	0+	0+	0+	0+	0+	0+	0+	0+	0+	0+	0+	0+	0+	0+	0+	0+	0+	22
	23	0+	0+	0+	0+	0+	0+	01	01	0+	0+	0+	0+	0+	0+	0+	01	01	01	0+	0+	23
	24	0+	0+	0+	0+	0+	0+	0+	0+	0+	0+	0+	0+	0+	0+	0+	0+	0+	0+	0+	0+	24
	25	0+	0+	0+	0+	0+	0+	0+	0+	0+	0+	0+	0+	0+	0+	0+	0+	0+	0+	0+	0+	25

Reprinted by permission from *Statistical Analysis for Business Decisions,* by William A. Spurr and Charles P. Bonini (Homewood, Ill.: Richard D. Irwin, 1977). Copyright © 1973, 1977 by William A. Spurr and Charles P. Bonini.

Table F. BINOMIAL DISTRIBUTION OF CUMULATIVE TERMS

Probability of r or more successes in n trials $= \sum\limits_{r}^{n} {_n}C_r p^r q^{n-r}$

n	r	.01	.02	.04	.05	.06	.08	.10	.12	.14	.15 ^{p}	.16	.18	.20	.22	.24	.25	.30	.35	.40	.45	.50	r
2	0	1	1	1	1	1	1	1	1	1	1	1	1	1	1	1	1	1	1	1	1	1	0
	1	020	040	078	098	116	154	190	226	260	278	294	328	360	392	422	438	510	578	640	698	750	1
	2	0+	0+	002	002	004	006	010	014	020	022	026	032	040	048	058	062	090	122	160	202	250	2
3	0	1	1	1	1	1	1	1	1	1	1	1	1	1	1	1	1	1	1	1	1	1	0
	1	030	059	115	143	169	221	271	319	364	386	407	449	488	525	561	578	657	725	784	834	875	1
	2	0+	001	005	007	010	018	028	040	053	061	069	086	104	124	145	156	216	282	352	425	500	2
	3	0+	0+	0+	0+	0+	001	001	002	003	003	004	006	008	011	014	016	027	043	064	091	125	3
4	0	1	1	1	1	1	1	1	1	1	1	1	1	1	1	1	1	1	1	1	1	1	0
	1	039	078	151	185	219	284	344	400	453	478	502	548	590	630	666	684	760	821	870	908	938	1
	2	001	002	009	014	020	034	052	073	097	110	123	151	181	212	245	262	348	437	525	609	688	2
	3	0+	0+	0+	0+	001	002	004	006	010	012	014	020	027	036	045	051	084	126	179	241	312	3
	4	0+	0+	0+	0+	0+	0+	0+	0+	0+	001	001	001	002	002	003	004	008	015	026	041	062	4
5	0	1	1	1	1	1	1	1	1	1	1	1	1	1	1	1	1	1	1	1	1	1	0
	1	049	096	185	226	266	341	410	472	530	556	582	629	672	711	746	763	832	884	922	950	969	1
	2	001	004	015	023	032	054	081	112	147	165	183	222	263	304	346	367	472	572	663	744	812	2
	3	0+	0+	001	001	002	005	009	014	022	027	032	044	058	074	093	104	163	235	317	407	500	3
	4	0+	0+	0+	0+	0+	0+	0+	001	002	002	003	004	007	010	013	016	031	054	087	131	188	4
	5	0+	0+	0+	0+	0+	0+	0+	0+	0+	0+	0+	0+	0+	001	001	001	002	005	010	018	031	5
6	0	1	1	1	1	1	1	1	1	1	1	1	1	1	1	1	1	1	1	1	1	1	0
	1	059	114	217	265	310	394	469	536	595	623	649	696	738	775	807	822	882	925	953	972	984	1
	2	001	006	022	033	046	077	114	156	200	224	247	296	345	394	442	466	580	681	767	836	891	2
	3	0+	0+	001	002	004	009	016	026	039	047	056	076	099	125	154	169	256	353	456	558	656	3
	4	0+	0+	0+	0+	0+	001	001	003	005	006	007	012	017	024	033	038	070	117	179	255	344	4
	5	0+	0+	0+	0+	0+	0+	0+	0+	0+	001	001	002	003	004	005	005	011	022	041	069	109	5
	6	0+	0+	0+	0+	0+	0+	0+	0+	0+	0+	0+	0+	0+	0+	0+	0+	001	002	004	008	016	6
7	0	1	1	1	1	1	1	1	1	1	1	1	1	1	1	1	1	1	1	1	1	1	0
	1	068	132	249	302	352	442	522	591	652	679	705	751	790	824	854	867	918	951	972	985	992	1
	2	002	008	029	044	062	103	150	201	256	283	311	368	423	478	530	555	671	766	841	898	938	2
	3	0+	0+	002	004	006	014	026	042	062	074	087	115	148	184	223	244	353	468	580	684	773	3
	4	0+	0+	0+	0+	0+	001	003	005	009	012	015	023	033	046	062	071	126	200	290	392	500	4
	5	0+	0+	0+	0+	0+	0+	0+	0+	001	001	002	003	005	007	011	013	029	056	096	153	227	5
	6	0+	0+	0+	0+	0+	0+	0+	0+	0+	0+	0+	0+	0+	001	001	001	004	009	019	036	062	6
	7	0+	0+	0+	0+	0+	0+	0+	0+	0+	0+	0+	0+	0+	0+	0+	0+	001	002	004	008	7
8	0	1	1	1	1	1	1	1	1	1	1	1	1	1	1	1	1	1	1	1	1	1	0
	1	077	149	279	337	390	487	570	640	701	728	752	796	832	863	889	900	942	968	983	992	996	1
	2	003	010	038	057	079	130	187	248	311	343	374	437	497	554	608	633	745	831	894	937	965	2
	3	0+	0+	003	006	010	021	038	061	089	105	123	161	203	249	297	321	448	572	685	780	855	3
	4	0+	0+	0+	0+	001	002	005	010	017	021	027	040	056	076	100	114	194	294	406	523	637	4
	5	0+	0+	0+	0+	0+	0+	0+	001	002	003	004	007	010	016	023	027	058	106	174	260	363	5
	6	0+	0+	0+	0+	0+	0+	0+	0+	0+	0+	0+	001	001	002	003	004	011	025	050	088	145	6
	7	0+	0+	0+	0+	0+	0+	0+	0+	0+	0+	0+	0+	0+	0+	0+	0+	001	004	009	018	035	7
	8	0+	0+	0+	0+	0+	0+	0+	0+	0+	0+	0+	0+	0+	0+	0+	0+	0+	001	002	004	8
9	0	1	1	1	1	1	1	1	1	1	1	1	1	1	1	1	1	1	1	1	1	1	0
	1	086	166	307	370	427	528	613	684	743	768	792	832	866	893	915	925	960	979	990	995	998	1
	2	003	013	048	071	098	158	225	295	366	401	435	501	564	622	675	700	804	879	929	961	980	2
	3	0+	001	004	008	014	030	053	083	120	141	163	210	262	316	371	399	537	663	768	850	910	3
	4	0+	0+	0+	001	001	004	008	016	027	034	042	062	086	114	148	166	270	391	517	639	746	4
	5	0+	0+	0+	0+	0+	0+	001	002	004	006	007	012	020	029	042	049	099	172	267	379	500	5
	6	0+	0+	0+	0+	0+	0+	0+	0+	001	001	002	003	005	008	010	025	054	099	166	254	6
	7	0+	0+	0+	0+	0+	0+	0+	0+	0+	0+	0+	001	001	001	004	011	025	050	090	7
	8	0+	0+	0+	0+	0+	0+	0+	0+	0+	0+	0+	0+	0+	0+	0+	0+	001	004	009	020	8
	9	0+	0+	0+	0+	0+	0+	0+	0+	0+	0+	0+	0+	0+	0+	0+	0+	0+	0+	001	002	9
10	0	1	1	1	1	1	1	1	1	1	1	1	1	1	1	1	1	1	1	1	1	1	0
	1	096	183	335	401	461	566	651	721	779	803	825	863	893	917	936	944	972	987	994	997	999	1
	2	004	016	058	086	118	188	264	342	418	456	492	561	624	682	733	756	851	914	954	977	989	2
	3	0+	001	006	012	019	040	070	109	155	180	206	263	322	383	444	474	617	738	833	900	945	3
	4	0+	0+	0+	001	002	006	013	024	040	050	061	088	121	159	201	224	350	486	618	734	828	4
	5	0+	0+	0+	0+	0+	001	002	004	007	010	013	021	033	048	067	078	150	249	367	496	623	5
	6	0+	0+	0+	0+	0+	0+	0+	001	001	002	004	006	010	016	020	047	095	166	262	377	6
	7	0+	0+	0+	0+	0+	0+	0+	0+	0+	0+	001	001	002	003	004	011	026	055	102	172	7
	8	0+	0+	0+	0+	0+	0+	0+	0+	0+	0+	0+	0+	0+	0+	002	005	012	027	055	8
	9	0+	0+	0+	0+	0+	0+	0+	0+	0+	0+	0+	0+	0+	0+	0+	001	002	005	011	9

Table F. BINOMIAL DISTRIBUTION OF CUMULATIVE TERMS (Continued)

Probability of r or more successes in n trials = $\sum\limits_{r}^{n} {}_nC_r p^r q^{n-r}$

n	r	.01	.02	.04	.05	.06	.08	.10	.12	.14	.15	.16	.18	.20	.22	.24	.25	.30	.35	.40	.45	.50	r
10	10	0+	0+	0+	0+	0+	0+	0+	0+	0+	0+	0+	0+	0+	0+	0+	0+	0+	0+	0+	0+	001	10
11	0	1	1	1	1	1	1	1	1	1	1	1	1	1	1	1	1	1	1	1	1	1	0
	1	105	199	362	431	494	600	686	755	810	833	853	887	914	935	951	958	980	991	996	999	1-	1
	2	005	020	069	102	138	218	303	387	469	508	545	615	678	733	781	803	887	939	970	986	994	2
	3	0+	001	008	015	025	052	090	137	191	221	252	316	383	449	513	545	687	800	881	935	967	3
	4	0+	0+	001	002	003	009	019	034	056	069	085	120	161	208	260	287	430	574	704	809	887	4
	5	0+	0+	0+	0+	0+	001	003	006	012	016	021	033	050	072	099	115	210	332	467	603	726	5
	6	0+	0+	0+	0+	0+	0+	001	002	003	004	007	012	019	028	034	078	149	247	367	500	6	6
	7	0+	0+	0+	0+	0+	0+	0+	0+	0+	0+	001	002	004	006	008	022	050	099	174	274	7	7
	8	0+	0+	0+	0+	0+	0+	0+	0+	0+	0+	0+	0+	001	002	004	012	029	061	113	8		8
	9	0+	0+	0+	0+	0+	0+	0+	0+	0+	0+	0+	0+	0+	0+	001	002	006	015	033	9		9
	10	0+	0+	0+	0+	0+	0+	0+	0+	0+	0+	0+	0+	0+	0+	0+	0+	001	002	006	10		10
	11	0+	0+	0+	0+	0+	0+	0+	0+	0+	0+	0+	0+	0+	0+	0+	0+	0+	0+	0+	11		11
12	0	1	1	1	1	1	1	1	1	1	1	1	1	1	1	1	1	1	1	1	1	0
	1	114	215	387	460	524	632	718	784	836	858	877	908	931	949	963	968	986	994	998	999	1-	1
	2	006	023	081	118	160	249	341	431	517	557	595	664	725	778	822	842	915	958	980	992	997	2
	3	0+	002	011	020	032	065	111	167	230	264	299	370	442	511	578	609	747	849	917	958	981	3
	4	0+	0+	001	002	004	012	026	046	075	092	111	155	205	261	320	351	507	653	775	866	927	4
	5	0+	0+	0+	0+	0+	002	004	009	018	024	031	049	073	102	138	158	276	417	562	696	806	5
	6	0+	0+	0+	0+	0+	0+	001	001	003	005	006	012	019	030	045	054	118	213	335	473	613	6
	7	0+	0+	0+	0+	0+	0+	0+	0+	001	001	002	004	007	011	014	039	085	158	261	387	7	7
	8	0+	0+	0+	0+	0+	0+	0+	0+	0+	0+	0+	001	001	002	003	009	026	057	112	194	8	8
	9	0+	0+	0+	0+	0+	0+	0+	0+	0+	0+	0+	0+	0+	0+	002	006	015	036	073	9		9
	10	0+	0+	0+	0+	0+	0+	0+	0+	0+	0+	0+	0+	0+	0+	0+	0+	001	003	008	019	10		10
	11	0+	0+	0+	0+	0+	0+	0+	0+	0+	0+	0+	0+	0+	0+	0+	0+	0+	0+	001	003	11		11
	12	0+	0+	0+	0+	0+	0+	0+	0+	0+	0+	0+	0+	0+	0+	0+	0+	0+	0+	0+	0+	12		12
13	0	1	1	1	1	1	1	1	1	1	1	1	1	1	1	1	1	1	1	1	1	0
	1	122	231	412	487	553	662	746	810	859	879	896	924	945	960	972	976	990	996	999	1-	1-	1
	2	007	027	093	135	181	279	379	474	561	602	640	708	766	815	856	873	936	970	987	995	998	2
	3	0+	002	014	025	039	080	134	198	270	308	346	423	498	570	636	667	798	887	942	973	989	3
	4	0+	0+	001	003	006	016	034	061	097	118	141	194	253	316	382	416	579	722	831	907	954	4
	5	0+	0+	0+	01	001	002	006	014	026	034	044	068	099	137	182	206	346	499	647	772	867	5
	6	0+	0+	0+	0+	0+	0+	001	002	005	008	010	018	030	046	068	080	165	284	426	573	709	6
	7	0+	0+	0+	0+	0+	0+	0+	0+	001	001	002	004	007	012	019	024	062	129	229	356	500	7
	8	0+	0+	0+	0+	0+	0+	0+	0+	0+	0+	001	001	002	004	006	018	046	098	179	291	8	8
	9	0+	0+	0+	0+	0+	0+	0+	0+	0+	0+	0+	0+	0+	001	001	004	013	032	070	133	9		9
	10	0+	0+	0+	0+	0+	0+	0+	0+	0+	0+	0+	0+	0+	0+	0+	001	003	008	020	046	10		10
	11	0+	0+	0+	0+	0+	0+	0+	0+	0+	0+	0+	0+	0+	01	0+	0+	001	004	011	11		11
	12	0+	01	0+	0+	0+	0+	0+	0+	0+	0+	0+	0+	0+	0+	0+	0+	0+	001	002	12		12
	13	0+	0+	0+	0+	0+	0+	0+	0+	0+	0+	0+	0+	0+	0+	0+	0+	0+	0+	0+	13		13
14	0	1	1	1	1	1	1	1	1	1	1	1	1	1	1	1	1	1	1	1	1	0
	1	131	246	435	512	579	689	771	833	879	897	913	938	956	969	979	982	993	998	999	1-	1-	1
	2	008	031	106	153	204	310	415	514	603	643	681	747	802	847	884	899	953	979	992	997	999	2
	3	0+	002	017	030	048	096	158	232	311	352	393	474	552	624	689	719	839	916	960	983	994	3
	4	0+	0+	002	004	008	021	044	077	121	147	174	235	302	372	443	479	645	779	876	937	971	4
	5	0+	0+	0+	0+	001	004	009	020	036	047	059	091	130	176	230	258	416	577	721	833	910	5
	6	0+	0+	0+	0+	0+	0+	001	004	008	012	016	027	044	066	095	112	219	359	514	663	788	6
	7	0+	0+	0+	0+	0+	0+	0+	001	001	002	003	006	012	020	031	038	093	184	308	454	605	7
	8	0+	0+	0+	0+	0+	0+	0+	0+	0+	0+	001	001	002	005	008	010	031	075	150	259	395	8
	9	0+	0+	0+	0+	0+	0+	0+	0+	0+	0+	0+	0+	001	002	002	008	024	058	119	212	9		9
	10	0+	0+	0+	0+	0+	0+	0+	0+	0+	0+	0+	0+	0+	0+	0+	002	006	018	043	090	10		10
	11	0+	0+	0+	0+	0+	0+	0+	0+	0+	0+	0+	0+	0+	0+	0+	001	004	011	029	11		11
	12	0+	0+	0+	0+	0+	0+	0+	0+	0+	0+	0+	0+	0+	0+	0+	0+	001	002	006	12		12
	13	0+	0+	0+	0+	0+	0+	0+	0+	0+	0+	0+	0+	0+	0+	0+	0+	0+	0+	001	13		13
	14	0+	0+	0+	0+	0+	0+	0+	0+	0+	0+	0+	0+	0+	0+	0+	0+	0+	0+	0+	14		14
15	0	1	1	1	1	1	1	1	1	1	1	1	1	1	1	1	1	1	1	1	1	0
	1	140	261	458	537	605	714	794	853	896	913	927	949	965	976	984	987	995	998	1-	1-	1-	1
	2	010	035	119	171	226	340	451	552	642	681	718	781	833	874	906	920	965	986	995	998	1-	2
	3	0+	003	020	036	057	113	184	265	352	396	439	523	602	673	736	764	873	938	973	989	996	3
	4	0+	0+	002	005	010	027	056	096	148	177	209	278	352	427	502	539	703	827	909	958	982	4

Table F. BINOMIAL DISTRIBUTION OF CUMULATIVE TERMS (Continued)

Probability of r or more successes in n trials $= \sum_{r}^{n} {}_nC_r p^r q^{n-r}$

n	r	.01	.02	.04	.05	.06	.08	.10	.12	.14	.15	.16	.18	.20	.22	.24	.25	.30	.35	.40	.45	.50	r
15	5	0+	0+	0+	001	001	005	013	026	048	062	078	117	164	219	281	314	485	648	783	880	941	5
	6	0+	0+	0+	0+	0+	001	002	006	012	017	023	039	061	090	127	148	278	436	597	739	849	6
	7	0+	0+	0+	0+	0+	0+	0+	001	002	004	005	010	018	030	046	057	131	245	390	548	696	7
	8	0+	0+	0+	0+	0+	0+	0+	0+	0+	001	001	002	004	008	013	017	050	113	213	346	500	8
	9	0+	0+	0+	0+	0+	0+	0+	0+	0+	0+	0+	0+	001	002	003	004	015	042	095	182	304	9
	10	0+	0+	0+	0+	0+	0+	0+	0+	0+	0+	0+	0+	0+	0+	001	001	004	012	034	077	151	10
	11	0+	0+	0+	0+	0+	0+	0+	0+	0+	0+	0+	0+	0+	0+	0+	0+	001	003	009	025	059	11
	12	0+	0+	0+	0+	0+	0+	0+	0+	0+	0+	0+	0+	0+	0+	0+	0+	0+	0+	002	006	018	12
	13	0+	0+	0+	0+	0+	0+	0+	0+	0+	0+	0+	0+	0+	0+	0+	0+	0+	0+	0+	001	004	13
	14	0+	0+	0+	0+	0+	0+	0+	0+	0+	0+	0+	0+	0+	0+	0+	0+	0+	0+	0+	0+	0+	14
	15	0+	0+	0+	0+	0+	0+	0+	0+	0+	0+	0+	0+	0+	0+	0+	0+	0+	0+	0+	0+	0+	15
16	0	1	1	1	1	1	1	1	1	1	1	1	1	1	1	1	1	1	1	1	1	1	0
	1	149	276	480	560	628	737	815	871	910	926	939	958	972	981	988	990	997	999	1-	1-	1-	1
	2	011	040	133	189	249	370	485	588	677	716	751	811	859	897	925	937	974	990	997	999	1-	2
	3	001	004	024	043	067	131	211	300	393	439	484	570	648	717	777	803	901	955	982	993	998	3
	4	0+	0+	003	007	013	034	068	116	176	210	246	322	402	481	558	595	754	866	935	972	989	4
	5	0+	0+	0+	001	002	007	017	035	062	079	099	146	202	265	334	370	550	711	833	915	962	5
	6	0+	0+	0+	0+	0+	001	003	008	017	024	032	053	082	119	164	190	340	510	671	802	895	6
	7	0+	0+	0+	0+	0+	0+	001	002	004	006	008	015	027	043	066	080	175	312	473	634	773	7
	8	0+	0+	0+	0+	0+	0+	0+	0+	001	001	002	004	007	013	021	027	074	159	284	437	598	8
	9	0+	0+	0+	0+	0+	0+	0+	0+	0+	0+	0+	001	001	003	006	007	026	067	142	256	402	9
	10	0+	0+	0+	0+	0+	0+	0+	0+	0+	0+	0+	0+	0+	001	001	002	007	023	058	124	227	10
	11	0+	0+	0+	0+	0+	0+	0+	0+	0+	0+	0+	0+	0+	0+	0+	0+	002	006	019	049	105	11
	12	0+	0+	0+	0+	0+	0+	0+	0+	0+	0+	0+	0+	0+	0+	0+	0+	0+	001	005	015	038	12
	13	0+	0+	0+	0+	0+	0+	0+	0+	0+	0+	0+	0+	0+	0+	0+	0+	0+	0+	001	003	011	13
	14	0+	0+	0+	0+	0+	0+	0+	0+	0+	0+	0+	0+	0+	0+	0+	0+	0+	0+	0+	001	002	14
	15	0+	0+	0+	0+	0+	0+	0+	0+	0+	0+	0+	0+	0+	0+	0+	0+	0+	0+	0+	0+	0+	15
	16	0+	0+	0+	0+	0+	0+	0+	0+	0+	0+	0+	0+	0+	0+	0+	0+	0+	0+	0+	0+	0+	16
17	0	1	1	1	1	1	1	1	1	1	1	1	1	1	1	1	1	1	1	1	1	1	0
	1	157	291	500	582	651	758	833	886	923	937	948	966	977	985	991	992	998	999	1-	1-	1-	1
	2	012	045	147	208	272	399	518	622	710	748	781	838	882	915	940	950	981	993	998	999	1-	2
	3	001	004	029	050	078	150	238	335	432	480	527	613	690	758	812	836	923	967	988	996	999	3
	4	0+	0+	004	009	016	042	083	138	207	244	284	367	451	533	611	647	798	897	954	982	994	4
	5	0+	0+	0+	001	003	009	022	045	078	099	122	178	242	313	388	426	611	765	874	940	975	5
	6	0+	0+	0+	0+	0+	001	005	011	023	032	042	069	106	151	205	235	403	580	736	853	928	6
	7	0+	0+	0+	0+	0+	0+	001	002	006	008	012	022	038	060	089	107	225	381	552	710	834	7
	8	0+	0+	0+	0+	0+	0+	0+	0+	001	002	003	006	011	019	032	040	105	213	359	526	685	8
	9	0+	0+	0+	0+	0+	0+	0+	0+	0+	0+	0+	001	003	005	009	012	040	099	199	337	500	9
	10	0+	0+	0+	0+	0+	0+	0+	0+	0+	0+	0+	0+	0+	001	002	003	013	038	092	183	315	10
	11	0+	0+	0+	0+	0+	0+	0+	0+	0+	0+	0+	0+	0+	0+	0+	001	003	012	035	083	166	11
	12	0+	0+	0+	0+	0+	0+	0+	0+	0+	0+	0+	0+	0+	0+	0+	0+	001	003	011	030	072	12
	13	0+	0+	0+	0+	0+	0+	0+	0+	0+	0+	0+	0+	0+	0+	0+	0+	0+	001	003	009	025	13
	14	0+	0+	0+	0+	0+	0+	0+	0+	0+	0+	0+	0+	0+	0+	0+	0+	0+	0+	0+	002	006	14
	15	0+	0+	0+	0+	0+	0+	0+	0+	0+	0+	0+	0+	0+	0+	0+	0+	0+	0+	0+	0+	001	15
	16	0+	0+	0+	0+	0+	0+	0+	0+	0+	0+	0+	0+	0+	0+	0+	0+	0+	0+	0+	0+	0+	16
	17	0+	0+	0+	0+	0+	0+	0+	0+	0+	0+	0+	0+	0+	0+	0+	0+	0+	0+	0+	0+	0+	17
18	0	1	1	1	1	1	1	1	1	1	1	1	1	1	1	1	1	1	1	1	1	1	0
	1	165	305	520	603	672	777	850	900	934	946	957	972	982	989	993	994	998	1-	1-	1-	1-	1
	2	014	050	161	226	294	428	550	654	740	776	808	861	901	931	952	961	986	995	999	1-	1-	2
	3	001	005	033	058	090	170	266	369	471	520	567	654	729	792	843	865	940	976	992	997	999	3
	4	0+	0+	005	011	020	051	098	162	238	280	323	411	499	582	659	694	835	922	967	988	996	4
	5	0+	0+	001	002	003	012	028	056	096	121	148	212	284	361	441	481	667	811	906	959	985	5
	6	0+	0+	0+	0+	0+	002	006	015	031	042	055	089	133	187	249	283	466	645	791	892	952	6
	7	0+	0+	0+	0+	0+	0+	001	003	008	012	017	031	051	080	117	139	278	451	626	774	881	7
	8	0+	0+	0+	0+	0+	0+	0+	001	002	003	004	009	016	028	046	057	141	272	437	609	760	8
	9	0+	0+	0+	0+	0+	0+	0+	0+	001	001	002	004	008	015	019	060	139	263	422	593		9
	10	0+	0+	0+	0+	0+	0+	0+	0+	0+	0+	0+	001	002	004	005	021	060	135	253	407		10
	11	0+	0+	0+	0+	0+	0+	0+	0+	0+	0+	0+	0+	0+	001	001	006	021	058	128	240		11
	12	0+	0+	0+	0+	0+	0+	0+	0+	0+	0+	0+	0+	0+	0+	001	006	020	054	119		12
	13	0+	0+	0+	0+	0+	0+	0+	0+	0+	0+	0+	0+	0+	0+	0+	001	006	018	048		13
	14	0+	0+	0+	0+	0+	0+	0+	0+	0+	0+	0+	0+	0+	0+	0+	0+	001	005	015		14
	15	0+	0+	0+	0+	0+	0+	0+	0+	0+	0+	0+	0+	0+	0+	0+	0+	0+	001	004		15
	16	0+	0+	0+	0+	0+	0+	0+	0+	0+	0+	0+	0+	0+	0+	0+	0+	0+	0+	001		16
	17	0+	0+	0+	0+	0+	0+	0+	0+	0+	0+	0+	0+	0+	0+	0+	0+	0+	0+	0+		17
	18	0+	0+	0+	0+	0+	0+	0+	0+	0+	0+	0+	0+	0+	0+	0+	0+	0+	0+	0+		18

Table F. BINOMIAL DISTRIBUTION OF CUMULATIVE TERMS (Continued)

Probability of r or more successes in n trials $= \sum\limits_{r}^{n} {}_nC_r p^r q^{n-r}$

(The column headed .16 is the central division of the probability scale p.)

n	r	.01	.02	.04	.05	.06	.08	.10	.12	.14	.15	.16	.18	.20	.22	.24	.25	.30	.35	.40	.45	.50	r
19	0	1	1	1	1	1	1	1	1	1	1	1	1	1	1	1	1	1	1	1	1	1	0
	1	174	319	540	623	691	795	865	912	943	954	964	977	986	991	995	996	999	1-	1-	1-	1-	1
	2	015	055	175	245	317	456	580	683	767	802	832	881	917	943	962	969	990	997	999	1-	1-	2
	3	001	006	038	067	102	191	295	403	509	559	606	691	763	822	869	889	954	983	995	1-	1-	3
	4	0+	0+	006	013	024	060	115	187	271	316	362	455	545	628	703	737	867	941	977	992	998	4
	5	0+	0+	001	002	004	015	035	069	116	144	176	248	327	410	494	535	718	850	930	972	990	5
	6	0+	0+	0+	0+	001	003	009	020	040	054	070	111	163	225	295	332	526	703	837	922	968	6
	7	0+	0+	0+	0+	0+	0+	002	005	011	016	023	041	068	103	149	175	334	519	692	827	916	7
	8	0+	0+	0+	0+	0+	0+	0+	001	003	004	006	013	023	040	063	077	182	334	512	683	820	8
	9	0+	0+	0+	0+	0+	0+	0+	0+	001	001	001	003	007	013	022	029	084	185	333	506	676	9
	10	0+	0+	0+	0+	0+	0+	0+	0+	0+	0+	0+	001	002	003	007	009	033	087	186	329	500	10
	11	0+	0+	0+	0+	0+	0+	0+	0+	0+	0+	0+	0+	0+	001	002	002	011	035	088	184	324	11
	12	0+	0+	0+	0+	0+	0+	0+	0+	0+	0+	0+	0+	0+	0+	0+	001	003	011	035	087	180	12
	13	0+	0+	0+	0+	0+	0+	0+	0+	0+	0+	0+	0+	0+	0+	0+	0+	001	003	012	034	084	13
	14	0+	0+	0+	0+	0+	0+	0+	0+	0+	0+	0+	0+	0+	0+	0+	0+	0+	001	003	011	032	14
	15	0+	0+	0+	0+	0+	0+	0+	0+	0+	0+	0+	0+	0+	0+	0+	0+	0+	0+	001	003	010	15
	16	0+	0+	0+	0+	0+	0+	0+	0+	0+	0+	0+	0+	0+	0+	0+	0+	0+	0+	0+	001	002	16
	17	0+	0+	0+	0+	0+	0+	0+	0+	0+	0+	0+	0+	0+	0+	0+	0+	0+	0+	0+	0+	0+	17
	18	0+	0+	0+	0+	0+	0+	0+	0+	0+	0+	0+	0+	0+	0+	0+	0+	0+	0+	0+	0+	0+	18
	19	0+	0+	0+	0+	0+	0+	0+	0+	0+	0+	0+	0+	0+	0+	0+	0+	0+	0+	0+	0+	0+	19
20	0	1	1	1	1	1	1	1	1	1	1	1	1	1	1	1	1	1	1	1	1	1	0
	1	182	332	550	642	710	811	878	922	951	961	969	981	988	993	996	997	999	1-	1-	1-	1-	1
	2	017	060	190	264	340	483	608	711	792	824	853	898	931	954	970	976	992	998	999	1-	1-	2
	3	001	007	044	075	115	212	323	437	545	595	642	725	794	849	891	909	965	988	996	999	1-	3
	4	0+	001	007	016	029	071	133	213	304	352	401	497	589	671	743	775	893	956	984	995	999	4
	5	0+	0+	001	003	006	018	043	083	137	170	206	285	370	458	544	585	762	882	949	981	994	5
	6	0+	0+	0+	0+	001	004	011	026	051	067	087	136	196	266	343	383	584	755	874	945	979	6
	7	0+	0+	0+	0+	0+	001	003	007	015	022	030	054	087	130	184	214	392	583	750	870	942	7
	8	0+	0+	0+	0+	0+	0+	001	002	004	006	009	018	032	054	083	102	228	399	584	748	868	8
	9	0+	0+	0+	0+	0+	0+	0+	0+	001	001	002	005	010	019	032	041	113	238	404	586	748	9
	10	0+	0+	0+	0+	0+	0+	0+	0+	0+	0+	0+	001	003	005	010	014	048	122	245	409	588	10
	11	0+	0+	0+	0+	0+	0+	0+	0+	0+	0+	0+	0+	001	001	003	004	017	053	128	249	412	11
	12	0+	0+	0+	0+	0+	0+	0+	0+	0+	0+	0+	0+	0+	0+	0+	001	006	020	057	131	252	12
	13	0+	0+	0+	0+	0+	0+	0+	0+	0+	0+	0+	0+	0+	0+	0+	0+	001	006	021	058	132	13
	14	0+	0+	0+	0+	0+	0+	0+	0+	0+	0+	0+	0+	0+	0+	0+	0+	0+	002	006	021	058	14
	15	0+	0+	0+	0+	0+	0+	0+	0+	0+	0+	0+	0+	0+	0+	0+	0+	0+	0+	002	006	021	15
	16	0+	0+	0+	0+	0+	0+	0+	0+	0+	0+	0+	0+	0+	0+	0+	0+	0+	0+	0+	002	006	16
	17	0+	0+	0+	0+	0+	0+	0+	0+	0+	0+	0+	0+	0+	0+	0+	0+	0+	0+	0+	0+	001	17
	18	0+	0+	0+	0+	0+	0+	0+	0+	0+	0+	0+	0+	0+	0+	0+	0+	0+	0+	0+	0+	0+	18
	19	0+	0+	0+	0+	0+	0+	0+	0+	0+	0+	0+	0+	0+	0+	0+	0+	0+	0+	0+	0+	0+	19
	20	0+	0+	0+	0+	0+	0+	0+	0+	0+	0+	0+	0+	0+	0+	0+	0+	0+	0+	0+	0+	0+	20
21	0	1	1	1	1	1	1	1	1	1	1	1	1	1	1	1	1	1	1	1	1	1	0
	1	190	346	576	659	727	826	891	932	958	967	974	985	991	995	997	998	999	1-	1-	1-	1-	1
	2	019	065	204	283	362	509	635	736	814	845	872	913	943	962	976	981	994	999	1-	1-	1-	2
	3	001	008	050	085	128	234	352	470	580	630	676	756	821	872	910	925	973	991	998	999	1-	3
	4	0+	001	009	019	034	082	152	240	338	389	440	538	630	710	779	808	914	967	989	997	999	4
	5	0+	0+	001	003	007	023	052	098	161	197	237	323	414	505	592	633	802	908	963	987	996	5
	6	0+	0+	0+	0+	001	005	014	033	063	083	106	162	231	308	391	433	637	799	904	961	987	6
	7	0+	0+	0+	0+	0+	001	003	009	020	029	039	068	109	160	222	256	449	643	800	904	961	7
	8	0+	0+	0+	0+	0+	0+	001	002	005	008	012	024	043	070	108	130	277	464	650	803	905	8
	9	0+	0+	0+	0+	0+	0+	0+	0+	001	002	003	007	014	026	044	056	148	294	476	659	808	9
	10	0+	0+	0+	0+	0+	0+	0+	0+	0+	0+	001	002	004	008	016	021	068	162	309	488	669	10
	11	0+	0+	0+	0+	0+	0+	0+	0+	0+	0+	0+	0+	001	002	005	006	026	077	174	321	500	11
	12	0+	0+	0+	0+	0+	0+	0+	0+	0+	0+	0+	0+	0+	001	001	002	009	031	085	184	332	12
	13	0+	0+	0+	0+	0+	0+	0+	0+	0+	0+	0+	0+	0+	0+	0+	001	002	011	035	091	192	13
	14	0+	0+	0+	0+	0+	0+	0+	0+	0+	0+	0+	0+	0+	0+	0+	0+	001	003	012	038	095	14
	15	0+	0+	0+	0+	0+	0+	0+	0+	0+	0+	0+	0+	0+	0+	0+	0+	0+	001	004	013	039	15
	16	0+	0+	0+	0+	0+	0+	0+	0+	0+	0+	0+	0+	0+	0+	0+	0+	0+	0+	001	004	013	16
	17	0+	0+	0+	0+	0+	0+	0+	0+	0+	0+	0+	0+	0+	0+	0+	0+	0+	0+	0+	001	004	17
	18	0+	0+	0+	0+	0+	0+	0+	0+	0+	0+	0+	0+	0+	0+	0+	0+	0+	0+	0+	0+	001	18
	19	0+	0+	0+	0+	0+	0+	0+	0+	0+	0+	0+	0+	0+	0+	0+	0+	0+	0+	0+	0+	0+	19
	20	0+	0+	0+	0+	0+	0+	0+	0+	0+	0+	0+	0+	0+	0+	0+	0+	0+	0+	0+	0+	0+	20
	21	0+	0+	0+	0+	0+	0+	0+	0+	0+	0+	0+	0+	0+	0+	0+	0+	0+	0+	0+	0+	0+	21

Table F. BINOMIAL DISTRIBUTION OF CUMULATIVE TERMS (Continued)

Probability of r or more successes in n trials $= \sum\limits_{r}^{n} {}_nC_r p^r q^{n-r}$

n	r	.01	.02	.04	.05	.06	.08	.10	.12	.14	.15	.16	.18	.20	.22	.24	.25	.30	.35	.40	.45	.50	r'
22	0	1	1	1	1	1	1	1	1	1	1	1	1	1	1	1	1	1	1	1	1	1	0
	1	198	359	593	676	744	840	902	940	964	972	978	987	993	996	998	998	1-	1-	1-	1-	1-	1
	2	020	071	219	302	384	535	661	760	834	863	888	926	952	970	981	985	996	999	1-	1-	1-	2
	3	001	009	056	095	142	256	380	502	612	662	707	785	846	892	926	939	979	994	998	1-	1-	3
	4	0+	001	011	022	040	094	172	267	372	425	477	578	668	746	810	838	932	975	992	998	1-	4
	5	0+	0+	002	004	009	027	062	115	186	226	270	362	457	550	637	677	835	928	973	992	998	5
	6	0+	0+	0+	001	002	006	018	041	077	100	127	191	267	351	439	483	687	837	928	973	992	6
	7	0+	0+	0+	0+	0+	001	004	012	026	037	050	085	133	193	263	301	506	698	842	929	974	7
	8	0+	0+	0+	0+	0+	0+	001	003	008	011	017	032	056	090	135	162	329	526	710	848	933	8
	9	0+	0+	0+	0+	0+	0+	0+	001	002	003	005	010	020	036	060	075	186	353	546	724	857	9
	10	0+	0+	0+	0+	0+	0+	0+	0+	0+	001	001	003	006	012	022	030	092	208	376	565	738	10
	11	0+	0+	0+	0+	0+	0+	0+	0+	0+	0+	0+	001	002	004	007	010	039	107	228	396	584	11
	12	0+	0+	0+	0+	0+	0+	0+	0+	0+	0+	0+	0+	0+	001	002	003	014	047	121	246	416	12
	13	0+	0+	0+	0+	0+	0+	0+	0+	0+	0+	0+	0+	0+	0+	0+	001	004	018	055	133	262	13
	14	0+	0+	0+	0+	0+	0+	0+	0+	0+	0+	0+	0+	0+	0+	0+	0+	001	006	021	062	143	14
	15	0+	0+	0+	0+	0+	0+	0+	0+	0+	0+	0+	0+	0+	0+	0+	0+	0+	002	007	024	067	15
	16	0+	0+	0+	0+	0+	0+	0+	0+	0+	0+	0+	0+	0+	0+	0+	0+	0+	0+	002	008	026	16
	17	0+	0+	0+	0+	0+	0+	0+	0+	0+	0+	0+	0+	0+	0+	0+	0+	0+	0+	0+	002	008	17
	18	0+	0+	0+	0+	0+	0+	0+	0+	0+	0+	0+	0+	0+	0+	0+	0+	0+	0+	0+	0+	002	18
	19	0+	0+	0+	0+	0+	0+	0+	0+	0+	0+	0+	0+	0+	0+	0+	0+	0+	0+	0+	0+	0+	19
	20	0+	0+	0+	0+	0+	0+	0+	0+	0+	0+	0+	0+	0+	0+	0+	0+	0+	0+	0+	0+	0+	20
	21	0+	0+	0+	0+	0+	0+	0+	0+	0+	0+	0+	0+	0+	0+	0+	0+	0+	0+	0+	0+	0+	21
	22	0+	0+	0+	0+	0+	0+	0+	0+	0+	0+	0+	0+	0+	0+	0+	0+	0+	0+	0+	0+	0+	22
23	0	1	1	1	1	1	1	1	1	1	1	1	1	1	1	1	1	1	1	1	1	1	0
	1	206	372	609	693	759	853	911	947	969	976	982	990	994	997	998	999	1-	1-	1-	1-	1-	1
	2	022	077	234	321	405	559	685	781	852	880	902	937	960	975	985	988	997	999	1-	1-	1-	2
	3	002	011	062	105	157	278	408	533	643	692	736	810	867	909	939	951	984	996	999	1-	1-	3
	4	0+	001	012	026	046	107	193	295	405	460	514	615	703	778	838	863	946	982	995	999	1-	4
	5	0+	0+	002	005	011	033	073	133	212	256	303	401	499	593	678	717	864	945	981	995	999	5
	6	0+	0+	0+	001	002	008	023	050	092	119	150	222	305	395	487	532	731	869	946	981	995	6
	7	0+	0+	0+	0+	0+	002	006	015	033	046	062	104	160	227	305	346	560	747	876	949	983	7
	8	0+	0+	0+	0+	0+	0+	001	004	010	015	022	042	072	113	166	196	382	586	763	885	953	8
	9	0+	0+	0+	0+	0+	0+	0+	001	003	004	007	014	027	048	078	096	229	444	612	780	895	9
	10	0+	0+	0+	0+	0+	0+	0+	0+	001	001	002	004	009	017	031	041	120	259	444	636	798	10
	11	0+	0+	0+	0+	0+	0+	0+	0+	0+	0+	001	003	005	011	015	055	142	287	472	661	11	11
	12	0+	0+	0+	0+	0+	0+	0+	0+	0+	0+	0+	0+	001	003	005	021	068	164	313	500	12	12
	13	0+	0+	0+	0+	0+	0+	0+	0+	0+	0+	0+	0+	0+	001	001	007	028	081	184	339	13	13
	14	0+	0+	0+	0+	0+	0+	0+	0+	0+	0+	0+	0+	0+	0+	0+	002	010	035	094	202	14	14
	15	0+	0+	0+	0+	0+	0+	0+	0+	0+	0+	0+	0+	0+	0+	0+	001	003	013	041	105	15	15
	16	0+	0+	0+	0+	0+	0+	0+	0+	0+	0+	0+	0+	0+	0+	0+	0+	001	004	015	047	16	16
	17	0+	0+	0+	0+	0+	0+	0+	0+	0+	0+	0+	0+	0+	0+	0+	0+	0+	001	005	017	17	17
	18	0+	0+	0+	0+	0+	0+	0+	0+	0+	0+	0+	0+	0+	0+	0+	0+	0+	0+	001	005	18	18
	19	0+	0+	0+	0+	0+	0+	0+	0+	0+	0+	0+	0+	0+	0+	0+	0+	0+	0+	0+	001	19	19
	20	0+	0+	0+	0+	0+	0+	0+	0+	0+	0+	0+	0+	0+	0+	0+	0+	0+	0+	0+	0+	0+	20
	21	0+	0+	0+	0+	0+	0+	0+	0+	0+	0+	0+	0+	0+	0+	0+	0+	0+	0+	0+	0+	0+	21
	22	0+	0+	0+	0+	0+	0+	0+	0+	0+	0+	0+	0+	0+	0+	0+	0+	0+	0+	0+	0+	0+	22
	23	0+	0+	0+	0+	0+	0+	0+	0+	0+	0+	0+	0+	0+	0+	0+	0+	0+	0+	0+	0+	0+	23
24	0	1	1	1	1	1	1	1	1	1	1	1	1	1	1	1	1	1	1	1	1	1	0
	1	214	384	625	708	773	865	920	953	973	980	985	991	995	997	999	999	1-	1-	1-	1-	1-	1
	2	024	083	249	339	427	583	708	801	869	894	915	946	967	980	988	991	998	1-	1-	1-	1-	2
	3	002	012	069	116	172	301	436	563	673	720	763	833	885	924	950	960	988	997	999	1-	1-	3
	4	0+	001	014	030	053	121	214	324	439	495	550	650	736	807	862	885	958	987	996	999	1-	4
	5	0+	0+	002	006	013	039	085	153	239	287	337	439	540	634	717	753	889	958	987	996	999	5
	6	0+	0+	0+	001	002	010	028	060	109	139	174	254	344	439	533	578	771	896	960	987	997	6
	7	0+	0+	0+	0+	0+	002	007	019	041	057	076	126	189	264	349	393	611	789	904	964	989	7
	8	0+	0+	0+	0+	0+	0+	002	005	013	020	028	053	089	138	199	234	435	642	808	914	968	8
	9	0+	0+	0+	0+	0+	0+	0+	001	004	006	009	019	036	062	099	121	275	474	672	827	924	9
	10	0+	0+	0+	0+	0+	0+	0+	0+	001	002	002	006	013	024	042	055	153	313	511	701	846	10
	11	0+	0+	0+	0+	0+	0+	0+	0+	0+	0+	001	002	004	008	016	021	074	183	350	546	729	11
	12	0+	0+	0+	0+	0+	0+	0+	0+	0+	0+	0+	0+	001	002	005	007	031	104	213	385	581	12
	13	0+	0+	0+	0+	0+	0+	0+	0+	0+	0+	0+	0+	0+	001	001	002	012	042	114	242	419	13
	14	0+	0+	0+	0+	0+	0+	0+	0+	0+	0+	0+	0+	0+	0+	0+	001	004	016	053	134	271	14

Table F. BINOMIAL DISTRIBUTION OF CUMULATIVE TERMS (Concluded)

Probability of r or more successes in n trials $= \sum\limits_{r}^{n} {}_nC_r p^r q^{n-r}$

n	r	.01	.02	.04	.05	.06	.08	.10	.12	.14	.15	P.16	.18	.20	.22	.24	.25	.30	.35	.40	.45	.50	r
24	15	0+	0+	0+	0+	0+	0+	0+	0+	0+	0+	0+	0+	0+	0+	0+	0+	001	005	022	065	154	15
	16	0+	0+	0+	0+	0+	0+	0+	0+	0+	0+	0+	0+	0+	0+	0+	0+	0+	002	008	027	076	16
	17	0+	0+	0+	0+	0+	0+	0+	0+	0+	0+	0+	0+	0+	0+	0+	0+	0+	002	010	032	17
	18	0+	0+	0+	0+	0+	0+	0+	0+	0+	0+	0+	0+	0+	0+	0+	0+	0+	0+	001	003	011	18
	19	0+	0+	0+	0+	0+	0+	0+	0+	0+	0+	0+	0+	0+	0+	0+	0+	0+	0+	0+	001	003	19
	20	0+	0+	0+	0+	0+	0+	0+	0+	0+	0+	0+	0+	0+	0+	0+	0+	0+	0+	0+	0+	001	20
	21	0+	0+	0+	0+	0+	0+	0+	0+	0+	0+	0+	0+	0+	0+	0+	0+	0+	0+	0+	0+	0+	21
	22	0+	0+	0+	0+	0+	0+	0+	0+	0+	0+	0+	0+	0+	0+	0+	0+	0+	0+	0+	0+	0+	22
	23	0+	0+	0+	0+	0+	0+	0+	0+	0+	0+	0+	0+	0+	0+	0+	0+	0+	0+	0+	0+	0+	23
	24	0+	0+	0+	0+	0+	0+	0+	0+	0+	0+	0+	0+	0+	0+	0+	0+	0+	0+	0+	0+	0+	24
25	0	1	1	1	1	1	1	1	1	1	1	1	1	1	1	1	1	1	1	1	1	1	0
	1	222	397	640	723	787	876	928	959	977	983	987	993	996	998	999	999	1-	1-	1-	1-	1-	1
	2	026	089	264	358	447	605	729	820	883	907	926	955	973	984	991	993	998	1-	1-	1-	1-	2
	3	002	013	076	127	187	323	463	591	700	746	787	853	902	936	959	968	991	998	1-	1-	1-	3
	4	0+	001	017	034	060	135	236	352	471	529	584	683	766	832	883	904	967	990	998	1-	1-	4
	5	0+	0+	003	007	015	045	098	173	267	318	371	477	579	672	752	786	910	968	991	998	1-	5
	6	0+	0+	0+	001	003	012	033	071	127	162	200	298	383	482	577	622	807	917	971	991	998	6
	7	0+	0+	0+	0+	001	003	009	024	051	070	092	149	220	303	393	439	659	827	926	974	993	7
	8	0+	0+	0+	0+	0+	001	002	007	017	025	036	066	109	166	235	273	488	694	846	936	978	8
	9	0+	0+	0+	0+	0+	0+	0+	002	005	008	012	025	047	079	123	149	323	533	726	866	946	9
	10	0+	0+	0+	0+	0+	0+	0+	0+	001	002	003	008	017	033	056	071	189	370	575	758	885	10
	11	0+	0+	0+	0+	0+	0+	0+	0+	0+	0+	001	002	006	012	022	030	098	229	414	616	788	11
	12	0+	0+	0+	0+	0+	0+	0+	0+	0+	0+	0+	001	002	004	008	011	044	125	268	457	655	12
	13	0+	0+	0+	0+	0+	0+	0+	0+	0+	0+	0+	0+	0+	001	002	003	017	060	154	306	500	13
	14	0+	0+	0+	0+	0+	0+	0+	0+	0+	0+	0+	0+	0+	0+	001	001	006	025	078	183	345	14
	15	0+	0+	0+	0+	0+	0+	0+	0+	0+	0+	0+	0+	0+	0+	0+	0+	002	009	034	096	212	15
	16	0+	0+	0+	0+	0+	0+	0+	0+	0+	0+	0+	0+	0+	0+	0+	0+	003	013	044	115	16
	17	0+	0+	0+	0+	0+	0+	0+	0+	0+	0+	0+	0+	0+	0+	0+	0+	001	004	017	054	17
	18	0+	0+	0+	0+	0+	0+	0+	0+	0+	0+	0+	0+	0+	0+	0+	0+	0+	001	006	022	18
	19	0+	0+	0+	0+	0+	0+	0+	0+	0+	0+	0+	0+	0+	0+	0+	0+	0+	0+	002	007	19
	20	0+	0+	0+	0+	0+	0+	0+	0+	0+	0+	0+	0+	0+	0+	0+	0+	0+	0+	0+	002	20
	21	0+	0+	0+	0+	0+	0+	0+	0+	0+	0+	0+	0+	0+	0+	0+	0+	0+	0+	0+	0+	21
	22	0+	0+	0+	0+	0+	0+	0+	0+	0+	0+	0+	0+	0+	0+	0+	0+	0+	0+	0+	0+	22
	23	0+	0+	0+	0+	0+	0+	0+	0+	0+	0+	0+	0+	0+	0+	0+	0+	0+	0+	0+	0+	23
	24	0+	0+	0+	0+	0+	0+	0+	0+	0+	0+	0+	0+	0+	0+	0+	0+	0+	0=	0+	0+	24
	25	0+	0+	0+	0+	0+	0+	0+	0+	0+	0+	0+	0+	0+	0+	0+	0+	0+	0+	0+	0+	25

Reprinted by permission from *Statistical Analysis for Business Decisions*, by William A. Spurr and Charles P. Bonini (Homewood, Ill.: Richard D. Irwin, 1977). Copyright © 1973, 1977 by William A. Spurr and Charles P. Bonini.

Table G. POISSON DISTRIBUTION OF INDIVIDUAL TERMS

$$f(r) = \frac{6^{-m}m^x}{r}$$

r	.001	.002	.003	.004	.005	.006	.007	.008	.009	.01	.02	.03	.04	.05	.06	.07	.08	.09	.10	.15	r
0	999	998	997	996	995	994	993	992	991	990	980	970	961	951	942	932	923	914	905	861	0
1	001	002	003	004	005	006	007	008	009	010	020	030	038	048	057	065	074	082	090	129	1
2													001	001	002	002	003	004	005	010	2

r	.20	.25	.30	.40	.50	.60	.70	.80	.90	1.0 m	1.1	1.2	1.3	1.4	1.5	1.6	1.7	1.8	1.9	2.0	r
0	819	779	741	670	607	549	497	449	407	368	333	301	273	247	223	202	183	165	150	135	0
1	164	195	222	268	303	329	348	359	366	368	366	361	354	345	335	323	311	298	284	271	1
2	016	024	033	054	076	099	122	144	165	184	201	217	230	242	251	258	264	268	270	271	2
3	001	002	003	007	013	020	028	038	049	061	074	087	100	113	126	138	150	161	171	180	3
4				001	002	003	005	008	011	015	020	026	032	039	047	055	063	072	081	090	4
5							001	001	002	003	004	006	008	011	014	018	022	026	031	036	5
6										001	001	001	002	003	004	005	006	008	010	012	6
7														001	001	001	001	002	003	003	7
8																			001	001	8

r	2.1	2.2	2.3	2.4	2.5	2.6	2.7	2.8	2.9	3.0 m	3.1	3.2	3.3	3.4	3.5	3.6	3.7	3.8	3.9	4.0	r
0	122	111	100	091	082	074	067	061	055	050	045	041	037	033	030	027	025	022	020	018	0
1	257	244	231	218	205	193	181	170	160	149	140	130	122	113	106	098	091	085	079	073	1
2	270	268	265	261	257	251	245	238	231	224	216	209	201	193	185	177	169	162	154	147	2
3	189	197	203	209	214	218	220	222	224	224	224	223	221	219	216	212	209	205	200	195	3
4	099	108	117	125	134	141	149	156	162	168	173	178	182	186	189	191	193	194	195	195	4
5	042	048	054	060	067	074	080	087	094	101	107	114	120	126	132	138	143	148	152	156	5
6	015	017	021	024	028	032	036	041	045	050	056	061	066	072	077	083	088	094	099	104	6
7	004	005	007	008	010	012	014	016	019	022	025	028	031	035	039	042	047	051	055	060	7
8	001	002	002	002	003	004	005	006	007	008	010	011	013	015	017	019	022	024	027	030	8
9				001	001	001	001	002	002	003	003	004	005	006	007	008	009	010	012	013	9
10							001	001	001	001	002	002	002	003	003	004	005	005	10
11												001	001	001	001	001	002	002	11
12																001	001	12

Table G. POISSON DISTRIBUTION OF INDIVIDUAL TERMS (Continued)

$$f(r) = \frac{6^{-m}m^x}{r}$$

r	4.1	4.2	4.3	4.4	4.5	4.6	4.7	4.8	4.9	5.0	5.1	5.2	5.3	5.4	5.5	5.6	5.7	5.8	5.9	6.0	r
0	017	015	014	012	011	010	009	008	007	007	006	006	005	005	004	004	003	003	003	002	0
1	068	063	058	054	050	046	043	040	036	034	031	029	026	024	022	021	019	018	016	015	1
2	139	132	125	119	112	106	100	095	089	084	079	075	070	066	062	058	054	051	048	045	2
3	190	185	180	174	169	163	157	152	146	140	135	129	124	119	113	108	103	098	094	089	3
4	195	194	193	192	190	188	185	182	179	175	172	168	164	160	156	152	147	143	138	134	4
5	160	163	166	169	171	173	174	175	175	175	175	175	174	173	171	170	168	166	163	161	5
6	109	114	119	124	128	132	136	140	143	146	149	151	154	156	157	158	159	160	160	161	6
7	064	069	073	078	082	087	091	096	100	104	109	113	116	120	123	127	130	133	135	138	7
8	033	036	039	043	046	050	054	058	061	065	069	073	077	081	085	089	092	096	100	103	8
9	015	017	019	021	023	026	028	031	033	036	039	042	045	049	052	055	059	062	065	069	9
10	006	007	008	009	010	012	013	015	016	018	020	022	024	026	029	031	033	036	039	041	10
11	002	003	003	004	004	005	006	006	007	008	009	010	012	013	014	016	017	019	021	023	11
12	001	001	001	001	002	002	002	003	003	003	004	005	005	006	007	007	008	009	010	011	12
13					001	001	001	001	001	001	002	002	002	002	003	003	004	004	005	005	13
14											001	001	001	001	001	001	001	002	002	002	14
15																	001	001	001	001	15

r	6.1	6.2	6.3	6.4	6.5	6.6	6.7	6.8	6.9	7.0	7.1	7.2	7.3	7.4	7.5	8.0	8.5	9.0	9.5	10.0	r
0	002	002	002	002	002	001	001	001	001	001	001	001	001	001	001						0
1	014	013	012	011	010	009	008	008	007	006	006	005	005	005	004	003	002	001	001		1
2	042	039	036	034	032	030	028	026	024	022	021	019	018	017	016	011	007	005	003	002	2
3	085	081	077	073	069	065	062	058	055	052	049	046	044	041	039	029	021	015	011	008	3
4	129	125	121	116	112	108	103	099	095	091	087	084	080	076	073	057	044	034	025	019	4
5	158	155	152	149	145	142	138	135	131	128	124	120	117	113	109	092	075	061	048	038	5
6	160	160	159	159	157	156	155	153	151	149	147	144	142	139	137	122	107	091	076	063	6
7	140	142	144	145	146	147	148	149	149	149	149	149	148	147	146	140	129	117	104	090	7
8	107	110	113	116	119	121	124	126	128	130	132	134	135	136	137	140	138	132	123	113	8
9	072	076	079	082	086	089	092	095	098	101	104	107	110	112	114	124	130	132	130	125	9
10	044	047	050	053	056	059	062	065	060	071	074	077	080	083	086	099	110	119	124	125	10
11	024	026	029	031	033	035	038	040	043	045	048	050	053	056	059	072	085	097	107	114	11
12	012	014	015	016	018	019	021	023	025	026	028	030	032	034	037	048	060	073	084	095	12
13	006	007	007	008	009	010	011	012	013	014	015	017	010	020	021	030	040	050	062	073	13
14	003	003	003	004	004	005	005	006	006	007	008	009	009	010	011	017	024	032	042	052	14
15	001	001	001	002	002	002	002	003	003	003	004	004	005	005	006	009	014	019	027	035	15
16		001	001	001	001	001	001	001	001	001	002	002	002	002	003	005	007	011	016	022	16
17									001	001	001	001	001	001	001	002	004	006	009	013	17
18																001	002	003	005	007	18
19																	001	001	002	004	19
20																		001	001	002	20
21																				001	21

Reprinted by permission from *Statistical Analysis for Business Decisions,* by William A. Spurr and Charles P. Bonini (Homewood, Ill.: Richard D. Irwin, 1977). Copyright © 1973, 1977 by William A. Spurr and Charles P. Bonini.

Table H. POISSON DISTRIBUTION OF CUMULATIVE TERMS

$$\sum_{r}^{\infty} \frac{6^{-m}m^r}{r}$$

r	.001	.002	.003	.004	.005	.006	.007	.008	.009	.01	.02	.03	.04	.05	.06	.07	.08	.09	.10	.15	r
0	1	1	1	1	1	1	1	1	1	1	1	1	1	1	1	1	1	1	1	1	0
1	001	002	003	004	005	006	007	008	009	010	020	030	039	049	058	068	077	086	095	139	1
2													001	001	002	002	003	004	005	010	2
3																				001	3

r	.20	.25	.30	.40	.50	.60	.70	.80	.90	1.0	1.1	1.2	1.3	1.4	1.5	1.6	1.7	1.8	1.9	2.0	r
0	1	1	1	1	1	1	1	1	1	1	1	1	1	1	1	1	1	1	1	1	0
1	181	221	259	330	393	451	503	551	593	632	667	699	727	753	777	798	817	835	850	865	1
2	018	026	037	062	090	122	156	191	228	264	301	337	373	408	442	475	507	537	566	594	2
3	001	002	004	008	014	023	034	047	063	080	100	121	143	167	191	217	243	269	296	323	3
4				001	002	003	006	009	013	019	026	034	043	054	066	079	093	109	125	143	4
5						001	001	002	004	005	008	011	014	019	024	030	036	044	053	5	
6								001	001	002	002	003	004	006	008	010	013	017	6		
7											001	001	001	002	003	003	005	7			
8														001	001	001	8				

r	2.1	2.2	2.3	2.4	2.5	2.6	2.7	2.8	2.9	3.0	3.1	3.2	3.3	3.4	3.5	3.6	3.7	3.8	3.9	4.0	r
0	1	1	1	1	1	1	1	1	1	1	1	1	1	1	1	1	1	1	1	1	0
1	878	889	900	909	918	926	933	939	945	950	955	959	963	967	970	973	975	978	980	982	1
2	620	645	669	692	713	733	751	769	785	801	815	829	841	853	864	874	884	893	901	908	2
3	350	377	404	430	456	482	506	531	554	577	599	620	641	660	679	697	715	731	747	762	3
4	161	181	201	221	242	264	286	308	330	353	375	397	420	442	463	485	506	527	547	567	4
5	062	072	084	096	109	123	137	152	168	185	202	219	237	256	275	294	313	332	352	371	5
6	020	025	030	036	042	049	057	065	074	084	094	105	117	129	142	156	170	184	199	215	6
7	006	007	009	012	014	017	021	024	029	034	039	045	051	058	065	073	082	091	101	111	7
8	001	002	003	003	004	005	007	008	010	012	014	017	020	023	027	031	035	040	045	051	8
9			001	001	001	001	002	002	003	004	005	006	007	008	010	012	014	016	019	021	9
10					001	001	001	001	001	002	002	003	003	004	005	006	007	008	10		
11											001	001	001	001	002	002	002	003	11		
12																001	001	001	12		

Reprinted by permission from *Statistical Analysis for Business Decisions,* by William A. Spurr and Charles P. Bonini (Homewood, Ill.: Richard D. Irwin, 1977). Copyright © 1973, 1977 by William A. Spurr and Charles P. Bonini.

158   THE MBA TOOLKIT

Table H. POISSON DISTRIBUTION OF CUMULATIVE TERMS (Continued)

$$\sum_{r}^{\infty} \frac{6^{-m}m^r}{r}$$

r	4.1	4.2	4.3	4.4	4.5	4.6	4.7	4.8	4.9	5.0	5.1	5.2	5.3	5.4	5.5	5.6	5.7	5.8	5.9	6.0	r
0	1	1	1	1	1	1	1	1	1	1	1	1	1	1	1	1	1	1	1	1	0
1	983	985	986	988	989	990	991	992	993	993	994	994	995	995	996	997	997	997	997	998	1
2	915	922	928	934	939	944	948	952	956	960	963	966	969	971	973	976	978	979	981	983	2
3	776	790	803	815	826	837	848	857	867	875	884	891	898	905	912	918	923	928	933	938	3
4	586	605	623	641	658	674	690	706	721	735	749	762	775	787	798	809	820	830	840	849	4
5	391	410	430	449	468	487	505	524	542	560	577	594	610	627	642	658	673	687	701	715	5
6	231	247	263	280	297	314	332	349	366	384	402	419	437	454	471	488	505	522	538	554	6
7	121	133	144	156	169	182	195	209	223	238	253	268	283	298	314	330	346	362	378	394	7
8	057	064	071	079	087	095	104	113	123	133	144	155	167	178	191	203	216	242	256	8	8
9	024	028	032	036	040	045	050	056	062	068	075	082	089	097	106	114	123	133	143	153	9
10	010	011	013	015	017	020	022	025	028	032	036	040	044	049	054	059	065	071	077	084	10
11	003	004	005	006	007	008	009	010	012	014	016	018	020	023	025	028	031	035	039	042	11
12	001	001	002	002	002	003	003	004	005	005	006	007	008	010	011	012	014	016	018	020	12
13			001	001	001	001	001	001	002	002	002	003	003	004	004	005	005	007	008	009	13
14									001	001	001	001	001	001	002	002	002	003	003	004	14
15															001	001	001	001	001	001	15
16																				001	16

r	6.1	6.2	6.3	6.4	6.5	6.6	6.7	6.8	6.9	7.0	7.1	7.2	7.3	7.4	7.5	8.0	8.5	9.0	9.5	10.0	r
0	1	1	1	1	1	1	1	1	1	1	1	1	1	1	1	1	1	1	1	1	0
1	998	998	998	998	998	999	999	999	999	999	999	999	999	999	999	1-	1-	1-	1-	1-	1
2	984	985	987	988	989	990	991	991	992	993	993	994	994	995	995	997	998	999	999	1-	2
3	942	946	950	954	957	960	963	966	968	970	973	975	976	978	980	986	991	994	996	997	3
4	857	866	874	881	888	895	901	907	913	918	923	928	933	937	941	958	970	979	985	990	4
5	728	741	753	765	776	787	798	808	818	827	836	844	853	860	868	900	926	945	960	971	5
6	570	586	601	616	631	645	659	673	686	699	712	724	736	747	759	809	850	884	911	933	6
7	410	426	442	458	473	489	505	520	535	550	565	580	594	608	622	687	744	793	835	870	7
8	270	284	298	313	327	342	357	372	386	401	416	431	446	461	475	547	614	676	731	780	8
9	163	174	185	197	208	220	233	245	258	271	284	297	311	324	338	407	477	544	608	667	9
10	091	098	106	114	123	131	140	150	151	170	180	190	201	212	224	283	347	413	478	542	10
11	047	051	056	061	067	073	079	085	092	099	106	113	121	129	138	184	237	294	355	417	11
12	022	025	028	031	034	037	041	045	049	053	058	063	068	074	079	112	151	197	248	303	12
13	010	011	013	014	016	018	020	022	024	027	030	033	036	039	043	064	091	124	164	208	13
14	004	005	005	006	007	008	009	010	011	013	014	016	018	020	022	034	051	074	102	136	14
15	002	002	002	003	003	003	004	004	005	006	006	007	008	009	010	017	027	041	060	083	15
16	001	001	001	001	001	001	002	002	002	002	003	003	004	004	005	008	014	022	033	049	16
17							001	001	001	001	001	001	001	002	002	004	007	011	018	027	17
18												001	001	001	001	002	003	005	009	014	18
19																001	001	002	004	007	19
20																	001	001	002	003	20
21																		001	002	21
22																			001	22

Program Listings

Basic program listings for a number of operations, financial, and statistical analyses are presented in the following pages. They may be entered as is on any Apple II series microcomputer. The few changes required for use on the IBM PC are noted at the end of each listing. These programs were written using ProDOS operating system.

Simple Moving Average

```
10      TEXT
11      REM  Author: Walter R. Hilker, III Date: December
             24, 1984 (revised)
12      REM  P = periods // I,N = moving periods // S(I) =
             period I actual demand // T = sum of demand
15      DIM S(100),S$(100)
20      REM  simple moving average
30      HOME
40      PRINT "Simple Moving Average"
45      PRINT ""
50      PRINT "To calculate a simple average, just input
                the number of values on which the average
                will be based, and the values themselves."
52      PRINT "After your first calculated average, ";:
                INVERSE : PRINT "TYPE X WHEN YOU WANT TO
                STOP.";: NORMAL
55      PRINT ""
60      INPUT "Your average will be based upon how many
                periods?";P
70      PRINT "": REM

75      LET N = P
80      LET J = 1: REM

89      REM  inputs actual data on which forecast is based
90      FOR I = J TO N
100       PRINT "Value for period ";I;: INPUT "   ";S(I)
110       NEXT I
120       GOTO 200: REM

129       REM  this makes forecast move
130     J = J + 1
140     N = N + 1
150     T = 0
160       PRINT "Value for period ";N;: INPUT "   ";S$(N)
165       IF S$(N) = "x" OR S$(N) = "X" THEN 400
170     S(N) = VAL (S$(N)): REM

199       REM  calculates simple moving average
200       FOR I = J TO N
210     T = S(I) + T
240       NEXT I
```

```
260     PRINT TAB( 40);"Forecast for period ";N + 1;
            " = ";T / P
280     GOTO 130
400     PRINT "Goodbye."
410     END
```

Note: Changes for IBM PC
```
10      SCREEN 0,0:WIDTH 80:COLOR 7,0
30      CLS
52      PRINT "After...average, ";:COLOR 0,7:PRINT
            "TYPE...STOP.";:COLOR 7,0
```

Weighted Average

```
11      REM  Author: Walter R. Hilker  Date: December 27,
            1984 (revised)
12      REM  W(I) = weight for period I // A = sum of
            weights // S(N) = Actual demand // T = sum of
            weighted demand
15      HOME
20      REM  Weighted Moving Average
30      DIM S(100),S$(100),W(100)
40      PRINT "Weighted Moving Average"
45      PRINT ""
50      PRINT "To calculate a weighted moving average,
                you'll need to input these data:"
55      PRINT ""
60      PRINT "    1] the number of periods on which you
                    want to base your average;"
70      PRINT "    2] weights, or levels of importance, for
                    each of those periods; and"
80      PRINT "    3] the values for each of those
                    periods."
85      PRINT ""
90      PRINT "For example, if you want your average to be
                based on three periods, the forecast for
                period n will always be calculated on
                periods (n-1), (n-2), and (n-3)."
95      PRINT ""
100     PRINT "The values on which your average is
                determined change, as you move forward in
```

```
                time. But the weights will stay constant
                for (n-1), (n-2), etc., because you"
110     PRINT "are calculating an average where recency,
                seasonality, or another time-related trend
                is evident."
115     PRINT ""
120     PRINT "After your first calculated average, ";:
                INVERSE : PRINT "TYPE X WHEN YOU WANT TO
                STOP.": NORMAL
125     J = 1
129     REM

130     REM   inputs weights on which forecasts will be
                based
135     PRINT ""
140     INPUT "Your weighted moving average will be based
                upon how many periods?"; N
150     PRINT ""
160     PRINT "This program will calculate the forecast
                for month ";N + 1
170     PRINT "": REM

180     REM   reverse step in the for/next loop to make
                the data input arrangement more logical for
                the user
190     FOR I = N TO J STEP - 1
200     PRINT "What weight should be assigned to period
                (n-";N - I + 1;")";: INPUT W(I)
210   A = W(I) + A
220     NEXT I
230     PRINT ""
240     FOR I = N TO J STEP - 1
250     PRINT "What is the value for period ";I;: INPUT
                S(I)
260     NEXT I
270     GOTO 400: REM

300   T = 0
310   J = J + 1
320   N = N + 1
340     PRINT "Actual value for month ":N:: INPUT S$(N)
349     REM   this makes the forecast move
350     IF S$(N) = "x" OR S$(N) = "X" THEN 500
360   S(N) = VAL (S$(N)): REM
```

```
399    REM   formula for weighted moving average
400    FOR I = N to J STEP - 1
410    T = (S(I) * W(I - J + 1)) / A + T
420    NEXT I
440    PRINT TAB(40);"Forecast for month ";N + 1;" = ";T
460    GOTO 300: REM

500    PRINT "Goodbye."
510    END
```

Note: Changes for IBM PC
```
15     SCREEN 0,0:WIDTH 80:COLOR 7,0:CLS
```

Linear Regression

```
10     REM   linear regression
11     REM   Author: Walter R. Hilker Date: December 27,
             1984 (revised)
12     REM   X = 'x' value // Y = 'y' value // XY = sum of
             xy // XSQUARE = sum of x^2 // SX = sum of x /
             / YSQUARE = sum of y^2 // SY = of y // B,A
             variables in line function Y=A+BX
13     REM   R = coefficient of correlation // N = number
             of periods
20     DIM X(100),Y(100)
30     TEXT
40     HOME : REM

50     PRINT "Linear Regression"
60     PRINT ""
70     PRINT "To determine the best-fitting line through
             your data points, you will need to input:"
80     PRINT ""
90     PRINT "   1] the number of data points to be used"
100    PRINT "   2] the 'x' and 'y' values for each data
                 point"
110    PRINT "": REM

119    REM   inputs data on which regression is based
120    INPUT "How many data points will you use?";N
```

```
125    FOR I = 1 TO N
130    PRINT "Type in x,y values for point #";I;: INPUT
           X(I),Y(I)
140    NEXT I: REM

149    REM  calculates variables for determining A,B
150    FOR I = 1 TO N
160 XY = X(I) * Y(I) + XY
170 XSQUARE = X(I) ^ 2 + XSQUARE
180 SX = X(I) + SX
190 YSQUARE = Y(I) ^ 2 = YSQUARE
200 SY = Y(I) + SY
210    NEXT I: REM

219    REM  y=a+bx
220 B = (XY - SX * SY / N) / (XSQUARE - SX ^ 2 / N)
230 A = SY / N - B * SX / N
235    REM

239    REM  output
240    PRINT "Y = ";A;" + ";B;"X"
250 R = (XY - SX * SY / N) / ((XSQUARE - SX ^ 2 / N) *
    (YSQUARE - SY ^ 2 / N)) ^ .5
260    PRINT "r = ";R
270    INPUT "To run another linear regression, type
            'Y':";Z$
280    IF Z$ = "Y" OR Z$ = "y" GOTO 120
290    PRINT "Goodbye."
300    END
```

Note: Changes for IBM PC
```
30     SCREEN 0,0:WIDTH 80:COLOR 7,0
40     CLS:REM
```

Exponential Smoothing

```
10     REM  exponential smoothing
11     REM  Author: Walter R. Hilker Date: December 27,
           1984 (revised)
```

```
12    REM  A = smoothing (alpha) factor // N = periods /
          / D(N) = actual demand // F(N) = forecasted
          demand
15   Y = 39
30   TEXT
40   HOME
45   REM

50   PRINT "Exponential Smoothing"
60   PRINT ""
70   PRINT "For running an exponentially smoothed
               forecast for period N, you need:"
80   PRINT ""
90   PRINT "   1] forecasted demand for period N-1"
100   PRINT "   2] actual demand for period N-1"
110   PRINT "   3] smoothing factor, 'a' — where 0.0 <
               a < 1.0"
120   PRINT "": REM
125   REM inputs data on which forecast is based
130   LET N = 1
140   INPUT "Enter smoothing factor: ";A
145   PRINT ""
150   PRINT "Enter forecast for period ";N;: INPUT F
155   PRINT ""
160   PRINT "Enter actual demand for period ";N;" (type
               X to quit)";: INPUT D$
162   IF D$ = "X" OR D$ = "x" THEN 700
165   D = VAL (D$)
170   GOSUB 220: REM exponential smoothing formula
185   REM this makes forecast move
190   N = N + 1
200   GOTO 160: REM

210   REM exponential smoothing formula
220   F = A * D - A * F + F
230   PRINT "Forecast for period ";N + 1;" = ";F
240   RETURN
700   INPUT "Do you want to change the alpha value?
               Type 'Y' or 'N':";Z$
710   IF Z$ = "Y" OR Z$ = "y" GOTO 720
715   GOTO 780
720   INPUT "New alpha value: ";A
725   N = N - 1
730   GOTO 170
```

166   THE MBA TOOLKIT

```
780    PRINT "Goodbye."
790    TEXT
800    END
```

Note: Changes for IBM PC
```
30     SCREEN 0,0:WIDTH 80:COLOR 7,0
40     CLS
790    CLS
```

Economic Order Quantity, Reorder Point, etc.

```
10     REM   economic order quantity, reorder point,
             optimal reorder time, total annual cost
11     REM   Author: Walter R. Hilker  Date: October 19,
             1984 (revised)
12     REM   D = annual demand // S = cost per order // H
             = holding (inventory) cost per unit // L =
             lead time // C = cost per unit // E = EOQ //
             R = reorder point
13     REM   T = recorder time // B = total annual cost //
             K = standard deviation of daily demand // V =
             standard deviation of demand during lead time
20     HOME
25     DIM K(100): REM

30     PRINT "To find economic order quantity, optimal
              rcorder point, recorder time and total
              annual cost, you will need to input:"
35     PRINT ""
40     PRINT "    1] Annual demand;"
45     PRINT "    2] Ordering cost;"
50     PRINT "    3] Inventory cost;"
55     PRINT "    4] Actual unit cost of the product
                  itself; and"
60     PRINT "    5] Required lead time for placing
                  orders."
65     PRINT ""
70     PRINT ""
75     REM

79     REM data inputs
```

```
80     INPUT "What is your annual demand?";D: INPUT "What
            is your cost per order?" ;S: INPUT " What
            is your annual inventory cost per unit?";H
85     INPUT "What is your required lead time, in days,
            for placing an order?";L: INPUT "What is
            the actual cost of each unit?";C
86     REM

89     REM EOQ formula
90   E = (2 * D * S / H) ^ .5
100    PRINT ""
110    PRINT "EOQ = "; INT (100 * E) / 100;" units."
120    PRINT ""
121    REM

130    REM reorder point formula
140  R = D * L / 365
150    PRINT "Reorder point = "; INT (100 * R) / 100;"
            units."
155    PRINT ""
156    REM

160    REM optimal reorder time formula
170  T = E / D
180    PRINT "Optimal reorder time = "; INT (1000 * T) /
            1000;" years, or"
190    PRINT "    "; INT ((T * 365) + .5);" days."
200    PRINT ""
201    REM

210    REM B = total annual cost
220  B = D * C + D * S / E + E * H / 2
230    PRINT "Total annual cost = $";B
300    INPUT "Do you wish to make new calculations? Type
            'Y' or 'N':";Z$
310    HOME
320    IF Z$ = "Y" OR Z$ = "y" THEN 80
349    REM

350    PRINT "Safety Stock"
360    PRINT ""
370    PRINT "To calculate safety stock, you will need
            to input the standard deviation of daily
            demand. Do you wish to find safety stock
            requirements?"
```

```
380    INPUT "Type 'Y' or 'N':";Z$
390    IF Z$ = "Y" or Z$ = "y" THEN 400
395    GOTO 700
400    PRINT "Data show that your reorder lead time is
                ";L;" days."
405    K = 0
410    INPUT "Does your standard deviation of daily
                demand vary from day to day? Enter 'Y' or
                'N':";Z$
420    IF Z$ = "Y" OR Z$ = "y" THEN 500: REM

430    INPUT "Enter standard deviation of daily
                demand:";K
440    V = (L * K ^ 2) ^ .5
450     GOTO 550: REM

500    FOR I = 1 TO L
510    PRINT "Enter standard deviation of demand, day
                ";I;: INPUT K(I)
520    K = K(I) ^ 2 + K
530     NEXT I
540    V = K ^ .5
545     PRINT "": REM

549    REM  shows safety stock and reorder point @
            90%,95%,99% confidence levels
550    PRINT "@ 90% Confidence Level: Safety Stock  =",
                INT (1.28 * V);" units"
560    PRINT "                          Reorder Point =",
                INT (D* L / 365 + 1.28 * V);" units"
565    PRINT ""
570    PRINT "@ 95% Confidence Level: Safety Stock  =",
                INT (1.645 * V);" units"
580    PRINT "                          Reorder Point =",
                INT (D * L / 365 + 1.645 * V);" units"
585    PRINT ""
590    PRINT "@ 99% Confidence Level: Safety Stock  =",
                INT (2.33 * V);" units"
600    PRINT "                          Reorder Point =",
                INT (D * L / 365 + 2.33 * V);" units"
605    PRINT ""
609    REM

610    INPUT "Do you want to adjust safety stock data?
                Enter 'Y' or 'N':";Z$
```

```
620     IF Z$ = "Y" OR Z$ = "y" THEN 400
629     REM
630     INPUT "Do you want to run further EOQ
              calculations?
              Type !Y! or !N!:";Z$
640     IF Z$ = "Y" OR Z$ = "y" THEN 70
700     PRINT "Goodbye."
710     END
```

Note: Changes for IBM PC
```
20      SCREEN 0,0:WIDTH 80:COLOR 7,0:CLS
310     CLS
```

Learning Curve

```
10      REM   learning curve
11      REM   Author: Walter R. Hilker   Date: October 19,
              1984
12      REM   Program calculates learning curve where nth
              iteration = data, line 40, at learning curve
              factors = data, line 80. // N = iteration //
              P = learning curve factor // K = time used in
              first iteration // N(17) = user's desired
              iteration
20      HOME
30      DIM N(1000),I(1000),Y(1000)
35      REM   reads nth iteration, standardized and
              included gratis
40      DATA 1,2,3,4,5,10,25,50,75,100,200,300,400,500,750,
              1000
50      FOR J = 1 TO 16
60      READ N(J)
70      NEXT J: REM

75      REM   reads selected learning curve factors
80      DATA .5,.75,.9
90      FOR I = 1 TO 3
100      READ P(I)
110      NEXT I: REM

120     PRINT "Learning Curve"
130     PRINT ""
140     PRINT "To calculate the learning curve, you will
              need to input:"
```

```
150    PRINT ""
160    PRINT ""      1] how long a process takes the first
                        time through;"
170    PRINT "     2] a percentage 'learning curve'
                        factor; and"
180    PRINT "     3] n, or the number of the iteration of
                        which you wish to estimate
                        completion."
190    PRINT "": REM

195    REM   input variables on which learning curve
                 calculations are based
200    INPUT "Please enter the learning curve factor
                (example: .85):";P(4)
210    INPUT "How many time units did the process take
                the first time?";K
220    INPUT "Please enter n -- the iteration you wish
                to estimate:";N(17)
225    GOSUB 255
230    INPUT "If you wish to make further learning curve
                calculations, type 'Y' or 'N':";Z$
240    IF Z$ = "Y" OR Z$ = "y" GOTO 190
250    GOTO 500
255    HOME : REM

259    REM   prints learning curve calculations
260    PRINT ,"Estimated Time to Completion:"
270    PRINT ""
280    PRINT "process #"," @ .5"," @ .75"," @ .9",
                " @"; P(4)
290    PRINT "---------","---------------------------
                ----------------------------"
300    FOR J = 1 TO 16
310    PRINT N(J),
320    FOR I = 1 TO 4
330    GOSUB 450
340    NEXT I
350    NEXT J
355    PRINT ""
360    PRINT N(17),: REM this is the nth iteration
            entered by user in line 200
370    FOR I = 1 TO 4
380    GOSUB 450
390    NEXT I
400    RETURN : REM
```

```
449    REM   learning curve calculations
450    PRINT K * N(J) ^ ( LOG (P(I)) / LOG (2)),
460    RETURN
500    PRINT "Goodbye."
510    END
```

Note: Changes for IBM PC
```
20     SCREEN 0,0:WIDTH 80:Color 7,0:CLS
255    CLS:REM
```

Financial Ratios

```
10     REM   FINANCIAL RATIOS
11     REM   Author: Walter R. Hilker Date: October 19,
          1984
12     REM   Variables defined in lines 100-210
13     REM   ONERR statements protect against division by
          zero
20     HOME
50     PRINT "Financial Ratios"
60     PRINT ""
70     PRINT "Please enter the proper value for each
             variable as it appears. If the value is
             unknown, enter 0."
80     PRINT "": REM

90     REM   inputs data to calculate ratios
100    INPUT "1. Accounts receivable: ";A
110    INPUT "2. Inventory: ";B
120    INPUT "3. Current assets: ";C
130    INPUT "4. Net fixed assets: ";D
140    INPUT "5. Total assets: ";E
150    INPUT "6. Current liabilities: ";F
160    INPUT "7. Total debt: ";G
170    INPUT "8. Owner!s equity: ";H
180    INPUT "9. Total sales: ";I
190    INPUT "10. Profit before taxes & interest
                charges: ";J
200    INPUT "11. Total interest charges: ";K
210    INPUT "12. Net income: ";L
220    PRINT "" ;: INPUT "To make changes, type 'Y':";Z$
```

```
230    IF Z$ = "Y" OR Z$ = "y" GOTO 100: REM

235    REM  calculates and prints ratios-ONERR protects
          against division by zero

240    HOME
250    PRINT "FINANCIAL RATIOS"
260    PRINT ""
270    PRINT "Liquidity:"
280    PRINT "Current = ";: ONERR GOTO 290
285    PRINT C / F: GOTO 300
290    GOSUB 1000
300    PRINT "Quick (Acid Test) = ";: ONERR GOTO 305
302    PRINT (C - B) / F: GOTO 310
305    GOSUB 1000
310    PRINT "" : REM

320    PRINT "Leverage:"
330    PRINT "Debt = ";: ONERR GOTO 335
332    PRINT G / E: GOTO 340
335    GOSUB 1000
340    PRINT "Times Interest Earned = ";: ONERR GOTO 345
342    PRINT J / K: GOTO 350
345    GOSUB 1000
350    PRINT "" : REM

360    PRINT "Activity:"
370    PRINT "Inventory Turnover = ";: ONERR GOTO 375
372    PRINT I / B: GOTO 380
375    GOSUB 1000
380    PRINT "Average Collection Period = ";: ONERR GOTO
          385
382    PRINT A / (I / 365): GOTO 390
385    GOSUB 1000
390    PRINT "Fixed Asset Turnover = ";: ONERR GOTO 395
392    PRINT I / D: GOTO 400
395    GOSUB 1000
400    PRINT "Total Asset Turnover = ";: ONERR GOTO 405
402    PRINT I / E: GOTO 410
405    GOSUB 1000
410    PRINT "" : REM

420    PRINT "Profitability:"
430    PRINT "Profit Margin on Sales = ";: ONERR GOTO
          435
```

```
432    PRINT L /I: GOTO 440
435    GOSUB 1000
440    PRINT "Return on Total Assets = ";: ONERR GOTO
           445
442    PRINT L / E: GOTO 450
445    GOSUB 1000
450    PRINT "Return on Owner's Equity = ";: ONERR GOTO
           455
452    PRINT L /H: GOTO 460
455    GOSUB 1000
457    PRINT "" : REM

460    INPUT "Do you want to run further ratios? Type
           'Y' or 'N':";Z$
470    IF Z$ = "Y" OR Z$ = "y" GOTO 20
500    PRINT "Goodbye."
510    END
1000   PRINT "N/A"
1010   RETURN
```

Note: Changes for IBM PC
```
20     SCREEN 0,0:WIDTH 80:COLOR 7,0:CLS
240    CLS
       In general, change ONERR GOTO nnn to ON ERROR GOTO
       nnn, and add RESUME after error recovery.
       Specifically:
280    PRINT "Current = ";:ON ERROR GOTO 290
291    RESUME 300
300    PRINT "Quick (Acid Test) = ";:ON ERROR GOTO 305
306    RESUME 310
330    PRINT "Debt = ";:ON ERROR GOTO 335
336    RESUME 340
340    PRINT "Times Interest Earned = ";:ON ERROR GOTO
           345
346    RESUME 350
370    PRINT "Inventory Turnover = ";:ON ERROR GOTO 375
376    RESUME 380
380    PRINT "Average Collection Period = ";:ON ERROR
           GOTO 385
386    RESUME 390
390    PRINT "Fixed Asset Turnover = ";:ON ERROR GOTO
           395
396    RESUME 400
400    PRINT "Total Asset Turnover = ";:ON ERROR GOTO
           405
406    RESUME 410
```

```
430     PRINT "Profit Margin on Sales = ";:ON ERROR GOTO
                435
436     RESUME 440
440     PRINT "Return on Total Assets = ";:ON ERROR GOTO
                445
446     RESUME 450
450     PRINT "Return on Owner's Equity = ";:ON ERROR
                GOTO 455
456     RESUME 457
```

Break-even Analysis

```
10      REM  Break-even analysis
11      REM  Author: Walter R. Hilker   Date: October 19,
            1984 (revised)
12      REM  P = price per unit // Q = unit quantity // F
            = fixed costs // V = variable costs per unit
20      HOME : REM

50      PRINT "Break-Even Analysis"
60      PRINT ""
70      PRINT "To find break-even, you'll need to input 3
                of these 4 values:"
80      PRINT ""
90      PRINT "   1] price per unit"
100     PRINT "   2] total quantity (in units)"
110     PRINT "   3] Total fixed costs"
120     PRINT "   4] variable costs per unit"
130     PRINT ""
140     PRINT "The program will solve for the fourth,
                missing variable."
150     PRINT "" : REM

159     REM  inputs variables to calculate breakeven
160     PRINT "Enter the following variables (if unknown,
                enter 0):"
170     PRINT ""
180     INPUT "Price per unit = ";P: INPUT "Total
                quantity (in units) = ";Q: INPUT "Total
                fixed costs = ";F: INPUT "Variable costs
                per unit = ";V
185     PRINT "" : REM
189     REM  if variable = 0, program forwards to
            calculation to solve for that unknown variable
```

```
190     IF P < > 0 GOTO 220
200     PRINT "Price per unit = $";F / Q + V
210     GOTO 300: REM
220     IF Q < > 0 GOTO 250
230     PRINT "Total quantity = ";F / (P - V);" units"
240     GOTO 300: REM

250     IF F < > 0 GOTO 280
260     PRINT "Total fixed costs = $";Q * (P — V)
270     GOTO 300: REM

280     PRINT "Variable costs per unit = $";P - F / Q
290     REM

300     INPUT "Do you want to find other break-evens?
                Type 'Y' or 'N':";Z$
310     IF Z$ = "Y" OR Z$ = "y" GOTO 150
340     PRINT "Goodbye."
350     END
```

Note: Changes for IBM PC

```
20      SCREEN 0,0:WIDTH 80:COLOR 7,0:CLS:REM
```

Present Value/Future Value

```
10      REM   present value/future value
11      REM   Author: Walter R. Hilker Date: October 19,
            1984 (revised)
12      REM   P = present value // F = future value // I =
            interest // N = periods
20      HOME : REM

50      PRINT "Present Value & Future Value"
60      PRINT ""
70      PRINT "To find PV or FV, enter three of the four
                following variables, and enter '0' for the
                variable for which you are solving. This
                program will calculate for that missing
                variable."
80      PRINT ""
90      PRINT "   1] Present value"
```

```
100    PRINT "   2] Future value"
110    PRINT "   3] Interest (expressed as a decimal)"
120    PRINT "   4] Number of periods"
130    PRINT "" : REM

139    REM  inputs variables for pv / fv calculations
140    INPUT "Present value = ";P: INPUT "Future value =
             ";F: INPUT "Interest (example: .12) = ";I:
             INPUT "Number of periods (n) = ";N
150    PRINT "" : REM

159    REM  if variable = 0, program advances to the
           calculation to solve for that unknown variable
160    IF P < > 0 GOTO 200
170  P = F / ((1 + I) ^ N)
180    PRINT "Present value = ";P
190    GOTO 300: REM

200    IF F < > 0 GOTO 240
210  F = ((1 + I) ^ N) * P
220    PRINT "Future value = ";F
230    GOTO 300: REM

240    IF I < > 0 GOTO 280
250  I = (F / P) ^ (1 / N) - 1
260    PRINT "Interest rate = ";I
270    GOTO 300: REM

280  N = LOG (F / P) / LOG (I + 1)
290    PRINT "Number of periods (n) = ";N
295    REM

300    INPUT "Do you want to make further present value
             or future value calculations? Type 'Y' or
             'N':";Z$
310    IF Z$ = "Y" OR Z$ = "y" GOTO 130
340    PRINT "Goodbye."
350    END
```

Note: Changes for IBM PC
```
20    SCREEN 0,0:WIDTH 80:COLOR 7,0:CLS:REM
```

Annuities

```
10    REM   PRESENT VALUE/FUTURE VALUE OF AN ANNUITY
11    REM   Author: Walter R. Hilker    Date: October 19,
          1984 (revised)
12    REM   P = present value // F = future value // I =
          interest // A = annuity // N = number of
          periods // U, L = upper & lower limits in
          binary search
20    HOME : REM

50    PRINT "Present Value & Future Value of an Annuity"
60    PRINT ""
70    PRINT "To find either PV or FV of an annuity
             (periodic payment), first select which you
             want to find."
80    INPUT "Please type either 'PV' or 'FV':";Z$
90    IF Z$ < > "PV" GOTO 650
100    HOME : REM

110    PRINT "Present Value of an Annuity"
120    PRINT ""
130    PRINT "Enter three of the four following
             variables, and enter 0 for the variable
             for which you are solving:"
140    PRINT "" : REM

145    REM   input variables for present value of annuity
150    INPUT "Present value = ";P: INPUT "Annuity = ";A:
             INPUT "Interest (example: .12) = ";I:
             INPUT "Number of periods (n) = ";N
160    PRINT "" : REM

165    REM   if variable = 0, program advances to perform
          calculation to solve for unknown variable
166    REM   present value
170    IF P < > 0 GOTO 210
180    P = A * (1 - 1 / (1 + I) ^ N) / I
190    PRINT "Present value = ";P
200    GOTO 600: REM

205    REM   annuity
210    IF A < > 0 GOTO 250
```

178   THE MBA TOOLKIT

```
220   A = (I*P) / (1 - (1 / (1 + I) ^ N))
230    PRINT "Annuity = ";A
240    GOTO 600: REM

245    REM  interest
250    IF I <  > 0 GOTO 540
260    IF P <  > A GOTO 280: REM lines 260,270 determine
                  if interest = 0%
270    IF N <  > 1 GOTO 280
275    PRINT "Interest = 0.00": GOTO 600
280    IF N < = 80 GOTO 290
285    PRINT "Sorry -- the computer gets migraines when
               'n' exceeds 80. Try changing your data.":
               GOTO 140
289    REM

290   I = - .0001: REM   screen for positive or negative
                  interest rate
300    GOSUB 500
310    IF B < C GOTO 400
315    REM

320   U = 1:L = 0: REM   beginning of positive interest
                  rate binary search
330   I = (U + L) / 2
340    GOSUB 500: REM

350    IF INT (B * 1000) > INT (C * 1000) GOTO 380
360    IF INT (B * 1000) < INT (C * 1000) GOTO 390
370    PRINT "Interest = "; INT ((I + .0005) * 1000)
            1000: GOTO 600
375    REM

380   U = I: GOTO 330
390   L = I: GOTO 330
395    REM

400   U = 0:L = - .9999: REM   beginning of negative
               interest rate binary search
410   I = (U + L) / 2
420    GOSUB 500: REM

430    IF INT (B * 1000) < INT (C * 1000) GOTO 460
440    IF INT (B * 1000) > INT (C * 1000) GOTO 470
450    PRINT "Interest = "; INT ((I + .0005) * 1000) /
            1000: GOTO 600
```

```
455    REM

460    U = I: GOTO 410
470    L = I: GOTO 410
480     REM

500    B = I * P: REM   shared trial-and-error calculation
                    for binary search
505     ONERR GOTO 530
510    C = A * (1 - 1 / ((1 + I) ^ N))
520     RETURN : REM

530     PRINT "Interest = 100% or greater.": GOTO 600
535     REM
539     REM  # of periods
540    N = - LOG (1 - P * I / A) / LOG (1 + I)
550     PRINT "Number of periods (n) = ";N
560     REM

600     INPUT "Do you want to run further PV/Annuity
                calculations? Type 'Y' or 'N':";Z$
610     IF Z$ = "Y" OR Z$ = "y" GOTO 140
630     INPUT "Do you want to run FV/Annuity
                calculations? Type 'Y' or 'N':";Z$
640     IF Z$ = "Y" OR Z$ = "y" GOTO 650
645     GOTO 1210
650     HOME = REM

660     PRINT "Future Value of an Annuity"
670     PRINT ""
680     PRINT "Enter three of the four following
                variables, and enter 0 for the variable
                for which you are solving:"
690     REM
695     REM  input variables for future value of annuity
700     INPUT "Future value = ";F: INPUT "Annuity = ";A:
                INPUT "Interest (example: .12) = ";I:
                INPUT "Number of periods (n) = ";N
710     PRINT "" : REM

715     REM  if variable = 0, program advances to perform
            calculations to solve for unknown variable
719     REM   future value
720     IF F < > 0 GOTO 760
730    F = A * ((1 + I) ^ N - 1) / I
```

180   THE MBA TOOLKIT

```
740    PRINT "Future value = ";F
750    GOTO 1150: REM

755    REM annuity
760    IF A <  > 0 GOTO 800
770   A = I * F / ((1 + I) ^ N - 1)
780    PRINT "Annuity = ";A
790    GOTO 1150: REM

795    REM  interest
800    IF I <  > 0 GOTO 1110
810    IF F <  > A GOTO 840: REM lines 810, 820
          determine if interest=0
820    IF N <  > 1 GOTO 840
830    PRINT "Interest = 0.00": GOTO 1150
840    IF N < = 80 GOTO 860
850    PRINT "Apologies: the computer gets physically
               ill when fed more than 80 n↓s. Please
               reenter data.": GOTO 690
855    REM

860    I = - .0001: REM screen for positive or negative
                    interest rate
870    GOSUB 1070
880    IF B > C GOTO 970
885    REM

890   U = 1:I = 0: REM  beginning of positive interest
                    rate binary search
900    I = (U + L) / 2
910    GOSUB 1070: REM

920    IF INT (B * 1000) > INT (C * 1000) GOTO 950
930    IF INT (B * 1000) < INT (O * 1000) GOTO 960
940    PRINT "Interest = "; INT ((I + .0005) * 1000) /
               1000: GOTO 1150
945    REM

950   L = I: GOTO 900
960   U = I: GOTO 900
965    REM

970   U = 0:L = - - .9999: REM  beginning of negative
                    interest rate binary search
980    I = (U + L) / 2
990    GOSUB 1070: REM
```

```
1000    IF INT (B * 1000) < INT (C * 1000) GOTO 1030
1010    IF INT (B * 1000) > INT (C * 1000) GOTO 1040
1020    PRINT "Interest = "; INT ((I + .0005) * 1000) /
              1000: GOTO 1150
1025    REM

1030    L = I: GOTO 980
1040    U = I: GOTO 980
1050    REM
1070    B = I * F: REM   shared trial-and-error calculation
                  for binary search
1075    ONERR GOTO 1100
1080    C = A * ((1 + I) ^ N - 1)
1090    RETURN : REM

1100    PRINT "Interest = 100% or greater.": GOTO 1150
1105    REM

1110    N = LOG (1 - A * I / P) / LOG (1 + I)
1120    PRINT "Number of periods (n) = ";N
1130    REM

1150    INPUT "Do you want to run further FV/Annuity
              calculations? Type 'Y' or 'N':";Z$
1160    IF Z$ = "Y" OR Z$ = "y" GOTO 690
1180    INPUT "Do you want to run PV/Annuity
              calculations? Type 'Y' or 'N':";Z$
1190    IF Z$ = "Y" OR Z$ = "y" GOTO 100
1210    PRINT "Goodbye."
1220    END
```

Note: Changes for IBM PC
```
20    SCREEN 0,0:WIDTH 80:COLOR 7,0:CLS:REM
100   CLS:REM
505   ON ERROR GOTO 530
530    PRINT "Interest = 100% or greater.":RESUME 600
650   CLS:REM
1075  ON ERROR GOTO 1100
1100   PRINT "Interest = 100% or greater.":RESUME 1150
```

Yield to Maturity

```
10    REM   yield to maturity
11    REM   Author: Walter R. Hilker   Date: December 27,
         1984 (revised)
12    REM   C = coupon rate // V = bond value // N =
         years to maturity // Y = yield to maturity
20    HOME : REM

50    PRINT "Yield to Maturity"
60    PRINT ""
70    PRINT "To calculate a bond's yield to maturity,
            enter:"
80    PRINT ""
90    PRINT "    1] The bond's coupon rate--the interest
                 rate payment on the bond;"
100   PRINT "    2] The value of the bond--the selling
                 price; and"
110   PRINT "    3] The years to maturity."
120   PRINT "" : REM

125   REM   inputs variables to calculate yield
130   INPUT "Enter the bond's coupon rate:";C: INPUT
            "Enter the value of the bond:";V: INPUT
            "Enter the years to maturity (maturity
            year - selling year):";N
135   REM

139   REM   yield to maturity formula
140   Y = (C + (1000 - V) / N) / ((1000 + V) / 2)
150   PRINT ""
160   PRINT "Yield to maturity = ";Y
165   REM

170   INPUT "Do you want to calculate another 'yield to
            maturity'? Type 'Y' or 'N':";Z$
180   IF Z$ = "Y" OR Z$ = "y" GOTO 120
200   PRINT "Goodbye."
210   END
```

Note: Changes for IBM PC
```
20    SCREEN 0,0:WIDTH 80:COLOR 7,0:CLS:REM
```

Weighted Average Cost of Capital

```
10     REM   weighted average cost of capital
11     REM   Author: Walter R. Hilker   Date: October 19,
          1984 (revised)
12     REM   T = tax rate // D = cost of debt before
          taxes // E = cost of equity // R = debt ratio
20     HOME : REM

50     PRINT "Weighted Average Cost of Capital"
60     PRINT ""
70     PRINT "To calculate WACC, input:"
80     PRINT ""
90     PRINT "   1] tax rate;"
100    PRINT "   2] cost of debt (before taxes);"
110    PRINT "   3] debt ratio; and"
120    PRINT "   4] cost of equity"
130    PRINT "" : REM

135    REM   inputs wacc variables
140    INPUT "Enter tax rate (example: .48) = ";T: INPUT
              "Enter cost of debt before taxes (example:
              .12) = ";D: INPUT "Enter cost of equity
              (example: .18) = ";E: INPUT "Enter debt
              ratio (example: .4) = ";R
145    PRINT "" : REM

149    REM   wacc formula
150    PRINT "Weighted Average Cost of Capital = ";(1 -
              T) * R * D + (1 - R) * E
160    INPUT "Do you want to calculate another WACC?
              Type 'Y' or 'N':";Z$
170    IF Z$ = "Y" OR Z$ = "y" GOTO 130
190    PRINT "Goodbye."
200    END
```

Note: Changes for IBM PC
```
20     SCREEN 0,0:WIDTH 80:COLOR 7,0:CLS:REM
```

184   THE MBA TOOLKIT

Net Present Value

```
10    REM    Net present value
11    REM    Author: Walter R. Hilker    Date: October 19,
      1984
12    REM  I = investment // K = cost of capital // R(I)
                              = dollar return for year I
                              // V-I = NPV

20    HOME : REM

50    PRINT "Net Present Value"
60    PRINT ""
70    PRINT "To calculate net present value (NPV), you
             will need to enter:"
80    PRINT ""
90    PRINT "   1] the initial outlay (investment);"
100   PRINT "   2] the cost of capital (k) with which
                 your NPV will be generated;"
110   PRINT "   3] the number of periods for the
                 investment, and the dollar return
                 for each period."
120   PRINT "" : REM

125   REM      input npv variables
130   INPUT "Enter the initial investment:";I: INPUT
             "Enter cost of capital (example: .15):";K:
             INPUT "Enter the number of periods (n):";N
135 V = 0
140   PRINT "" : REM

145   REM  iterations for each year's dollar return on
           investment
150   FOR J = 1 TO N
160   PRINT "What is the dollar return in year ";J;:
             INPUT R(J)
165   REM  calculates sum of present values of
           investment returns
170 V = R(J) / (1 + K) ^ J + V
180   NEXT J: REM

189   REM  output
190   PRINT "Net Present Value = ";V - I
200   PRINT ""
210   INPUT "Do you want to determine another NPV? Type
             'Y' or 'N':";Z$
```

```
220    IF Z$ = "Y" OR Z$ = "y" GOTO 120
240    PRINT "Goodbye."
250    END
```

Note: Changes for IBM PC
```
20    SCREEN 0,0:WIDTH 80:COLOR 7,0:CLS:REM
```

Internal Rate of Return

```
10    REM    internal rate of return
11    REM  Author: Walter R. Hilker   Date: December 27,
         1984 (revised)
12    REM  U,L = upper & lower limits for IRR binary
         search // I = initial investment // N = number
         of periods of expected cash flow // F(A) =
         expected future cash flow for each period // V
         = sum of present values for each future cash
         flow
20    DIM F(100)
30    HOME : REM

50    PRINT "Internal Rate of Return"
60    PRINT ""
70    PRINT "To calculate internal rate of return (IRR),
             you will need to input:"
80    PRINT ""
90    PRINT "   1] the initial outlay (investment)"
100    PRINT "   2] the number of periods for the
                  investment"
110    PRINT "   3] the expected future cash flow for
                  each period"
120    PRINT "" : REM

125    REM    inputs data to calculate IRR
130    INPUT "Please enter the amount of the initial
              investment:";I
140    INPUT "Please enter the number of periods of
              expected cash flow:";N
145    PRINT ""
149    REM    loop for inputting returns on investment
```

```
150    FOR A = 1 TO N
160    PRINT "What is the expected future cash flow for
                period ";A;: INPUT F(A)
170    NEXT A: REM

175    REM   binary search for IRR (interest)
180    U = 2:L = 0
190    K = (U + L) / 2
195    V = 0
200    GOSUB 500
210    IF INT (V*1000) > INT (I*1000) GOTO 300
220    IF INT (V*1000) < INT (I*1000) GOTO 320
230    PRINT "Internal Rate of Return = ";( INT
                (K*100000)) / 100000
235    REM

240    INPUT "Do you want to determine another IRR? Type
                'Y' or 'N':";Z$
250    IF Z$ = "Y" OR Z$ = "y" GOTO 120
280    PRINT "Goodbye."
290    END : REM

300  L = K
310    GOTO 190
320  U = K
330    GOTO 190: REM

499    REM   summation of present values of returns on
            investment
500    FOR A = 1 TO N
510    V = F(A) / (1 + K) ^ A + V
520    NEXT A
530    RETURN
```

Note: Changes for IBM PC

```
30     SCREEN 0,0:WIDTH 80:COLOR 7,0:CLS:REM
```

Mean, Standard Deviation, and Standard Error of the Mean

```
10     REM  MEAN, STANDARD DEVIATION, STANDARD ERROR OF
            THE MEAN
```

```
11    REM  Author: Walter R. Hilker   Date: December 27,
         1984 (revised)
12    REM  N = number of entries // X(I) = data for Ith
         entry // F(I) = frequency of X(I) // T = sum of
         x // U = sum of x ^ 2 // S = standard
         deviation
30    HOME : REM

50    PRINT "Mean, Standard Deviation, Standard Error of
               the Mean"
60    PRINT ""
70    PRINT "To find these three statistical measures,
               enter all data points for x. If the data
               are grouped (e.g., frequency of x @ 3 is
               12), your data entry will be greatly
               simplified."
75    PRINT "" : REM

79    REM   inputs data points
80    INPUT "How many data points will you enter?";N
85    PRINT ""
89    REM   inputs whether data are grouped or ungrouped.
         If grouped, program asks for frequency of each
         data point
90    INPUT "Are your data ungrouped or grouped? Enter
               '1' for ungrouped, '2' for grouped:";Z
100    IF Z = 1 GOTO 180: REM

105    REM   data entry, grouped data
110    FOR I = 1 TO N
120    PRINT "Enter x(";I;"):";: INPUT X: PRINT "Enter
               frequency of ";X;":";: INPUT F
130   T = X * F + T: REM t = sum of x
140   U = X ^ 2 * F + U: REM u = sum of x ^ 2
150   I = I + F - 1
160    NEXT I
170    GOTO 250: REM

175    REM   data entry, ungrouped data
180    FOR I = 1 TO N
190    PRINT "Enter x(";I;"):";: INPUT X
200   T = X + T: REM t = sum of x
210   U = X ^ 2 + U: REM u = sum of x ^ 2
220    NEXT I: REM

249    REM    output
```

```
250    PRINT "Mean (x) = ";T / N
255    S = ((U - T ^ 2 / N) / (N - 1)) ^ .5
260    PRINT "Standard deviation (x) = ";S
265    PRINT "Standard error of the mean = ";S / N ^ .5
270    INPUT "Do you want to make new calculations? Type
               'Y' or 'N':";Z$
280    IF Z$ = "Y" OR Z$ = "y" GOTO 290
285    GOTO 320
290    T = 0:U = 0
300    GOTO 75
320    PRINT "Goodbye."
330    END
```

Note: Changes for IBM PC
```
30    SCREEN 0,0:WIDTH 80:COLOR 7,0:CLS:REM
```

Binomial Probability

```
10     REM    BINOMIAL PROBABILITY
11     REM   Author: Walter R. Hilker Date: December 27,
          1984 (revised)
12     REM  P = probability of success in 1 attempt // S
          = number of successes // A = number of attempts
          // C = combination // B = binomial probability
30     HOME : REM

40     PRINT "Binomial Probability"
60     PRINT ""
70     PRINT "To determine binomial probability, first
               decide if the probability will be based on
               cumulative or individual terms."
80  FD = X
100    PRINT ""
110    PRINT "Next, you'll need to input:"
120    PRINT ""
130    PRINT "   1] the number of attempts;"
135    PRINT "   2] the number of successes; and"
140    PRINT "   3] the probability of success in one
               attempt."
141    REM

142    REM  inputs probability, number of attempts,
          number of successes
```

```
145     PRINT "" :INPUT "What is the probability of
                success in one attempt (0 < p <
                1.0)?";P
150     INPUT "Enter the number of attempts:";A: INPUT
                "Enter the number of successes:";S
160   T = 0
165     PRINT ""
170     IF Z = 1 GOTO 300
175     REM

180     PRINT "As this binomial probability will be
                calculated on a cumulative basis, please
                enter whether you wish it to be upwardly
                cumulative (e.g., 3 or more successes in 5
                attempts) or downwardly cumulative (e.g.,
                3 or fewer successes)"
190     INPUT "Enter '+' for upwardly cumulative, '-' for
                downwardly cumulative:";Z$
200     IF Z$ <  > "-" GOTO 220
210     GOTO 260: REM

219     REM    loop for upwardly cumulative binomial
                distribution
220     FOR I = S TO A
230     GOSUB 400
240     NEXT I
250     GOTO 600: REM

259     REM    loop for downwardly cumulative binomial
                distribution
260     FOR I = S TO 0 STEP - 1
270     GOSUB 400
280     NEXT I
290     GOTO 600: REM

299     REM    calculation for individual bionimal
                distribution
300   I = S
310     GOSUB 400
320     GOTO 600: REM

399     REM    factorial loops
400   N = I
410     GOSUB 1000
420   FI = X
430   N = A
440     GOSUB 1000
```

190   THE MBA TOOLKIT

```
450    FA = X
460    N = A - I
470     GOSUB 1000
480    FD = X
490     GOSUB 2000
500    T = B + T
510     RETURN : REM

599     REM    outputs
600     IF Z = 1 GOTO 700
605     PRINT ""
610     PRINT "Cumulative probability = ";T
620     PRINT "":INPUT "Do you want to calculate another
                 binomial probability? Type 'Y' or
                 'N':";Z$
630     IF Z$ = "Y" OR Z$ = "y" GOTO 640
635     GOTO 680
640     HOME :INPUT "Do you want to calculate an
                 individual or cumulative probability? Type
                 '1' for individual, '2' for cumulative:";Z
650     GOTO 145
680     PRINT "Goodbye."
690     END
700     PRINT "Individual probability = ";T
710     GOTO 620: REM

999     REM    factorials
1000    X = 1
1010     FOR J = 1 TO N
1019     ONERR GOTO 1050
1020    X = J * X
1030     NEXT J
1040     RETURN
1050     PRINT "Sorry, 'Attempts' variable must be kept
                 at or below 33 or the computer explodes."
1060     GOTO 150
1070     REM

1999    REM    calculates combination, binomial
                 probability
2000    C = FA / (FI*FD)
2010    B = (P ^ I * (1 - P) ^ (A - I))*C
2020     RETURN
```

Note: Changes for IBM PC
```
30     SCREEN 0,0:WIDTH 80:COLOR 7,0:CLS:REM
640    CLS: INPUT " Do you . . . for cumulative:";Z
```

```
1019    ON ERROR GOTO 1050
1060    RESUME 150
```

Poisson Distribution

```
10      REM    poisson distribution
11      REM   Author: Walter R. Hilker Date: October 19,
           1984 (revised)s
12      REM   M = mean number of successes per unit // S =
           actual number of successes experienced per unit
           // L,H = low, high ranges for cumulative
           poisson // P(S) = poisson probability
20      DIM F(40),P(40)
30      HOME : REM

40      PRINT "Poisson Distribution"
50      PRINT ""
60      PRINT "To calculate poisson distribution, first
               decide if the probability will be based on
               individual or cumulative terms."
70      INPUT "Type '1' for individual, '2' for
               cumulative:";Z
80      PRINT ""
90      PRINT "Next, you'll need to input:"
100      PRINT ""
110     PRINT "    1] the mean (average) number of
                    successes per unit measured;"
120     PRINT "    2] the number of successes actually
                    experienced"
130     PRINT "" : PRINT "Poisson will calculate the
                    probability of your selected number of
                    experiences based on the mean number of
                    successes per unit measured."
140     PRINT "" : REM

149     REM    inputs data for poisson calculations
150     INPUT "What is the mean # of successes per
               unit?";M
160     IF Z <  > 1 GOTO 240
165     REM
```

```
169    REM    individual poisson
170    INPUT "Please enter the actual number of
               successes:";S
180    GOSUB 400
200    PRINT "" : PRINT "p(";S;") = ";P(S)
210    GOTO 600: REM

220    REM    cumulative poisson
240    PRINT ""
250    PRINT "For cumulative poisson, enter low, high
               ranges of the actual number of successes
               you're interested in. For instance, if you
               wanted the poisson probabilities for 5, 6,
               7, and 8 successes, you would enter
               '5,8'."
260    INPUT "Please enter low, high ranges:";L,H
270    T = 0
280    FOR S = L TO H
290    GOSUB 400: REM

300    REM sums Poisson probabilities
310    T = P(S) + T
320    NEXT S
330    P(S) = T
340    GOTO 200: REM

399    REM factorial loop
400    X = 1
410    FOR J = 1 TO S
420    ONERR GOTO 480
430    X = J * X
440    NEXT J: REM

445    REM    poisson calculations
450    P(S) = EXP ( - M) * M ^ S / X
460    RETURN
480    PRINT "Sorry, '";S;"' successes variable too
               large to calculate.": GOTO 150
590    REM

600    INPUT "Do you want to calculate another poisson
               distribution? Type 'Y' or 'N':";Z$
610    IF Z$ = "Y" OR Z$ = "y" GOTO 620
615    GOTO 650
620    INPUT "Type '1' for individual, '2' for
               cumulative:";Z
```

```
630   GOTO 150
650   PRINT "Goodbye."
660   END
```

Note: Changes for IBM PC
```
30   SCREEN 0,0:WIDTH 80:COLOR 7,0:CLS:REM
420   ON ERROR GOTO 480
480   PRINT "Sorry . . . to calculate.":RESUME 150
```

Friedman Statistic

```
10   REM   Friedman statistic
11   REM   Author: Walter R. Hilker Date: October 19,
        1984 (revised)
12   REM  K = number of items ranked, number of ranks /
        / A = sum of squares of ranks times votes // W
        = check for data integrity
20   HOME : REM

50   PRINT "Friedman Statistic"
60   PRINT "": PRINT "To determine the Friedman
                        statistic, enter:"
70   PRINT ""
80   PRINT "   1] The number of items rank-ordered;"
90   PRINT "   2] The sample size; and"
100   PRINT "   3] The frequency of each item at each
                    rank level."
110   PRINT "": REM

115   REM    inputs variables for Friedman calculations
120   INPUT "Please enter # of items rank-ordered:":K
150   FOR I = 1 TO K
160   PRINT "Name of item #";I;":";: INPUT A$(I)
170   NEXT I: REM

240   INPUT "Please enter sample size:";N
250   FOR I = 1 TO K
260  T = 0
265  W = 0
270   FOR J = 1 TO K
280   PRINT "Enter frequency of ";A$(I);" at rank
            #:";J;: INPUT R(I,J)
```

```
285   REM    sums each level!s rankings
290   T = R(I,J) * J + T
295   W = R(I,J) + W
300   NEXT J
305   IF   W < > N GOTO 5050: REM checks for integrity of
                                ranking data
309   REM    sums squares of each item's rank score
310   A = T ^ 2 + A
320   NEXT I: REM

329   REM    Friedman calculation
330   F = (12 / (N * K * (K + 1))) * A - 3 * N * (K + 1)
340   PRINT ""
350   PRINT "Friedman statistic = ";F
360   PRINT "Compare 'F' to Chi-square tables, for ";K
             - 1;" degrees of freedom"

370   PRINT "and your selected level of significance."
380   INPUT "Do you wish to calculate another Friedman
             statistic? Type 'Y' or 'N':";Z$
390   IF Z$ = "Y" OR Z$ = "y" GOTO 110
420   PRINT "Goodbye."
430   END : REM

499   REM    ONERR safeguard for data integrity
500   PRINT "WARNING: frequencies do not equal sample
             size. They should. If they don't, the
             Friedman statistic will be misleading. Do
             you wish to continue? Type 'Y' or 'N':";:
             INPUT Z$
510   IF Z$ = "Y" OR Z$ = "y" GOTO 310
520   GOTO 380
```

Note: Changes for IBM PC
```
20    SCREEN 0,0:WIDTH 80:COLOR 7,0:CLS:REM
```

z-Test

```
10    REM    z test
11    REM    Author: Walter R. Hilker Date: October 19,
          1984 (revised)
```

```
12    REM  (P(1), P(2) = sample proportions // N =
         sample size // S = standard deviation of sample
         // Z = z value
20    HOME : REM

50    PRINT "z Test for Proportions"
60    PRINT ""
70    INPUT "Do you want to compare one sample to a
            norm, or two independent samples to each
            other? Type '1' for one sample to a norm,
            '2' for two independent samples:";K
75    IF K = 2 GOTO 170
79    REM

80    PRINT ""
85    PRINT "To find z for comparing one sample's
            proportion to a norm, enter:"
90    PRINT ""
100    PRINT "   1] observed proportion of your sample;"
110    PRINT "   2] expected proportion of the norm;
                  and"
120    PRINT "   3] sample size (n)."
130    PRINT "" : REM

135    REM  input variables for z test, one sample vs.
         norm
140    INPUT "Please enter observed proportion:";P(1):
            INPUT "Please enter expected
            proportion:";P(2): INPUT "Please enter
            your sample size:";N
145    REM  standard deviation of the sample calculation
150   S = (P(2) * (1 - P(2)) / N) ^ .5
155    PRINT ""
160    GOTO 250: REM

170    PRINT "To find z for comparing proportions from
            two independent samples, enter:"
180    PRINT ""
190    PRINT "   1] proportions of sample 1 and sample
                  2; and"
200    PRINT "   2] sizes of sample 1 and sample 2."
210    PRINT "" : REM

215    REM  inputs variables for z test, 2 independent
         samples
```

196   THE MBA TOOLKIT

```
220    INPUT "Please enter proportion of sample
             1:";P(1): INPUT "Please enter proportion
             of sample 2:";P(2): INPUT "Please enter
             size of sample 1:";N(1): INPUT "Please
             enter size of sample 2:";N(2)
225    REM    weighted proportion
230    P(0) + (P(1) * N(1) + P(2) * N(22)) / (N(1) +
       N(2))
235    REM    pooled standard deviation
240    S = (P(0) * (1 - P(0)) * (1 / N(1) + 1 / N(2))) ^
       .5
245    PRINT "" : REM

249    REM    z value calculation
250    Z = ABS (P(1) - P(2)) / S
255    PRINT ""
260    PRINT "z = ";Z
265    Print "" :PRINT "Compare to value in z tables,
             adjusting appropriately for 1- or 2-
             tailed tests.
267    PRINT ""
270    INPUT "Do you want to calculate another z-value?
             Type 'Y' or 'N':";Z$
280    IF Z$ = "Y" OR Z$ = "y" GOTO 20
300    PRINT "Goodbye."
310    END
```

Note: Changes for IBM PC
```
20     SCREEN 0,0:WIDTH 80:COLOR 7,0:CLS:REM
```

t-Test

```
10     REM    t-test
11     REM    Author: Walter R. Hilker    Date: December
             27, 1984 (revised)
12     REM    M = mean of samples // D = degrees of
       freedom // T = t-value // S = standard deviation /
       / N = sample size // F = F-variable for equal
       variances // B,C used to determine equality of
       variances (F-test)
B,C used to determine equality of variances (F-test)
30     DATA x,y
40     HOME : REM
```

```
50    PRINT "t-test"
55    PRINT ""
60    PRINT "To find t for your sample of metric data,
              first select if you are comparing one
              independent group to an existing norm, or
              two independent groups."
70    PRINT "" : REM

80    INPUT "Type '1' for comparing 1 group of data to a
              norm, or '2' for comparing two independent
              groups:";K
85    HOME
90    IF K = 2 GOTO 250
91    REM  k variable states if simple t-test (k=1) or
          independent t-test(k=2)
95    REM

100   PRINT "To find t for comparing a group of data to
               a norm, enter:": PRINT ""
110   PRINT "    1] each 'x' value;"
115   PRINT "    2] frequency of each 'x' value;"
120   PRINT "    3] sample size; and"
125   PRINT "    4] mean of the existing norm."
150   PRINT "" : REM

155   REM  inputs data for t-test, 1 sample vs. norm
160   INPUT "Enter mean of the existing norm:";M(0)
161   REM  m(0) equals mean of existing norm for simple
          t-test
170   GOSUB 1000: REM goes to data input loop
175   REM

180   REM   calculate simple t, degrees of freedom
190   T = (M(1) - M(0)) / (S(1) / N(1) ^ .5)
191   REM  t=difference of means divided by standard
              deviation of the sample
200   D = N(1) - 1
201   REM   d=degrees of freedom for simple t-test
210   GOTO 2000: REM

250   REM   independent groups t-test
260   PRINT " ": PRINT "To find t for your two
                  independent samples, enter:": PRINT ""
270   PRINT "    1] each 'x' value, and its
                  corresponding frequency;"
```

198   THE MBA TOOLKIT

```
275    PRINT "    2] each 'y'value, and its corresponding
               frequency;"
280    PRINT "    3] sample size for n(x) and n(y)."
300    PRINT ""
310    PRINT "This program will help you determine
               whether the variances of x and y are equal
               or unequal, so you can select the proper
               t-test."
320    GOSUB 1000: REM goes to data input loop
325    REM
329    REM  to calculate f-test for equal variances,
         larger s^2 must be in numerator
330    IF S(1) ^ 2 > S(2) ^ 2 GOTO 360
340    IF S(1) ^ 2 = S(2) ^ 2 GOTO 370
350    PRINT "F = ";S(2) ^ 2 / S(1) ^ 2:B = N(2) - 1:C =
               N(1) - 1
355    GOTO 380
360    PRINT "f = ";S(1) ^ 2 / S(2) ^ 2:B = N(1) - 1:C =
               N(2) - 1
365    GOTO 380
370    PRINT "F = 1.00":B = N(1) - 1:C = N(2) - 1
380    PRINT ""
385    PRINT "Compare 'F' to F tables, using ";B;" as
               numerator degrees of freedom, and"
390    PRINT C;"as denominator degrees of freedom. If
               your F is greater than the F value in
               the tables, then variances are equal."
395    PRINT "" :INPUT "Enter '=' if you judge variances
               to be equal, or '0' if variances are
               unequal:";Z$
400    IF Z$ <> "=" GOTO 460
401    REM  in line 400, user selects independent groups
         t-test for equal or for unequal variances
405    REM

410    REM   t-test equal variances
419    REM   d = degrees of freedom
420    D = N(1) + N(2) - 2
429    REM   p = pooled variance
430    P = (S(1) ^ 2 * (N(1) - 1) + S(2) ^ 2 * (N(2) -
         1)) / D
439    REM   t-test formula
440    T = ABS (M(1) - M(2)) / ((S(1) ^ 2 / N(1) + S(2) ^
         2 / N(2)) ^ .5)
450    GOTO 2000: REM
```

PROGRAM LISTINGS   **199**

```
460    REM    t-test unequal variances
469    REM    a = abbreviation for calculating t-test,
          degrees of freedom
470  A = (S(1) ^ 2 / N(1) + S(2) ^ 2 / N(2))
479    REM    t-test
480  T = ABS (M(1) - M(2)) / A ^ .5
489    REM    b = abbreviation for calculating degrees of
             freedom
490  B = (S(1) ^ 2 / N(1)) / A
499    REM    d = degrees of freedom
500  D = 1 / (B ^ 2 / (N(1) - 1) + ((1 - B ^ 2) / (N(2)
     - 1)))
510    GOTO 2000: REM

999    REM    data input loop
1000   FOR I = 1 TO K
1005 U = 0:V = 0
1010   READ A$(I)
1015   PRINT "" :PRINT "Do you want to label ";A$(I);"?
                 Type 'Y' or 'N':";: INPUT Z$
1020   IF Z$ = "Y" OR Z$ = "y" GOTO 1030
1025   GOTO 1040
1030   GOSUB 3000
1040   PRINT "Enter sample size, n(";A$(I);"):";: INPUT
             N(I)
1045   PRINT ""
1050   FOR J = 1 TO N(I)
1060   PRINT A$(I);"(";J;") = ";: INPUT X
1070   PRINT "Frequency of ";A$(I);"(";J;") = ";: INPUT
             F
1080 U = X * F + U: REM u = sum of x
1090 V = X ^ 2 + F + V: REM v = sum of x^2
1100 J = J + F - 1
1110   NEXT J: REM
1120   REM    calculate mean, standard deviation,
          variance
1130 M(I) = U / N(I): PRINT "Mean of ";A$(I);" =
                            ";M(I)
1140 S(I) =( ABS (V - U ^ 2 / N(I)) / (N(I) - 1)) ^
             .5: PRINT "Standard deviation of ";A$(I);"
             = ";S(I)
1150   PRINT "Variance of ";A$(I);" = ";S(I) ^ 2
1160   NEXT I
1170   RETURN : REM

1999   REM    sayonara
```

200   THE MBA TOOLKIT

```
2000    PRINT "t = ";T
2010    PRINT ""
2020    PRINT "Compare with t-tables at ";D;" degrees of
                freedom.": PRINT ""
2030    INPUT "Do you want to calculate another t-test?
                Type 'Y' or 'N':";Z$
2040    IF Z$ = "Y" OR Z$ = "y" GOTO 2050
2045    GOTO 2070
2050    RESTORE
2060    GOTO 40
2070    PRINT "Goodbye."
2080    END
2090    REM

2999    REM    labelling of variables
3000    PRINT "What label would you like to assign
                ";A$(I);: INPUT B$(I)
3010    A$(I) = B$(I)
3020    RETURN
```

Note: Changes for IBM PC
```
40    SCREEN 0,0:WIDTH 80:COLOR 7,0:CLS:REM
85    CLS
```

Glossary of Accounting, Finance, and Marketing Terms

abandonment value Amount that can be realized by liquidating a project before its economic life ceases.

absorption costing Method of costing where all costs related to the manufacture of the product are allocated to the product cost. Also called "full costing."

accounting cycle Six transaction steps in annual cycle: (1) journalize transactions, (2) debits & credits to ledgers, (3) worksheet, (4) financial statements, (5) adjusting/closing entries, (6) after-closing trial balance.

accounting equation Assets = liabilities + owner's equity. Or, owner's equity = assets − liabilities.

accounting period Span of time covered by an accounting statement. Usually one year, but can be quarterly or semi-annually.

accounting principles Those principles of accounting that are "generally accepted" by the Financial Accounting Standards Board (FASB).

accounts payable A liability that is generated by the purchase of goods or services on credit.

accounts receivable A current asset generated by the extension of goods or services on credit to someone else.

accrual basis of accounting Recognize revenue in the period in which it is earned. Deduct expenses used to generate the revenue in that period, irrespective of timing of actual cash receipts or expenditures.

accumulated depreciation A contra-asset account related to a depreciable asset account.

acid test ratio A measure of liquidity. (Current assets − inventories) ÷ current liabilities. Also called "quick ratio."

activity ratios Ratios that measure how effectively a firm is utilizing its resources. Includes inventory turnover, average collection period, fixed asset turnover, and total asset turnover.

actual costing The only costs allocated to the product using this method are actual direct labor, direct materials, and factory overhead.

advertising Sponsor-paid communication of a product or service in a manner that will entice a potential customer to purchase, subscribe, or otherwise expend toward that product or service. See **publicity**.

aging schedule Shows how long accounts receivable have been outstanding.

amortize To liquidate or reduce indebtedness on an installment basis. A mortgage payment is an example of a loan that is amortized.

annuity A series of payments of a fixed amount for a specified number of years.

appropriations That portion of retained earnings not available for cash dividends.

arbitrage Process of buying undervalued assets and selling them at a higher value.

assets Economic resources owned by a business (e.g., cash, accounts receivable, buildings, equipment, etc.).

auditing Impartial review of an accounting system.

average collection period Average time that it takes to collect accounts receivable.

balance sheet The financial statement that portrays the financial composition of a firm at a particular time.

balloon payment Situation where final payment on amortized debt is larger than other preceding payments. Final payment is the balloon.

beta coefficient. Measure of a firm's risk. Indicates extent to which returns on a firm's stock move with the market. Also called risk coefficient.

bond Debt instrument used to secure funds by firm offering the bond. Investment instrument for those buying. A *debenture bond* is unsecured; the value rests on credit of the corporation. A *serial bond* has varying maturity dates. A *callable bond* can be paid off by the issuing corporation before maturity date. A *convertible bond* has the option to be exchanged for common stock.

bond valuation Value of bond is annual interest payment (cash flows) plus principal due (maturity value) when the bond matures.

book value The book value of an asset is the cost less accumulated depreciation. The book value per share of common stock is the total stockholders equity divided by the number of common shares outstanding. As opposed to market value (or carrying value).

break-even point The point at which your total accumulated salary equals the salary you could have made had you not gone to graduate school. Point at which costs equal revenues.

broker Someone who negotiates the purchase, sale, or other such expenditure, between two parties.

budget Summary statement of quantitative plans for reaching financial and operational goals.

business entity Economic unit that enters into business transactions.

call Option to buy a share of stock at a specified price within a specified time period. It also refers to the process of redeeming a bond before it reaches maturity.

call provision A provision to redeem a bond before maturity.

call premium The additional price tagged onto a bond when it is called.

capital Another term for money. Usually associated with long-range financing.

capital asset pricing mode (CAPM) Method to calculate the cost of equity capital.

capital budgeting Long-range planning for proposed capital outlays, the potential returns, and how to finance them.

capital structure Composition of the permanent long-term financing of a firm. Includes debt (bank and bonds), preferred and common stock, and other owner's equity (retained earnings).

capitalization rate Discount rate a firm uses to do its capital budgeting; the percentage rate used to find the present value of the future cash payments.

carrying costs Costs of holding inventory, including costs for storage space, brokerage, insurance, obsolescence, and deterioration. Carrying costs are factored at the cost of capital to arrive at the cost to the firm. Example: $1 mm in inventory $\times$ 12% (cost of capital) = $120K carrying cost for holding the inventory for one year.

cash budget Schedule of a firm's projected cash flows (or lack thereof). Everyone should have one, if only to say they've done it.

certainty equivalents The rate of return required to make an uncertain (risky) investment opportunity equally attractive as a certain (conservative) investment.

coefficient of variation Standard deviation $\div$ mean.

commercial paper Short term promissory notes (unsecured) of large firms. Usually issued in large denominations ($1 MM+). Rate of interest is slightly below prime rate.

committed costs Fixed costs associated with plant, equipment, etc.

common stock Offerings by a firm for ownership rights in the firm in exchange for the market value of each share. Shareholders have right to vote for firm's directors and other ownership rights. Stocks and bonds are also referred to as "securities."

compensating balance The required minimum checking account balance for a firm. Usually 15 to 20% of outstanding loans.

compound value Interest building on interest.

consumers' goods Products that are intended to be used by household consumers. See **industrial goods.**

contra-asset account Account that has a credit balance and is offset against an asset account (e.g., accumulated depreciation, allowance for doubtful accounts).

contra-liability account Account that has a debit balance and is offset against a liability account (e.g., discount on notes payable).

contribution margin The percent of sales dollars available to cover fixed expenses, or (sales − variable expenses) $\div$ sales.

convenience goods Frequently purchased products for the household consumer that are selected with little or no comparison or consideration. Includes staples, such as milk, as well as impulse items such as snack foods. See also **shopping goods, speciality goods.**

conversion feature on preferred stock Feature that enables owner of preferred stock to exchange the stock for shares of common at stipulated price.

convertibles Securities (bonds and preferred stock) that one can exchange for common stock at specified ratio.

cost accounting That phase of accounting that deals with the collecting and interpreting of cost data.

cost of capital A firm's cost on the money it uses or would use. Used in capital budgeting analysis.

cost of goods sold Just like it sounds. Deducted from revenues to reveal gross profit.

cost-revenue analysis Study of how revenues and costs behave in response to changes in level of business activity (e.g., break-even analysis, contribution margin, profit volume, etc.).

cost variances Difference between budgeted or planned costs and actual costs.

credit A term meaning "loan." Convention places credit on the right-hand side of the ledger. Generally credit is an increase in liability or revenue account, or a decrease in asset or expense account.

current assets Term applied to assets that are easier to liquidate. Includes cash, accounts receivable, marketable securities, inventories—anything normally converted into cash within one year.

current ratio A measure of liquidity. Current assets ÷ current liabilities.

debit A term meaning "owed." Convention puts debits on the left side of the ledger. Generally refers to an increase in asset or expense account, or a decrease in liability or revenue account.

debt ratio Total debt (i.e., current liabilities + bonds) ÷ total assets.

deficit Negative amount of retained earnings.

demographics The study of the characteristics of human populations, such as age, sex, annual income, race, etc.

depletion Similar to depreciation, only it applies to natural resources.

depreciation Allowance made for the loss in value of an asset or resource. Usually allocated over a specified time frame.

direct sales Selling of a product or service by the producer directly to the consumer or retailer, without middlemen.

discretionary income Personal income minus costs associated with a given standard of living; money that is available for use at one's own discretion; play money.

discount, cash Reduction of invoice for prompt payment. Example: 2/10 net 30. Firm is given a 2% discount if it pays bill within 10 days; it must pay full bill within 30.

discounted cash flow A capital budgeting technique for determining the present value of future cash payments by using the discount rate.

discounting accounts receivable Or "pledging of accounts receivable." Means by which a firm can generate short-term financing by using the accounts receivable as collateral.

disposable income Personal income minus taxes and other compulsory deductions.

distribution The system that takes the product from the manufacturer to the consumer. Five common strategies:

manufacturer-customer

> manufacturer-retailer-customer
>
> manufacturer-wholesaler-customer
>
> manufacturer-wholesaler-retailer-customer
>
> manufacturer-broker-wholesaler-retailer-customer

dividends Distribution of cash or stock by a corporation to its shareholders. Dividends are paid from net profits (although dividends can also be paid if the company suffers a loss). Preferred shareholders have first rights to dividends.

double-entry methods Commonly used accounting method. Derives name from fact that equal debit and credit entries are made for every transaction.

doubtful accounts, allowance for Estimated amount deducted from accounts receivable on the balance sheet. Allows for uncollectible funds.

durable goods Goods that last through several uses, e.g., cars, musical instruments, household tools. See also **services.**

earned surplus Another term for retained earnings.

earnings before interest and taxes (EBIT) Sales − cost of goods sold − operating expenses.

earnings per share (EPS) Net income ÷ no. of common shares outstanding. One measure of firm's financial strength and investment potential.

efficiency variance Standard price (of resource) × (actual quantity of inputs − standard quantity of inputs allowed).

equity Segment of company's resources held or financed by the owners. Also called owner's equity, net worth, or total equity. Consists of common and preferred stock, paid-in capital, and retained earnings.

equity ratio total equity ÷ total assets.

ex dividend date Date on which right to current dividend no longer accompanies a stock.

expected return The rate of return a firm expects to realize from an investment.

expenses Cost of goods and services used in the process of obtaining revenue.

factoring Method whereby a firm sells its accounts receivable to a financial institution to generate some cash.

financial accounting Accounting procedures directed towards interested parties external to the firm. Contrasted to managerial accounting, which is for internal users of accounting data.

financial leverage Concept of using debt to "expand" the firm's operation. Total debt ÷ total assets. Leverage is correlated with the degree of risk a firm presents as an investment. The higher the leverage, the higher the risk.

financial structure How assets are financed, either through debt or equity. This is depicted by the balance sheet, which shows the liabilities and owner's equity on the right-hand side, and the assets being financed on the left-hand side.

fiscal year Any 12-month accounting period adopted by a business.

fixed assets Non-liquid, depreciable assets such as plant, equipment, land, etc.

fixed costs Costs that do not change over time despite fluctuations in business activity.

float Amount of money tied up in checks written but not yet cashed or collected.

F.O.B. (Free on Board) "FOB shipping point" means seller places material on "free" and buyer pays transportation charges. "FOB destination" means the seller pays the shipping cost.

focus groups A form of marketing research in which several panels of target respondents discuss products, strategies, and/or other researchable issues.

full costing See **absorption costing.**

general journal The original record of accounting entries used in the first step in the accounting cycle.

general ledger Name for group of accounts called ledger accounts.

going-concern assumption A rule governing a business enterprise that it will be a continuing operation.

goodwill A calculation of the company's future earnings that exceed the normal earnings in the industry, or net purchase price minus book value. May be due to good name, established clientele, etc. Recognized as having a negotiable value only when purchased from or sold to another entity.

gross profit Sales minus cost of goods sold. Also called gross margin.

holding companies Corporations whose main purpose is owning the common stock of other companies.

hurdle rate The minimum acceptable rate of return for capital budgeting projects.

imputed costs Opportunity or outlay costs.

income Earnings that a firm generates on its sales, or revenues minus expenses.

income statement Financial statement that displays how effectively the firm utilized its resources in generating income.

incremental cash flow Net cash proceeds attributable to an investment project. For example, the thousands of dollars you will generate by reading this book.

indenture Agreement between bond issuer and bond holders.

indirect costs Expenses that cannot be directly allocated to one particular department. General company expenses, e.g., "building expense."

industrial goods Products that are intended to be used by industry in the manufacturing of other products or in the offering of services.

inflation The rise in the general level of prices. "Too much money chasing too few goods."

insolvency The condition of not being able to meet one's financial obligations. Sometimes referred to as "Chapter 13."

intangible assets Assets with no physical substance, e.g., goodwill.

interim statements Financial statements issued on monthly, quarterly, or semi-annual basis.

internal financing Retained earnings + depreciation. Used in capital budgeting analysis.

internal rate of return (IRR) The rate (percentage) that equates the present value of future cash flows to the cost of the investment.

inventory All goods owned and held for sale in regular course of business. There are three types: raw materials, work-in-process, and finished goods.

inventory profits "Shadow" or fictitious profits generated through use of FIFO inventory valuation method. Capitalizes on increased cost of goods by subtracting old inventory costs rather than replacement costs from revenues.

journal Chronological record showing each transaction before it is posted in specific ledger accounts.

ledger A group of accounts. If one ledger is maintained, it is referred to as the general ledger; if several are maintained, they are called subsidiary ledgers.

leverage ratios Measures proportion of funds supplied by creditors vis-à-vis funds supplied by owners. Includes debt ratio, times interest earned, and fixed charge coverage.

liabilities Debts the company or individual has incurred.

line of credit An open account of loanable funds from a bank or other financial institution to a firm, up to a certain level. For example, a firm may have a line of credit of $5 million with a bank.

liquidity Describes a firm's cash position (or assets readily converted into cash) and its ability to meet its obligations.

liquidity ratios Measurements that depict how readily a firm could meet its financial obligations. Includes current ratio and quick ratio.

make/buy decisions Company makes decision to manufacture in-house (internally) or buy from external source.

mapping Showing graphically where a product fits in among its competitors. The graph can be made of any number of axes, with each axis representing an attribute relevant to the products. Where each product fits on the graph is determined by the degree to which it contains each of the attributes. For instance, a two-axes (X-Y) graph of soft drinks might show the X axis to represent sweet taste to bitter taste, and the Y axis high carbonation to low carbonation. A graph using n axes might also include axes representing color, calorie level, age appeal, etc.

margin of safety Dollar amount by which actual sales exceed break-even sales volume.

margin requirements Requirements for purchasing additional shares of stock with less than full financing. "Buying on margin" enables an investor to leverage himself without turning over the total funds involved.

marginal cost Cost of additional unit. Marginal cost of capital is cost of an additional dollar of new funds.

marginal efficiency of capital A schedule depicting internal rate of return on investment opportunities.

market demand The sales (or other performance measure) of a product or service that is achieved under particular market conditions, e.g., promotion, packaging, distribution, advertising, competitors' marketing efforts, etc.

market forecast The anticipated sales of a product or service, based on a particular level of company marketing effort.

market indifference curve Line that graphically depicts the risk premium required for the level of risk expected.

market potential The level of market demand that could be achieved under ideal conditions.

market share A company's sales divided by its industry's sales. Can be stated in actual or forecasted terms.

market value Of inventories: What it would cost to replace the inventory in today's market; current replacement cost. Of stock: Current stock market price, or value if sold today.

marketing information systems A process within the company that handles and disseminates information from inside and outside the company for the benefit of marketing in its decision-making needs.

marketing mix The four elements of the marketing mix are:

1. Product (quality, features/options/attributes, style, brand name, packaging, product line, warranty/guarantee, service level, other services and benefits generated by the product). See **product life cycle.**

2. Place (distribution, coverage, locations of outlets, sales territories, inventory levels, transportation methods and costs, other influences on a product's availability to its consumers). See **distribution.**

3. Price (level of price, discounts/allowances, payment terms, position relative to comparable products or services, other effects on the acceptability of a product's cost to its consumers). See **pricing.**

4. Promotion (advertising, personal selling, sales promotion, publicity, public relations, concurrent events, and other methods that affect the demand for and interest in a product). See **advertising, publicity.**

master budget Overall financial and operations plan for upcoming fiscal period. Includes the program to achieve that plan.

matching concept Process where costs are "matched" to revenues. Cost becomes an expense.

maturity value Principal plus interest on a note payable.

money market Financial markets in which funds are borrowed or loaned for short periods. Capital markets are long-term funds.

mortgage A pledge of designated property to secure a loan.

natural business year Fiscal year ending at low point of annual activity.

net present value method (NPV) Method of ranking investment proposals. See **discounted cash flow.** NPV = present value of future earnings discounted at marginal cost of capital − present value of the cost of the investment.

net worth Assets − liabilities. Same as owner's equity or net assets.

notes payable Current liability arising from promise to pay for goods or services received.

operating costs Costs incurred in the daily operations of a business.

operating cycle Time between purchase of merchandise or material and conversion of merchandise into revenue.

operating leverage Extent to which fixed costs are used in a firm's operation. The higher the percentage of fixed costs, the more operating leverage the firm can gain as sales volume increases.

opportunity cost Lost benefit of not pursuing course of action; the rate of return on an alternative investment.

outlay costs Actual cash disbursements.

out-of-pocket costs Costs incurred during the current accounting period.

owner's equity Net amount that owners have claim to. Assets − liabilities, or net worth.

paid-in capital Premium on capital stock. Part of owner's equity.

par value Arbitrary amount (nominal value) assigned to each share of stock. Usually a small amount for common stock (e.g., $1), but a meaningful amount for preferred.

partnership Business owned by two or more individuals who are subject to unlimited liability.

payback period Capital budgeting technique for evaluating investment proposals. Payback period equals the number of years it takes a firm to recover initial investment.

payout ratio Percentage of a firm's earnings paid out in dividends.

penetration A pricing strategy where the price yields a minimum profit. Used to establish a customer base and brand loyalty, after which the price is raised to achieve a more acceptable profit level. See also **skimming.**

percent of sales method Used for forecasting and trend analysis. All items on the balance sheet are calculated as a ratio of sales. Also used for pro forma statements.

period costs Costs not directly or easily allocatable to a specific product or group of products, e.g., salary of a night watchman. These costs are not charged against cost of goods sold, but are written off as operating expenses during the period in which they are incurred.

perpetual inventory system Continuous record of inventory kept by adding to or reducing raw materials, work in process, and finished goods on a daily basis.

periodic inventory system Merchandise on hand counted periodically to determine inventory levels.

perpetuity Stream of equal future payments expected to continue forever.

pooling of interests Acquisitions that take place through exchange of stock.

portfolio effect Extent to which variation in the returns on a combination of assets (portfolio) is less than the variations of the individual assets.

portfolio theory Idea that by combining a certain group of investments or assets a firm can offset the riskiness of the overall investment. Portfolio theory deals with finding optimal portfolios or those that offer best possible return at a given risk level.

position statement Balance sheet.

preemptive right Right of stockholders to maintain a certain percentage of ownership in a company by purchasing that percentage of additional shares offered.

present value Value in today's monetary terms of a future payment or receipt. Derived by discounting at cost of capital or another appropriate discount rate.

price variance (Actual unit price − standard unit price) × actual quantity of goods.

pricing An element of the marketing mix that states how much customers will pay for goods or services, based on market conditions, expectations and manipulations.

prime rate Interest rate that major banks charge their best and biggest customers.

pro forma Projected financial statements such as income statements or balance sheets. Used for evaluating financial impact under various assumptions or scenarios.

product costs Costs that become part of goods in process and finished good inventories. They are deductible from revenue in the period that products are sold.

product life cycle The theory that products pass through four stages:

1. Introduction: high advertising, low awareness, no competition, growing sales. Objective: establish interest, awareness and availability.

2. Growth: high advertising, increasing awareness, heavy competition, high growth in sales. Objectives: minimize costs and maximize market share.

3. Maturity: diminished advertising, high awareness, competitive shakeout, peaked sales. Objectives: extend life, maintain market share.

4. Decline: little or no advertising, lower awareness, little competition, dropping sales. Objective: fish or cut bait.

product line A group of products that are related in use, distribution, or marketing. For example, kitchen appliances. *Width of line* refers to the number of types of products (e.g. toasters, blenders, microwave ovens, can openers, electric knives); *depth of line* refers to the number of products of any one type (e.g. several microwave ovens of varying sizes, functions, capabilities).

product mix A group of products that are related only in that they are manufactured or sold by the same concern. The company whose product line of kitchen appliances is described above may also sell no-wax floors, over-the-counter drugs, radios and sausages; their collection of products would be their "mix." It would also be their headache.

profitability ratios Measures of the relationship of profits to other financial gauges. Includes profit margin/sales, return on assets, return on equity (ROE), and return on investment (ROI)

proprietorship Business owned by one person.

psychographics The study of an individual's interests, values, life styles, activities and opinions that help to classify him/her with others in the population.

publicity Events, news and "press releases" that can affect a product much like advertising, but, unlike advertising, are not paid for by its sponsor. Publicity can be positive or negative.

reference groups Groups of people whose opinions and behavior affect your own.

retained earnings Portion of company's income not paid out in dividends. Used for reinvestment or held as cash.

return on assets (Net income + interest expense) ÷ total assets.

return on equity (ROE) Net income ÷ owner's equity. See **return on investment.**

return on investment (ROI) Net income ÷ total amount invested. Sometimes used synonymously with ROE. However, ROI may apply to a specific project, whereas ROE usually applies to the return from the total company investments.

risk The probability that actual future returns will fall below expected returns. Risk is a function of the standard deviation of expected returns.

risk premium The difference between the required rate of return on a risky asset and the rate on a risk-free asset.

segmentation Breaking up the marketplace into groups (defined by demographics, needs, wants, tastes, and attitudes), in order to target a product or service efficiently at those segments who desire it most.

semi-variable costs Costs that change in response to change in volume by less than the proportionate amount.

sensitivity analysis "What if" technique. Measures expected value changes under certain assumptions and scenarios.

services Nontangible benefits that consumers purchase or contract with, e.g., carpet cleaning, plumbing. See also **durable goods.**

shopping Goods Consumers' products that require "shopping around"—comparing price, suitability, and other considerations. Examples: furnishings, major appliances, used cars.

sinking fund An amount set aside to meet financing commitments (e.g., bond issue).

skimming Setting a product's price at the highest possible level in order to establish market share and then drop its price, or to get in and out of the market quickly. In either case, the intent is to maximize return on investment rapidly. See **penetration, threshold.**

social class A classification of peoples more specific than either culture or subculture. Commonly used to refer to Warner's Index of Status Characteristics, which identified six classes based on occupation, source of income, house type and dwelling area. They are:

Upper upper class (0.5% of the sample)

Lower upper class (1.5%)

Upper middle class (10.0%)

Lower middle class (33.0%)

Upper lower class (40.0%)

Lower lower class (15.0%)

solvency Ability to meet financial obligations.

sources and uses of funds statement Financial statement depicting how funds are being utilized, as well as interrelationships among funds.

specialty goods Goods that certain consumers make a special effort to buy because of the goods' peculiar benefits or attributes. Goods that carry social status are typically specialty goods, e.g., high-tech electronic equipment and designer wear. See also **convenience goods, shopping goods.**

standard costs Predetermined cost estimates for labor, factory overhead, and material used as basis for costing. Used as proxy for actual costs. Actual costs are later measured against standard costs. See **variances.**

standard deviation Measures the variation of results or observations from the mean. In finance it is used as a risk coefficient to depict how much variation from "normal" risk a particular investment or asset involves.

strategic planning The evaluation of the corporate mission in terms of how day-to-day operations and activities can satisfy that mission.

subcultures Small segments of society to which an individual belongs and that affect his or her behavior or attitudes. Subcultures may be defined by age, nationality, income, geography, religion, or other delineations.

subordinated debentures Bonds that have claim on assets after "senior" debt has been paid, in the event of liquidation.

subscription price Price for stock in a rights offering.

sunk cost Cost that has already been incurred. This cost is no longer relevant to future decisions.

synergy Situation where the whole is greater than the sum of the parts. Important theory in merger analysis.

systematic risk Risk that cannot be eliminated through diversification.

tender offers Situation where one firm offers to buy stock of another firm by going directly to the shareholders.

terminal value Value of an asset at some future end date.

test market An evaluative exercise in which a new product is marketed in one or a few markets as a means to gauge its strengths, weaknesses, and overall acceptability for the total market.

threshold A price level beyond which a product experiences a sharp dropoff in market acceptance. Can be a low-end or high-end threshold. See **skimming.**

times interest earned (Profit before taxes + interest charges) ÷ interest charges. Measures the margin by which a firm can cover its interest charges.

trend analysis Review of historical financial data to project future positioning.

underwriting Process of issuing new corporate securities. Also, the function of bearing the risk of adverse price fluctuations.

unsystematic risk Portion of a firm's risk associated with random events. Unlike systematic risk, this portion can be reduced or eliminated through diversification. An example of reducing unsystematic risk would be to take a welding course while you're in the MBA program.

utility theory Deals with relationships among money, income, happiness (utility), and the willingness to accept risks.

variances Deviations of actual results from budgeted or standard results.

warrant Long-term option to buy a stated number of shares of common stock at a specified price.

weighted average cost of capital Average cost of debt, common stock, and preferred stock. It is weighted by the proportional amount of each component.

working capital Gross working capital is the firm's total current assets. Net working capital = current assets − current liabilities.

yield Rate of return on an investment.

Glossary of Economics Terms

Economics per se *has not been presented as a separate subject in this book, mainly because it is not one that can readily be presented in handbook fashion or reduced to a few simple axioms or formulas. We're also inclined to agree with Thomas Carlisle that it is a "dismal science" and requires mental deep waders to even test its waters. Nevertheless, since economic terms seem to crop up relatively frequently in the practice of business, we felt a glossary of economic terms might come in handy. In these pages you can learn, for instance, the not inconsiderable difference between full employment and zero unemployment and the translation of the oft-heard yet elusive phrase* ceteris paribus.

absolute price Amount of money that must be spent to acquire one unit of a commodity.

aggregate demand function Relates level of desired expenditure to the level of income. AD = C + I, where C = desired consumption and I = desired investment. Income is at equilibrium when aggregate demand equals income.

antitrust laws Laws that restrict or curtail the development of monopolies on the basis that competition produces good results.

arc elasticity Ratio of percentage change in quantity demanded to percentage change in price for a particular price change. Elasticity varies along the demand curve. The midpoint of the relevant range covered by the demand curve is used as the basis for the elasticity calculation.

average cost. Also average total cost Cost per unit. Total cost of production divided by number of units produced. Average total cost is a combination of average fixed cost and average variable cost.

average product Total product divided by the number of units of labor.

average propensity to consume. Total consumption divided by total income.

average propensity to save Total savings divided by total income.

average revenue Revenue per unit sold. Total revenue divided by number of units sold.

balance of payments Accounts that keep track of transactions between countries. A deficit signifies that the reserves are being diminished. A surplus indicates that reserves are rising.

balance of trade The balance of payments on tangible goods.

balanced budget Situation where revenues are equal to government spending.

balanced budget multiplier The percentage of balanced budget government spending that results in a change in income. So when revenues equal spending, the balanced budget multiplier is the change in income divided by the change in spending *or* the change in income divided by the change in revenues.

barriers to entry Restrictions that prohibit new firms from entering an industry. Every good monopoly shouldn't be without a few.

black market Where goods are sold illegally.

Bretton-Woods Agreement A system for international monetary payments established at Bretton Woods, New Hampshire, in 1944. The agreement is well known for establishing a gold exchange standard whereby U.S. dollars were convertible into gold at $35 an ounce.

capacity Level of output that corresponds to the minimum short-run average total cost.

capitalized value Another term for present value, or the value of an asset after the present value of its income stream has been determined. One simplified way to determine capitalized value is to divide the level cash flow by the capitalization rate (such as WACC, discount rate, or whatever the firm is using). For example, if cash flow $(F) = \$10,000$ and capitalization rate $(R) = 10\%$, the capitalized value $= F/R = \$10,000/.10 = \$100,000$.

cartel A group of producers that form a cooperative and attempt to "control" the market by agreement on the restriction of output. OPEC is an example.

central bank The regulatory financial institutions in a country. The Federal Reserve System is the central bank for the U.S.

ceteris paribus Latin phrase meaning "other things being equal." It is often used to describe the relation among economic variables.

closed economies Systems that do not engage in trade with foreign countries.

closed shop A business where employment of non-union members is restricted. Prohibited in 1948 by Taft-Hartley Act.

collusion Agreement between two or more sellers to set a common market price or act in any way similar to a "multipartner" monopoly. This is verboten behavior in business.

commodity Goods and services generated by the resources or factors of production of a firm.

complement good (or service). Also complementary good Any good or service that is used jointly with another good or service. For example, gasoline is a complement good of automobiles.

conspicuous consumption The purchase of goods for snob appeal, rather than for the inherent value of the good.

constant dollars Dollars as measured in "real" terms taking into account inflation-adjusted purchasing power. In measuring constant dollars, one year is established as the base year and dollars in succeeding years are evaluated against purchasing power in the base year.

Consumer Price Index (CPI) An index that measures the changes in prices of consumer goods (such as gas, food, mortgages). The year 1967 is used as the base year, with a base value of 100.0. Used as an indicator of inflation.

consumption Act of utilizing goods and services to satisfy needs.

cost push Theory of inflation that attributes the rise in price to upward spiraling costs (e.g., wage costs).

credit rationing Situation where lending institutions restrict the amount of money available to businesses. This results in "tight money."

cross elasticity of demand The percentage change in quantity demanded of one good divided by the percentage change in price of another good.

crowding-out effect A reduction in expenditures by private firms and households caused by an increase in government spending.

demand curve Curve depicting the quantity of commodities demanded at various prices.

demand deposits Bank deposits that can be withdrawn at any time the customer desires. Checking accounts are an example.

demand-pull inflation Changes in price are a result of changes in aggregate demand. When demand exceeds ability of economy to produce, prices are bid upward; this is demand-pull inflation.

derived demand Pertains to the demand for factors of production (resources such as labor, raw materials, etc.). The demand is "derived" because the resources are required to produce the commodities the business sells.

diminishing returns An economic "law" that holds that if constant increments of a variable factor are applied to a given quantity of fixed factors, the additional output received will eventually decrease.

discount rate The rate of interest the Federal Reserve Bank charges on loans to its member banks. This is one variable used to adjust the money supply.

disposable income Personal income minus personal income taxes.

Dow Jones Industrial Average Average stock market index of thirty major industrial firms.

economics The study of the allocation of scarce resources to produce goods and services that satisfy wants.

economies of scale Advantages to be gained by an increase in size or volume of production and the subsequent lower costs associated with those two factors.

elasticity of demand The percentage change in quantity demanded divided by the percentage change in price. This calculation measures the responsiveness of demand to changes in price. Perfectly elastic demand is when demand elasticity equals 1.0. See **inelastic demand.**

elasticity of supply The percentage change in quantity supplied divided by the percentage change in price.

equilibrium Point at which supply equals demand.

equilibrium income Situation where the national income has a temdency neither to increase nor to decrease.

equilibrium price Price toward which actual market price tends to gravitate.

expansionary monetary policy Effort by the Federal Reserve to "loosen up" the money supply and increase the level of aggregate demand. In so doing, interest rates decline, *ceteris paribus*.

externalities Effect on third parties of production in which they are not directly involved. (e.g., impact of water pollution from a paper mill on the local fishing industry).

factors of production Resources used by a firm to produce the commodities that consumers desire. Includes labor, land (minerals, fuel), capital (machinery, buildings), and entrepreneurs (the organizers).

FDIC Federal Deposit Insurance Corporation. Government agency that insures specified amounts placed in FDIC-member banks.

Federal Reserve System The central bank of the United States. The Fed (as it is known) has the capacity to affect the money supply (and thereby influence interest rates, inflation, and unemployment) in three ways: (1) the discount rate, (2) the reserve ratio, and (3) open market monetary policy.

fiat money Money declared by government order to be legal tender.

fiscal policy The use of government spending and tax policies to influence employment and national income.

floating exchange rates Rates left free to be determined by the forces of demand and supply.

free market economy. Also capitalist economy Economy where the allocation of resources is determined chiefly by the decisions of individual firms and households.

frugal economy An economy in which firms and households consider future needs. Savings and investments occur along with consumption.

full employment Situation where approximately 6% of the labor force is unemployed. Full employment and zero unemployment are not synonymous.

Giffen good An inferior good for which an increase in price leads to an increase in demand.

gold standard See **Bretton Woods Agreement.**

good Tangible commodity produced by a firm for the satisfaction of consumers' needs.

Gross National Product (GNP) Dollar value of final goods and services produced in the country.

holding company A corporation organized to hold the stock of one or more other corporations.

hyperinflation Situation where inflation increases at rates of 50%, 100%, or higher.

income-consumption line Line that graphically demonstrates how household purchases react to changes in income while relative prices are held constant.

incremental cost Marginal cost.

indifference curve Curve that demonstrates the points at which a consumer or household is indifferent in selecting various combinations of goods. For example a consumer may be indifferent (i.e., receives the same satisfaction between choices) in selecting 4 mango melons and 6 kiwi fruit, or 3 mango melons and 8 kiwi fruit.

inelastic demand When elasticity is less than one. For example, if a 1% increase in price causes a less than 1% decrease in quantity demanded, the price elasticity of demand will be less than one. In other words, inelastic demand is when the market is not very responsive to price.

inferior good Consumption of the good decreases in response to a rise in income. A common example is margarine. If income rises, people may switch to butter and decrease their consumption of margarine.

inflation An increase in the price of goods and services that is not accompanied by a proportional increase in the quality or quantity of those goods and services.

invisibles Services that cannot be seen or touched (e.g., insurance, tourist expenditures, etc.).

joint profit maximization Strategy of oligopolies whereby all firms in the group maximize their collective profits.

Keynesian Related to economic theory developed by John Maynard Keynes. The main premise behind Keynesian economics is that the economy, left by itself, will not produce full employment. Keynesians believe fiscal policy is more influential than monetary policy in shaping the economy.

kinked demand curve Applies to oligopolies. The "kink" in the demand curve suggests that the firm has two demand curves. The seller may be unwilling to change price because of anticipated poor results in either lowering or raising prices.

labor A service rendered in the production of other goods and services. One of the factors of production.

laissez faire An economic policy that promotes free-market enterprise with little or no government interference. The loose translation of the French phrase is "let (them) do."

limit price The lowest price at which a firm can enter a market and not incur a loss.

liquidity preference Preference to hold assets in the form of money (liquid capital) rather than interest-earning wealth.

long-run average cost curve (LRAC) Curve that plots the lowest costs attainable for factors of production at various levels of output, when all factors are variable.

long-run supply curve Demonstrates the points of equilibrium between the marginal revenue curve and the long-run marginal cost curve.

long-run profit maximizing A sales-maximizing strategy that may not result in short-term profit maximization; since higher sales will result in higher growth, the long-term result is maximized profits.

Lorenz curve An income distribution curve that depicts the percentage of total income accounted for by given proportions of the nation's families (e.g., the upper 20% of the nation's families may account for 40% of the nation's total income).

M1 Term used to describe currency in circulation plus demand deposits.

M2 M1 plus money market funds plus mutual funds.

M3 M2 plus large time deposits.

macroeconomics The study of the determination of economic aggregates, or the "big picture" approach. Includes study of aggregate demand, total output, total employment, price level, etc., and how they interact.

marginal cost The increase in total cost caused by producing one more unit.

marginal efficiency of capital The rate of return earned on the last dollar of capital utilized.

marginal efficiency of investment schedule A graph (curving downward) that relates the level of investment to the rate of interest.

marginal product The change in product resulting from the use of one more unit of the variable factor; e.g., $MP_L = \Delta TP/\Delta L$, where TP = total product and L = labor.

marginal propensity to consume The change in consumption divided by the change in income.

marginal propensity to save Change in total saving divided by the change in income.

marginal revenue The change in total revenue resulting from the sale of one additional unit.

microeconomics Study of the allocation of resources and the distribution of income as affected by the price system and government policies.

minimum efficient scale The smallest size a plant can be and still achieve economies of scale.

mixed economy An economic system where some decisions are made by households and businesses (free market) and some decisions are made by the central authority or government (command economy).

monetarism A school of economic thought that believes that variations in the money supply are the major cause of cyclical fluctuations and inflation.

money A generally accepted medium of exchange.

money supply The total amount of money in the economy at any moment.

monopoly Situation where one producer or seller controls the output of the entire market.

multiplier A term used to describe the effect of an increase in expenditure on national income. Because the increase in national income exceeds the increase (on a dollar-for-dollar basis) in expenditure, the dynamic is called the multiplier effect. The ratio of income increase to expenditure increase is the multiplier.

neo-Keynesians Contemporary economists who support the economic philosophy of John Maynard Keynes.

nonprice competition Market competition that does not use price as a point of differentiation or strategy (e.g., advertising).

oligopoly Situation where a handful of firms in essence "control the market" and, by their very size, make entry into the market nearly impossible.

open market operations The most important method by which the Federal Reserve controls the money supply. Deals with the buying and selling of government securities in the financial markets.

Pareto-optimality An economic condition where no entity can be made better off without making another entity worse off. In other words, if a business or individual prospers, it does so at the expense of another.

perfect competition Conditions necessary for perfect competition include a large number of buyers and sellers, homogeneous product, perfect information, and no barriers to entry.

perpetuity Situation where interest is paid on a bond every year forever.

Phillips curve A downward-sloping curve that depicts the level of unemployment vis à vis the rate of inflation. The Phillips curve relates to "demand-pull" inflation. This means that the lower the unemployment rate, *ceteris paribus,* the higher the rate of inflation because, for a given level of goods on the market, there is more money chasing them.

price ceiling The highest permissible price producers can legally charge based on price standards established by the government.

price elasticity See demand elasticity.

price parity Measures the prices farms (and farmers) received for goods against the prices they paid for the goods.

price taker One of the assumptions of perfect competition. A price-taking firm has to accept the prevailing price on the market, because it can alter its rate of production and sales without seriously affecting the price of the product.

production possibility curve A downward-sloping curve that depicts all the possible combinations of production given that all available resources are fully employed.

profit maximization Assumed to be a firm's objective in guiding its decisions. In other words, the motivation behind the firm's actions.

public sector The government or central authority.

quantity theory of money Theory of the relation between money and the price level.

real capital Physical assets such as equipment, plant, inventories, raw materials.

real income The quantity of goods and services that can be purchased with money income. In other words, real income is adjusted for inflation and represents actual purchasing power.

reserve ratio Percentage of deposits that a bank holds on reserve in its vaults or on deposit with the central bank.

required reserve ratio Another tool the Federal Reserve uses to influence the money supply. The Fed controls the amount that member banks must keep on reserve.

resource allocation What economics (and life) are all about.

scarcity The "limited" part of the definition of economics. In other words, resources are scarce and hence need allocation.

social cost Measure of the value of the best alternative uses of resources available to society.

speculative motive One of three motives for the demand for money. The other two are transaction and precautionary. The speculative demand reflects the need for cash in the optimal portfolio of financial assets.

stagflation Economic situation with concurrent high unemployment and high inflation.

supply Quantity of goods that firms are willing and able to sell. Supply is the quantity available, not the quantity sold.

supply curve Upward-sloping curve depicting the commodity levels available at various prices.

tariff A tax applied on imports usually on a percentage-of-value basis.

total cost Aggregate cost of producing a given level of output.

total revenue Total amount received by a firm for the product or service sold.

transfer payments Payments to individuals or institutions that are not generated by current productive activity. Examples are social security, welfare, pensions, veteran's benefits, and unemployment insurance.

unemployment See **full employment.**

union shop Operating with a union shop, the firm may hire anyone at the union wage, and the employee must join the union within a specified amount of time.

value added The difference between the value of the firm's final product and the value of the inputs the firm purchased to make the product. In other words, the value the firm added to the output through its involvement in the process.

velocity of circulation The number of times a given unit of money changes hands during a given time period.

zero elasticity The quantity demanded does not change when the price changes.

zero unemployment When the entire work force is employed. Don't hold your breath.

Bibliography

American Marketing Association. *Marketing Definitions: A Glossary of Marketing Terms.* Compiled by the Committee on Definitions, Ralph S. Alexander, Chairman. Chicago, IL, 1960.

Bierman, Harold, Jr., Charles P. Bonini, and Warren H. Hausman. *Quantitative Analysis for Business Decisions.* 5th ed. Homewood, IL: Richard D. Irwin, Inc., 1977.

Chase, Cochrane, et al. *Solving Marketing Problems with Visicalc.* Radnor, PA: Chilton Book Co., 1984.

Chase, Cochrane, and Kenneth L. Barasch. *Marketing Problem Solver.* 2nd ed. Radnor, PA: Chilton Book Co., 1977.

Chase, Richard B., and Nicholas J. Aquilano. *Production and Operation Management: A Life Cycle Approach.* Rev. ed. Homewood, IL: Richard D. Irwin, Inc., 1977.

Colberg, Marshall R., Bascomb R. Forbush, and Gilbert L. Whitaker Jr. *Business Economics: Principles and Cases,* 6th ed. Homewood, IL: Richard D. Irwin, Inc., 1980.

Davidson, William R., Alton F. Doody, and Daniel J. Sweeney. *Retailing Management.* 4th ed. New York: The Ronald Press Co., 1975.

Fallon, William K., ed. *AMA Management Handbook.* 2nd ed. New York: AMACOM, 1983.

Gordon, M., "The Savings, Investment and Valuation of a Corporation," *Review of Economics and Statistics,* February, 1962, pp. 37–51.

Hansen, Harry L. *Marketing: Text, Technique and Cases.* 3rd ed. Homewood IL: Richard D. Irwin, Inc., 1967.

Horngren, Charles T., *Cost Accounting: A Managerial Emphasis.* 5th ed. Englewood Cliffs, NJ: Prentice-Hall, 1982.

Ibbotson, Roger G., and Rex A. Sinquefield. *Stocks, Bonds, Bills and Inflation: The Past and the Future.* 1982 edition. Financial Analyst Research Foundation, Charlottesville, VA.

Johnson, Charles E., Robert F. Meigs, and Walter B. Meigs. *Accounting: The Basis for Business Decisions.* 5th ed. New York: McGraw-Hill, 1982.

Kotler, Philip. *Marketing Management: Analysis, Planning and Control.* 4th ed. Englewood Cliffs, NJ: Prentice-Hall, 1980.

Luther, William M. *The Marketing Plan.* New York: AMACOM, 1982.

Lipsey, Richard C., and Peter O. Steiner. *Economics.* 5th ed. New York: Harper & Row, 1978.

McCarthy, E. Jerome. *Basic Marketing: A Managerial Approach.* 7th ed. Homewood, IL: Richard D. Irwin, Inc., 1981.

Pope, Jeffrey L. *Practical Marketing Research.* New York: AMACOM, 1981.

Richards, Larry E., and Jerry J. LaCava. *Business Statistics: Why and When.* 2nd ed. New York: McGraw-Hill, 1983.

Shapiro, Benson P. *Sales Program Management: Foundation and Implementation.* New York: McGraw-Hill, 1977.

Shelly, Gary P., and Thomas J. Cashman. *Introduction to BASIC Programming.* Brea, CA: Anaheim Publishing Co., 1982.

Spurr, William A., and Charles P. Bonini. *Statistical Analysis for Business Decisions.* Rev. ed. Homewood, IL: Richard D. Irwin, Inc., 1977.

Vichas, Robert P. *Complete Handbook of Profitable Marketing Research Techniques.* Englewood Cliffs, NJ: Prentice-Hall, 1982.

Weston, J. Fred, and Eugene F. Brigham. *Managerial Finance.* 6th ed. Hinsdale, IL: The Dryden Press, 1978.

Wonnacott, Paul. *Mucroeconomics.* Homewood, IL: Richard D. Irwin, Inc., 1974.

Wilcox, Clair, and William G. Shepherd. *Public Policies Toward Business.* 5th ed. Homewood, IL: Richard D. Irwin, Inc., 1975.

Index